598 Kap OF
Kaplan, Gisela T.
Birds : their habits and
skills $ 15.95

OCT 1 1 2002

Birds

PROFESSOR GISELA KAPLAN is a researcher at the University of New England, Armidale, NSW and lectures in Biological Sciences and Education. She has written over ten books and rehabilitates native Australian birds, especially birds of prey. Her current research includes the vocal behaviour of the Australian magpie. She is also active in the protection of native wildlife and in animal welfare.

LESLEY ROGERS is Professor of Neuroscience and Animal Behaviour at the University of New England. She has conducted ground-breaking research on the brain structure and behaviour of chickens. Her research on animal behaviour extends to a wide range of avian species and other vertebrate species.

Other books by the authors published by Allen & Unwin:

Minds of Their Own (1997)
Not Only Roars & Rituals (1998)
The Orang-utans (1999)

BIRDS

Their habits and skills

Gisela Kaplan & Lesley J. Rogers

First published in 2001

Copyright © Gisela Kaplan & Lesley J. Rogers 2001

All rights reserved. No part of this book may be reproduced or transmitted in any form or by any means, electronic or mechanical, including photocopying, recording or by any information storage and retrieval system, without prior permission in writing from the publisher. The Australian Copyright Act 1968 (the Act) allows a maximum of one chapter or 10 per cent of this book, whichever is the greater, to be photocopied by any educational institution for its educational purposes provided that the educational institution (or body that administers it) has given a remuneration notice to Copyright Agency Limited (CAL) under the Act.

Allen & Unwin
83 Alexander Street
Crows Nest NSW 2065
Australia
Phone: (61 2) 8425 0100
Fax: (61 2) 9906 2218
Email: info@allenandunwin.com
Web: www.allenandunwin.com

National Library of Australia
Cataloguing-in-Publication entry:
Kaplan, Gisela.
Birds: their habits and skills.

Bibliography.
Includes index.
ISBN 1 86508 376 3.

1. Birds—Identification. 2. Birds. I. Rogers, Lesley J. (Lesley Joy), 1943– . II. Title.

598

Set in 11.5/14.5 pt Adobe Garamond by Midland Typesetters, Maryborough, Vic.
Printed by Griffin Press, South Australia

10 9 8 7 6 5 4 3 2 1

To Mike Cullen,
late Emeritus Professor of Zoology at
Monash University, Melbourne, who was
respected worldwide for his research on birds—
in memory of his work and friendship

CONTENTS

PREFACE

One day Gisela Kaplan collected a little eagle who was suffering from an impacted crop that prevented food from reaching her stomach. Judging by her very serious condition, this adult female had been without fluids or food for some time and would die without immediate treatment. A crop wash was required (given under licence). A saline solution, held in a syringe, was transported several centimetres down the oesophagus to the crop via a small pipe or rod inserted through the mouth. The procedure was quite risky considering the fully conscious state of the eagle. The large beak had to be opened, kept open with one hand and, with the other hand, the pipe had to be manoeuvred down the bird's throat without causing injury. The first treatment succeeded.

This little eagle received the cropwash treatment and volunteered to be a patient.

A few hours later another crop wash was due. The bird cast her eye over the equipment and, settling back without struggle, she opened her beak voluntarily and allowed the pipe to be inserted. Thanks to the eagle's willingness, many crop washes could be administered and, eventually, she was totally cured and released. Her level of cooperation was dumbfounding in a context so utterly unfamiliar to her.

We have been fortunate in getting to know many birds personally, even intimately, and we have been both impressed and moved by how they are able to communicate and incorporate us into their world. Partly because of these experiences, we wanted to write about birds, although we are far from being the first to do so. The vast number of people who study, observe and are fascinated by birds today will ensure that we periodically have to update our records and take stock of what we understand about them. It is still true though to say that we know far too little about them.

In this book we bring together some of the known facts about birds. We also draw on our own research and our own personal experiences. Birds are now typically studied in relatively disparate disciplines. In this book we have tried to 'reassemble' birds by bringing together ecological, physiological and behavioural knowledge about them. We would like the reader to experience birds as individual organisms living in a physical world and in a biological and social context.

We have written this book for a wide audience of bird lovers, for students and academics, and for those who simply like watching birds in their backyards and wish they knew more about them. In doing so we have touched on many fields, asking how birds do things, why, and how well 'equipped' they are to succeed and survive. Like most people, we share a concern for their future welfare at a time when everyone is keenly aware of the waves of extinction of mammals but might forget that bird species are just as much at risk. The *2000 Red List*, published by the International Union for the Conservation of Nature (IUCN) in the year 2000, identified more than 18 200 species at risk, including hundreds of avian species located in South-East Asia and Australia.

The increasing number of studies that focus on why some avian species are perilously close to extinction and others are declining is helping us to understand their needs and dangers and, hopefully, to turn around the slide into oblivion. Birds are excellent indicators of the health of an environment and we need to understand these sentinels of our future.

The study of behaviour was our focus and therefore sensory perception plays a large role in our book. We have also considered how birds develop and how they have evolved. Each species has its own specialisations and its own history. While we can give only a glimpse of the rich variety of bird behaviours, and describe some of their dazzling displays and rituals, we have emphasised that, in each generation, learning and even culture may be an intrinsic part of a species' survival. Inevitably, some areas could not be covered in the detail that some would wish. Bird migration and navigation, for instance, have become large and specialised topics in their own right and detailed accounts are readily available elsewhere.

We have also written this book to contribute to the ever-increasing number of voices saying that birds are not only complex but endowed with some remarkable qualities. Among these qualities are the abilities to think abstractly and to strategise, to memorise events, faces, people, places, food sources and contexts. More than ever we are asking how much birds know, and what makes them capable of greatly innovative behaviour.

We are grateful to Professor Hugh Ford for his advice and generous assistance with compiling the list of scientific names, and to Craig Lawlor for preparing some of the figures. We also thank our publisher, Ian Bowring, and editor, Colette Vella, as well as the rest of the team at Allen & Unwin, for their advice and ongoing good collaboration.

Gisela Kaplan & Lesley J. Rogers
May 2001

part I
DIVERSITY

chapter 1

SPECIAL FEATURES OF BIRDS

Birds are so much a part of our lives, even in cities, that we can barely imagine what it would be like without them. Recently, we suffered a devastating hailstorm in Armidale, New South Wales. Buildings and power poles were mangled. Trees were stripped of their leaves and branches broken as if they were matchsticks. Unexpectedly, the worst part of our experience was not the storm itself but the aftermath. We were struck by the quiet, a stillness of foreboding or mourning, and then we realised what was missing. There were no sounds of insects or birds. Not a single tone or indication of life could be heard. We realised how much background noise, including the songs and calls of birds, was part of our subconscious, how much we really lived with the birds in our garden and how very important they were to us.

Birds signal life. They also indicate that the environment is healthy.[1] After a forest fire, there is the same deadly stillness. Some birds succumb to the flames, others manage to migrate to safe areas. Some even return days later to scavenge among the devastation.

A miracle happened the day after the hailstorm. A pair of tawny frogmouths that Gisela Kaplan had raised some time earlier flew over to us with their first offspring in tow. Their small, fragile bodies had survived the assault of huge hailstones. What strategy had they adopted for protection? Slowly, other birds returned. They too were unharmed. There is no point in saying that birds are tough. Sheep and even horses had been killed

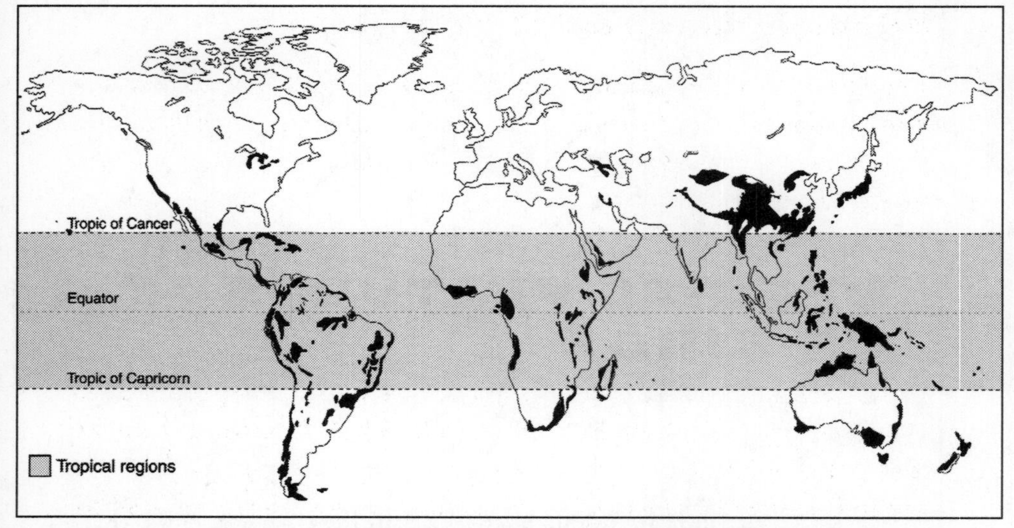

Figure 1.1 The distribution of significant ecosystems in which bird diversity is highest (black areas) shows the importance of the tropics. The middle line is the equator and the dotted lines indicate the tropical and subtropical regions.

that afternoon. We were impressed because we had witnessed an example of the outstanding success, ecologically speaking, of the class *Aves*. Birds are small enough to hide and skilful enough to do their hiding in a manner that avoids dangerous exposure. In a forest fire, they fly away. In a flood they stay in the treetops. Fragile they might be, but they have many resources and, as a class of animals, have adapted to living in almost every ecological niche on earth.

The class *Aves* is larger than the class *Mammalia*. Over 9000 avian species inhabit the earth but we have substantial information for only a fraction of these species. Today their number is shrinking but birds still occupy every niche of the planet. The highest concentration of birds of different species is found in wetlands and rainforests which are located around the tropical belts and in the southern hemisphere (see Figure 1.1). But even in areas that are relatively impoverished by a lack of bird species, such as parts of northern Europe, birds feature as a significant part of human life; at times, they have become icons and part of the national consciousness of a people.

Adaptive features of birds

Birds come in all shapes, sizes and colours and are adapted to an enormously wide range of ecological circumstances. Despite their differences, they all have several features in common. All birds have two legs and two wings, all have feathers and a beak and most of them are equipped to fly. Some, like the migratory birds, have the ability to fly extraordinary distances to enable them to move between suitable feeding grounds and breeding sites. Fascination with birds' ability to fly has occupied a branch of ornithology and scientists and birdwatchers for as long as written records have been kept.[2] We know, for instance, that birds were studied during the era of the Egyptian Pharaohs 5000 to 6000 years ago. One of the most famous bird lovers of the early modern period was Leonardo da Vinci. He was so fascinated by birds that he dissected them, drew them and studied them in great detail. They provided the model in his quest for human flight.

Beaks, wings and feathers are unique to birds (except for the platypus with its bill and the extinct theopod dinosaurs which had feathers) so we consider these unique features first.

The beak

The beak, or bill, is the bird's main equipment for preening, feeding and attacking. The bill is adapted primarily for feeding and we know this by comparing the shape of the bill (bill morphology) with the actual feeding habits of the species (Figure 1.2). For instance, Australia's cockatoos have extremely strong and massively constructed beaks, and this makes them capable of cracking hard-shelled nuts and extracting banksia and casuarina kernels. Honeyeaters and hummingbirds have slender beaks that are often curved, perfect for inserting into narrow flowers to extract nectar. In general, bills are specialised for grasping and manipulating food items.[3] While most adaptations of the bill for feeding have taken a long time to evolve, there are well documented instances when adaptations have taken place over a few generations in conditions of intense competition and/or changes in food availability. The most studied of these adaptations is the Galápagos finch, living in the very place where Darwin first conceived his theory of evolution. Here, scientists were able to see with their own eyes, from one season to the next, how fast evolution can work. One year, a

Figure 1.2 The variety of bird beaks: (top row, left to right) the beak of the Australian glossy black cockatoo is capable of cracking hard nuts; the South African Marico sunbird has a long curved beak to access nectar from flowers; the zebra finch beak is capable of dealing with hard seeds despite the bird's small size; the long beak of the African ground hornbill allows the bird to feed on poisonous insects and snakes far away from its body; (bottom row, left to right) the Australian wedge-tailed eagle has a beak designed for tearing flesh; the sturdy beak of a seed eater (guinea fowl); the sacred kingfisher has a long, strong beak, designed to capture and hold prey of its own body size.

drought caused most of the finches' common food items to disappear, leaving behind only a very hard-shelled fruit. The finches with the strongest bills were able to crack the surface of the fruit and they survived. The others perished. The survivors had offspring with the same strong beaks. Within one generation, a selection was made for a specific beak shape and strength.[4]

By developing wings, birds forfeited hands, quite a substantial handicap, one would think. Instead, the beak took over many of the functions of arms and hands. Birds use the beak to pick up, hold, throw and transport items such as twigs, stones and grasses. The beak is used for building nests, for wrestling with competitors and also for preening. Preening and scratching are particularly important for a bird's survival. Preening involves the removal of debris and a waterproofing process, achieved by spreading over the feathers an oil derived from a preening gland located at the base of the tail feathers. Preening and scratching are also essential for defence against ectoparasites,[5] such as lice, that live on the outside of the body (as compared to internal parasites) and feed on the body of the host. Without regular preening, birds would soon suffer from parasite overload, reducing their own chances of survival as well as their chances of reproducing successfully.[6]

Bills and beaks may be well designed for feeding but not necessarily for preening.[7] This is particularly noticeable in species with unwieldy beaks, such as the toucans and the hummingbirds. The beaks of toucans and hummingbirds are about the size of the bird's body and are impossible to use for preening all parts of the body. In fact, the beak of the sword-billed hummingbird exceeds the length of its entire body. Despite this, the parasite load on these birds is no larger than in birds with beaks of a size and shape better suited to preening, because they have developed other anti-parasite strategies to compensate for their beak limitations. To remove the ectoparasites, they rub against surfaces such as tree branches, sun themselves or bathe in the dust.[8] They use their feet for scratching to remove parasites. Even self-medication by ingestion or by keeping certain plants at the nest site may be used to inhibit ectoparasite build-up.[9] Self-grooming (auto-grooming) with the beak and feet may have its limitations if not all parts of the body can be reached but these too can be overcome. Birds that live in social groups have developed mutual grooming as an important social activity, just as in primates. This 'allogrooming' may well maintain a level of control over ectoparasites greater than can be achieved by self-grooming.

The feet

Many birds use their feet, as well as their beaks, for foraging and hunting. Chickens and many ground-dwelling birds scratch the ground to locate food, uncovering seeds or insects that live under leaf litter. Some of the ground-nesting species that do not sit on their own eggs, such as mallee fowl and the brush turkey, also use their feet to scratch their nest mounds to maintain the correct temperature for their eggs. Birds of prey use their talons exclusively to catch, immobilise and kill their prey. While their strong beaks are designed for tearing flesh once the prey is dead, the hunting bird captures its prey with outstretched legs to obtain the maximum impact of the weight and speed of the raptor. This technique is used for capture both on land and over water. Fish owls, such as Pel's fishing owl, and fish eagles can time their hunt so precisely that they can take a fish from under the surface of the water while still in flight. The sharp claws ensure that the slippery prey cannot get away. Falcons that specialise in feeding on birds hunt on the wing (in the air) and they too use impact and outstretched legs to secure their prey. Peregrine falcons dive-bomb their victims at hair-raising speeds.

Occasionally, birds use tools to help them forage but these tools, such as small sticks, are usually held by the beak not the feet. Combinations of foot and beak are also used to manipulate food. Many parrot species of the world feed by holding the food in one foot and manipulating it with the beak and tongue. Raptors often hold down the carcass of their captured prey with a foot while they prise off pieces of the meat. These are prime functions of the feet.

Avian feet are also designed to suit the surface on which they are used. Swimming birds, such as ducks, have webbed feet. Some species walk on floating leaves and have long toes to give them a broader surface area. The feet of perching birds are padded and their toes positioned so that they can grip branches. Birds that feed on vertical tree surfaces have feet with long sharp nails for better grip. Some species, such as cockatoos and rainforest pigeons, have so much power in their grip that they can hang upside down suspended by one foot in order to reach the desired food.

The wings

The wing is a forelimb and an adaptation to flight that is unique to class Aves (Figure 1.3). The bones of the wing reveal their reptilian ancestry. From the shoulder to the elbow (the humerus) and from elbow to wrist (radius to ulna) the bones of all vertebrates look quite similar, including those of birds. Only the hand shows a distinctly different adaptation in birds. In vertebrates with paws or hands, the metacarpal bones are shaped into fingers. In birds, they are fused and taper off into one bone (the end part is called *manus*, Latin for 'hand'). Unlike the 'hands' of reptiles and the paws of many mammals, the bird-wing 'hand' cannot be moved up and down but has lateral rotation for wing beating.

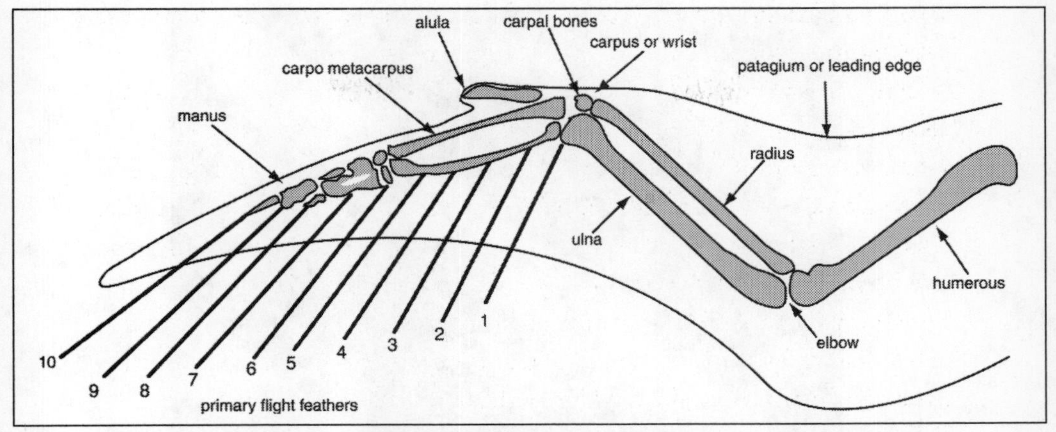

Figure 1.3 The bone outline of a wing. The upper and lower arm are very similar to that of humans. Below the wrist, there are some important differences, both in mobility and in the fusion of bones of the 'hand' into one finger.

There is a large but invisible difference between mammalian bones and avian bones—a bird's bones are not filled with marrow but with air. Mammalian bones are heavy which would impede flight or make it impossible. The bones of birds are hollow and this gives them a lightness that is a very important adaptation to flight.

The wings of birds are covered in specialised feathers that help to carry the birds in flight. Feathers are part of the entire covering (called the 'integument') that divides the skin from the surrounding air.[10] In fact, feathers are the main part of the bird's integument, although scales on the legs and horny protrusions on the head also form a part. How feathers evolved is an interesting study, one that is not yet agreed upon.[11] The architecture of the feathers is not the same in all birds and not all birds possess the same number of feathers. A small songbird may have 1000 feathers while a large bird, such as a swan, can have more than 25 000.[12]

The function of feathers, however, is the same in all bird species. In addition to their role in flight, they provide insulation against cold, heat and rain. They protect the skin and they are replaceable. To fulfil these various functions, birds have several different types of feathers on their body (Figure 1.4). The flight feathers on the upper part of the wing (manus) are called primaries. In the ulna area, there are the secondary feathers. There are also downy feathers for insulation and feathers

Figure 1.4 This is a twelve-times enlargement of one section of a goshawk's feather. The three visible large rods across the image are the small branches, growing from the mainstem of the feather. Note that these branches again have small branches—the barbs—which connect the sections and give each feather the strength to withstand air pressure.

specialised in shape and colour for displaying during courtship (such as the tail feathers of the peacock) or for threat displays (as in the yellow bittern, for instance). Some feather types are age-dependent. Altricial species—that is, birds that are immature at hatching, grow up in a nest and are fed by parents—have no tail feathers or primary feathers before fledging. Adults have no downy feathers covering all of their bodies, as nestlings do, although some remain and some of the different feather types are indicated by a colour change from chick to adult.

Perhaps the most ingenious aspect of feather structure is how the feathers of the wing can withstand immense air pressure during flight without being torn apart. Each feather is a separate unit but gaps may also occur between strands of a single feather. It is possible to prise the single strands of a feather apart, yet they hold firmly when in flight. This is because each strand of a feather has small protrusions, called barbs, which intermesh with the barbs and smaller branches of the next strand of the feather. While light in weight, these hooked cross-connections cling together so strongly that they prevent air from ripping them apart in flight (Figure 1.4).

Since wings are needed for flight, landing and even balance, the feathers are replaced (a process called 'moulting') at regular intervals but never all at once. A few feathers can be shed without disabling flight. The new feathers start to form underneath the existing feathers and slowly push out the old ones. The shape of the wings also helps to maintain a moulting bird's ability to fly. Wings are always concave in shape and this is important for aerodynamics.[13]

The form of the wings is also shaped according to the environment in which the bird lives. The albatross, gliding most of the time across oceans, has long, slender wings whereas birds negotiating between tree branches have short, broad wings. Some species have lost the ability to fly; they may have lived on islands where they have faced no predators. These flightless birds retain only vestigial wings that are rarely used, or they may be adapted for swimming instead of flying. A penguin, for example, 'flies' in the water.

Food and foraging

Birds occupy both a vertical plane and a horizontal plane above ground level. Not all birds forage for food at the same level above ground. Shorebirds, waders, ducks and other waterbirds may feed well below the surface of the water or even at the bottom of a shallow lake, swamp, lagoon or river. Other species, such as kingfishers, skim just below the surface of the water, and swifts and martins skim just above its surface. Some species feed well above ground or sea level. In tropical rainforests we have at least a three-tiered, if not a four-tiered, vertical environment which, at each level, extends horizontally as well. First, there is the upper canopy, occurring only in ancient and intact rainforests, made up of very tall trees that may be hundreds of years old. In this layer we often find the really large birds such as toucans or hornbills. At the top of the canopy, they have access to the airspace for taking off and landing and they are able to locate large branches that provide easily accessible roosting and landing spots.

Fruit-eaters living in the upper canopy, like hornbills, have the task of dispersing seeds; they enable seeds in the very top of the canopy to be carried some way off before being dropped for germination.

The next layer of the forest, the main canopy, is often the top layer in regenerated forest. It houses a variety of birds that require shelter and also feed on fruit. Examples include fruit doves and the topknot pigeon. The next layer down is a sub-canopy, housing many smaller songbirds and sunbirds. Finally, there is the understorey. This is subdivided into a region used by the birds that occupy a range above ground (up to 10 metres) and an area for the birds that live and forage on the forest floor. Many of these species living at different levels of the forest never meet. Their particular niche in the forest may remain unique to them and provide all the resources they require. H.L. Bell showed some years ago, in the lowland rainforest of New Guinea, that even very similar sized birds of similar weight range (8–35 grams) and with a varied diet of insects can be ecologically segregated in the rainforest.[14] Such birds include fantails and gerygones. Some fantails are found on the ground floor, grey-breasted rufus fantails in the understorey, the yellow-bellied gerygone in the sub-canopy and another gerygone (the fairy gerygone) in the main or even the upper canopy.

Sharing out the resources among the species is an important aspect of survival. Some of this partitioning is the result of adaptation that has occurred over evolutionary time. In other cases there is evidence of competition. If a species dares to leave its layer of the forest, it may be attacked and shown its place by others. Rainforest birds have a well developed community structure that helps to minimise competition and enhance full use of resources. Even mangrove forests, which do not reach great heights, are 'zoned' for different species according to foraging requirements.[15]

Where birds forage may also be determined by sex. It has been known for some time that bark-foraging species such as woodpeckers, treecreepers and sittellas divide up their feeding range according to gender. R.A. Noske showed, for instance, that sittella males (which have larger beaks) feed much more often on trunks and main branches of trees than do females.[16]

Within a species, and in individual birds, there may also be a variety of foraging strategies according to their specific needs in the life cycle or in a certain season, which lead to the bird being in different locations and using different methods of food acquisition. The north-western crow on Diana Island in British Columbia, Canada, for example, exhibits two types of foraging behaviour depending on the availability of food and the amount of food required. Only during nesting do parent crows forage at low tide as the water recedes. Apparently, it is easier to find food at low tide and so less energy is expended on basic requirements and the surplus energy can be spent on obtaining extra food for their young.[17]

Foraging space is not only divided up according to vertical, horizontal and other locational cues but also according to time of day. There are exclusive daytime feeders (diurnal species), there are dawn and dusk feeders (twilight or crepuscular species) and there are those that are classified as night-time feeders (nocturnal species). So airspace and ground space are utilised over a 24-hour period and some birds get exclusive use of some hours over others. The species that occupy broad daylight live in an entirely different world from those that wake and feed at night. As Graham Martin has shown so well, the number of species capable of switching between day and night is relatively small as each requires specific adaptations of sight, hearing and other senses to be able to use the different conditions of illumination effectively.[18]

Birds have developed very sophisticated strategies to make sure they get the food they need. They must know where food can be found as well as the appropriate techniques for extracting it. Being able to occupy a niche in nature, and finding a niche that is not wanted by every other bird as well has resulted in very specific requirements for breeding, feeding and even roosting. As later chapters show, the social organisation of birds, the types and location of nests and different ways of rearing their young ensure a diversity of habits that is sufficient to allow the coexistence of many species. Nests may occupy the ground, the scrub, branches on trees, holes in trees, edges of cliffs, sand dunes, or the rocky shores of many coastlines. In an average inland property in Australia there may be as many as 50 to 80 bird species occupying the same area. In national parks, the species occupation rate may increase to 120 or even more.

While birds occupy large parts of the globe, many species have become so specialised that any reduction in their essential resources can immediately threaten their survival. Birds of the sea (pelagic birds) and those of the shore require undisturbed beaches for nesting but, with increasing beach cultures around the world, they find their terrain being contested by humans. Wetland birds require the continuous existence of shallow waters, but many wetlands are at risk because the water is being diverted to irrigate farms and support industry. Most bird species need shelter and roosting sites, whether in grasslands, open woodlands, rainforests or near the sea. As a result of the destruction of their habitat much of the diversity of bird species has become confined to small areas of the world,[19] the areas with the richest variety of species occurring mainly in tropical regions. Here birds coexist with many other animals and plants (as Figure 1.1 showed) because, as yet, resources for feeding and shelter are not in short supply.

Territory

Habitat selection varies according to species but not all habitat selection involves 'territory'. Many species remain itinerant, at least to some extent. Albatrosses, as is legendary, are eternal wanderers, the seas being their true home. They may spend years flying at sea, rarely even landing on the water's surface. Only for breeding purposes do they come back to land and reunite with a lifelong breeding partner. Other bird species are true nomads that never call a plot their own, choosing a nesting site that they will defend just for the period of raising their young. Then there are the seasonal travellers, the birds that migrate across vast expanses of land and sea. A wide variety of species belongs in this category, including shore-birds, water birds, raptors, songbirds and even very small passerines.

Birds may stay in one place or move into a home range on a seasonal basis. The latter are said to be semi-nomadic. Most parrots are semi-nomadic: they go where they can find seeds. Fruit-eating birds, likewise, go to where the trees are fruiting, and this may be sporadic and require quite long-distance travel. Semi-nomadic birds may also be found in tropical rainforests around the world.

A very large group of avian species, however, is territorial and sedentary, meaning that they choose an area and remain in it permanently for as long as life circumstances permit. Territorial behaviour is of great interest in all living organisms. It is found in invertebrates, fish, amphibians, reptiles, birds and mammals—in short, in most living organisms. Territoriality involves a range of behaviours that has been established in each species over evolutionary time.

Countless researchers have investigated territoriality. Classic studies are concerned with the biological significance of the territories of birds.[20] The questions of territory size, shape, choice and neighbourhood have all featured in research although the fascination with defence and aggression has probably outweighed all other aspects of territoriality. Even so, the processes by which territory is actually established and secured are still not well understood.[21]

Establishing a territory can be hard work, requiring continuous vigilance to defend and maintain it. There may be a different set of problems in the centre of a territory as against the fringe of it, called the centre-edge effect,[22] and the territory may never be secure from takeover by intruders.[23] Fighting or vigilance flying requires a continuous high output of energy and this raises the question of what advantage territoriality can confer over semi-nomadic or highly nomadic living. Most birds can fly and hence could take advantage of their mobility. By opting to remain in one territory, they voluntarily forfeit some of the advantages of being able to fly. Presumably, flight enables birds to choose a territory after surveying possible sites elsewhere. The advantages and disadvantages of one lifestyle over another must balance out. For example, territoriality in its broadest sense is a form of resource partitioning that secures a constant supply of food. Territoriality may thus be the best way of surviving in one locality but not in another.

With their unique physical features and diverse adaptive behaviours, birds present us with the continual challenge of unravelling their complexities and diversity. A hundred years ago, people were not fully aware that birds have very specialised needs and that everything we humans do can have a detrimental effect on them. Now that we know this we are in a position where we can actively plan the prevention of any further decline of bird numbers and species. To do this well, we need to study their behaviour. Without this knowledge, we cannot begin to be effective protectors of their needs.

chapter 2

THE EVOLUTION OF BIRDS

During the late Jurassic period, about 150 million years ago, the first bird left a fossil record. At that time the climate of Europe was tropical and palm-like trees surrounded shallow lagoons. The ancient bird met its death in one of these lagoons and there, in the fine mud at the bottom of the lagoon, it formed an exquisite fossil to be unearthed in the limestone quarry at Solnhofen, Germany, in the 1880s.[1] This specimen was called *Archaeopteryx lithographica*. It was remarkable on two counts. First, it had features of both birds and reptiles and so formed the 'missing link' in the evolutionary branch from reptiles to birds. Second, it was discovered just two years after Charles Darwin published his book, *The Origin of Species*, outlining the theory of evolution. The fossil of a single feather had been found a year earlier and also dated to the late Jurassic (150 million years ago) but *Archaeopteryx* was the first full fossil to be discovered. Subsequently, more fossils of ancient birds came to light, all found in nearby regions in Bavaria, Germany[2] and today there are seven known fossils of *Archaeopteryx*.[3]

Archaeopteryx had reptilian jaws and teeth and a reptile-like tail. It also had feathers remarkably similar to those of modern birds. The fine grain of the Solnhofen limestone preserved such detail of the feathers that even the interlocking barbs can be seen in the fossils.[4] These feathers made wings and they were also present on the tail. In many ways *Archaeopteryx* resembled the present-day pheasant coucal of Australia and New Guinea, not only in size but also in general bone and feather construction.[5] The structure of the tail was, however, different in *Archaeopteryx*: the feathers projected out from a long tail. *Archaeopteryx* also had three clawed fingers on the leading side of its wings and these were movable. It might have used these claws in climbing trees just as the young hoatzins of South America do today.[6] If a nestling hoatzin falls out of the nest, it uses its claws to climb back to safety. In fact, wing claws are not uncommon in modern tree-climbing birds (e.g. woodpeckers), especially at nestling stage.

It seems that *Archaeopteryx* was not a strong flier, although it was no larger than a pigeon or a chicken. Its rather small size should have assisted flying, but all the fossils of *Archaeopteryx*, except one, lack the sternum of birds that evolved later. The sternum is the breastbone, a large bone extending from the chest to the abdomen. The powerful flight muscles (pectoral muscles) are anchored to the sternum in modern birds. These extremely large muscles enable birds to fly by flapping their wings. One fossil of *Archaeopteryx*, believed to be the least ancient of the seven fossils, has a sternum to which pectoral muscles could have been attached. This specimen of *Archaeopteryx* may well have had powered flight.

Some pectoral muscles are also attached to the furcula, the wishbone formed by fusion of the collarbones. *Archaeopteryx* had a furcula but, although this might have meant that it had some pectoral muscles for flight, it would not have provided sufficient anchorage for large pectoral muscles. *Archaeopteryx* also lacked the air sacs characteristic of flying birds. These are bags of air extending from the lungs and into the bones through small openings and they are used to supply oxygen during the extreme energy demands of flight.

Archaeopteryx, therefore, did not have all the characteristics necessary for flight as seen in modern birds, even though it had feathers.[7] It has even been suggested that the feathers were merely for insulation and not used in flying at all. Birds are able to maintain their body temperature in ways that reptiles cannot, but the fossil records cannot tell us whether *Archaeopteryx* was bird-like or reptile-like in this characteristic. Having feathers is not the ultimate clue to the ability to fly. Although it used to be thought that *Archaeopteryx* was the very first feathered creature to evolve, recently discovered fossils show that dinosaurs—probably quite unrelated to the ancient birds—also had feathers.[8] These dinosaurs walked the earth in the late Jurassic and early Cretaceous periods. They did not fly, as can be seen by their bone structure, particularly the bones of the hind limbs. Therefore, having feathers and being able to fly are two characteristics that need not always go together. Feathers might well have evolved in the first instance to provide insulation or to fulfil some function other than flight. Then, later, they were used for flight.

Archaeopteryx was well adapted for running, as were the dinosaur theropods, the carnivorous dinosaur reptiles from which, many believe, birds evolved. The pelvis and hind limbs of *Archaeopteryx* were constructed for running but, in contrast to the dinosaur theropods, *Archaeopteryx* already had a bird-like arrangement of its toes—three long toes facing forwards and one backwards. Together with its clawed fingers, these toes could have been used to climb trees and, in particular, to perch on branches.

The long tail of *Archaeopteryx* with its many vertebral bones would have counterbalanced the forward part of its body. In modern birds the tail is very short and the vertebral bones are fused to form what is called a pygostyle. It was thought that the pygostyle was found only in birds but it now appears that pygostyle-like structures evolved independently at least three times in the theropod dinosaur, but not necessarily in the ancestors of birds.[9] The evolution of the pygostyle required matching enlargement of the pelvis and the hind-limb muscles to replace the loss of the counterbalancing tail, and this is another characteristic typical of birds.

These changes occurred over evolutionary time to give rise to birds as we know them today. A number of fossils, not quite as old as those of *Archaeopteryx*, have been discovered in China and these belong to another genus, *Confuciusornis*.[10] They are the oldest beaked birds known. Most of the specimens have teeth but there are some without teeth,[11] which suggests they ate plants rather than animals—*Archaeopteryx* used its teeth to eat meat. Apart from these differences, *Confuciusornis* was very similar to *Archaeopteryx*, although smaller. The existence of these two distinct forms of ancient birds suggests that even more avian forms were living at that time and indicates the diversity even of ancient birds. They must all have evolved from feathered creatures that had evolved well before both *Archaeopteryx* and *Confuciusornis*. Feathers were, in fact, widespread in the theropod dinosaurs.[12] Recently found specimens of theropod dinosaurs, known as *Caudipteryx* spp., have unmistakable imprints of feathers as well as other features of birds, including one backward-facing toe.[13]

Becoming airborne

It is not known whether *Archaeopteryx* could fly but it probably did, at least for short distances. We can make reasoned guesses about how it might have done so but there is no conclusive evidence about flying in *Archaeopteryx* because the behaviour of a species leaves no fossil record.

First, we should look at the methods that animals other than birds use to become airborne. Even though birds have the most astounding abilities of flight, they are not the only creatures to take to the air. Some existing species of frogs, snakes, lizards and mammals launch themselves from a height and glide for considerable distances in the air. They do so by using skin flaps on the sides of their bodies or by extending broad, sail-like limbs. The gliders of Australia are typical examples of this kind of 'flight'. Some of the ancient reptiles living in the late Triassic period more than 200 million years ago used this method of flying. A fossil record of a flying reptile (a saurian) called *Protoaxis texensis* has been dated to that time.[14] It could represent one of the first steps towards the evolution of birds, but many ancient reptiles had flaps of skin or long scale-like structures that they could have used for gliding or even more sustained flying.

Archaeopteryx could have used its feathers to aid gliding after climbing up a high tree, using its finger claws, and then launching itself into the air. This is known as the 'trees-down' hypothesis. Alternatively, it could have used its wings to obtain lift-off after running fast on the ground with wings flapping. This is known as the 'ground-up', or cursorial, hypothesis. *Archaeopteryx* might, for example, have used running and flapping flight to catch insects.[15] This hypothesis links wing use to feeding and takes into account the fact that *Archaeopteryx* had teeth and fed on meat, either exclusively or among other things. It might have used the feathers simply to provide air resistance (drag) when pouncing on prey.[16] Pouncing might then have turned into swooping as feathers and flight muscles provided better lift-off. Evolving to be smaller in size would have been another factor essential for becoming airborne but that occurred after the time of *Archaeopteryx*. In fact, it seems that *Archaeopteryx* was unable to become fully airborne after running and flapping flight because, given its construction, to provide sufficient energy for take-off it would have needed to run much faster than possible.

Another suggestion, no longer popular, is that *Archaeopteryx* used its winged forelimbs rather like fans to trap insects as it ran along the ground.[17] Later, wings evolved and were used in flying. This hypothesis is similar to the idea that feathers first evolved for insulation, in the sense that feathers are said to have first appeared for purposes other than flying. Another alternative is that feathers first evolved for performing the visual displays used in social communication and were only later used for flying.[18] As we see later, modern birds use their feathers to communicate, with often spectacular visual displays.[19] It is possible that the first feathered creatures (ancient birds and theropod dinosaur) used their feathers in similar ways to communicate with other members of their species. Evidence that dinosaurs formed groups supports the idea that they may have communicated using vocalisations or visual displays.[20]

None of these hypotheses about the first uses of feathers can help us to decide whether *Archaeopteryx* was a ground-up or a trees-down flier. It is a matter of putting the many pieces of evidence together and coming up with the most plausible hypothesis, but there is no overwhelming evidence to determine whether *Archaeopteryx* glided down from above or flapped its way up from a running start on the ground. We can say, however, that only the 'trees-down' hypothesis finds a good use for its hooked finger claws—used to climb up trees.[21] Claws could, of course, be used in a number of different ways—some other ancient birds too large to fly had claws, which they must have used for purposes other than climbing.

Birds of the Cretaceous period

The Cretaceous period extends from about 146 million years ago to 65 million years ago (Figure 2.1). In the early Cretaceous period there was a blossoming of many different kinds of birds, referred to as a 'radiation' of different species.[22] It seems that *Archaeopteryx* and *Confuciusornis* may have died out even before the early Cretaceous period and thus were evolutionary dead-ends—they did not give rise to the next step in the evolution of birds.[23] However, ancient birds similar to *Archaeopteryx*

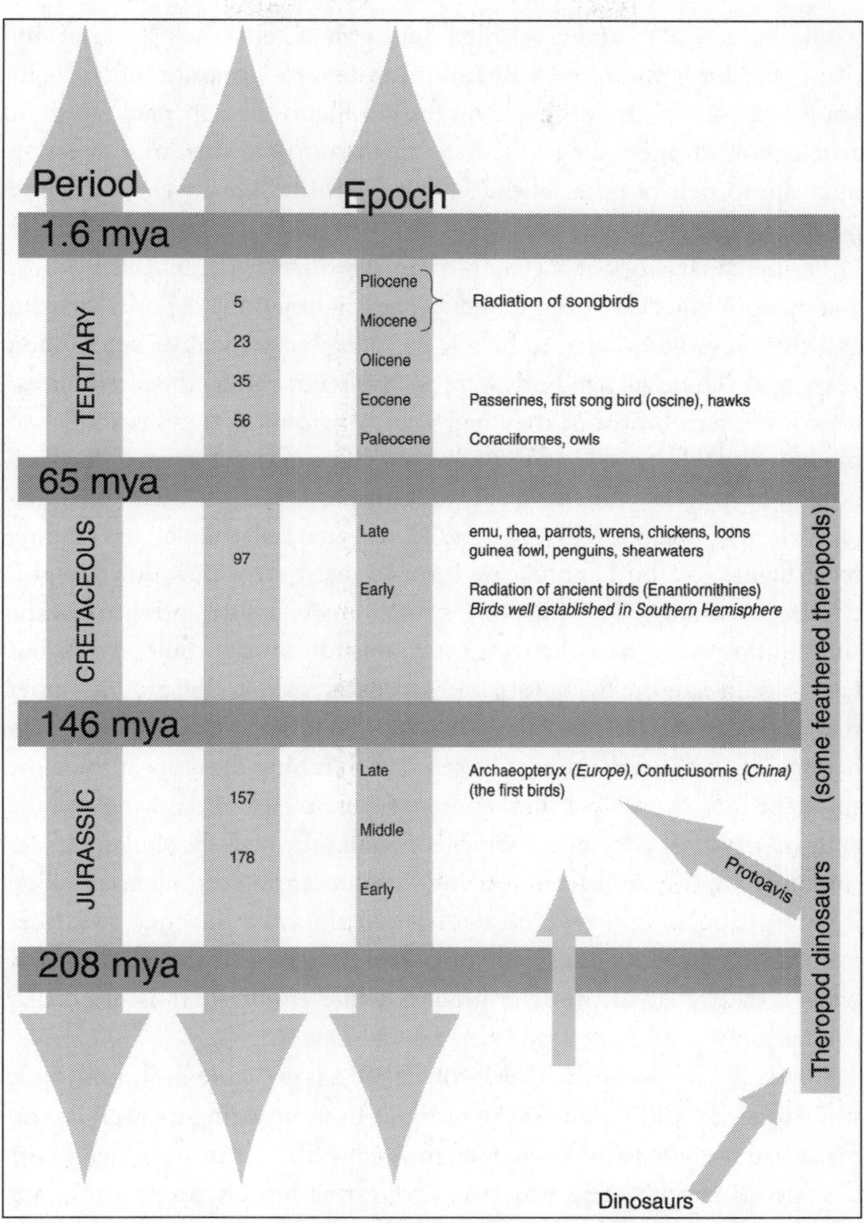

Figure 2.1 Evolutionary timeline, showing the time of evolution of different species of birds. Column 1 refers to the geological period; column 2 indicates the years (in millions) from the present in which the main geological epochs (column 3) occurred. Note the time of the mass extinction at 65 million years ago, and the evolution of birds prior to this time, as well as after it.

would have evolved and diversified during the Cretaceous. These primitive flying birds were called Enantiornithines, or 'opposite birds'.[24] The name 'opposite birds' was based on fossil evidence that appeared to show articulation of one joint in the foot, the tarsometatarsus, in a direction opposite to that of other birds.[25] These 'opposite birds' were capable of powered flight.

Feathered skeletons of ancient birds intermediate between *Archaeopteryx* and modern birds have been found recently in limestone deposits in Spain and they have been dated to belong to birds that were alive 125 million years ago.[26] These ancient birds were probably not among the direct ancestors of modern birds but they had many anatomical features similar to modern birds. They still had teeth and several primitive features of the skull bones but in one of the fossils[27] it was possible to see that there were tufts of feathers on the bird's first fingers. These tufts, called alulas, aid landing from flight. As a bird approaches for landing, it must slow down, and it does so by rotating its wings to a steeper angle. This rotation stops the smooth flow of air over the wing's surface and causes turbulence. Turbulence would stall the flying bird and cause it to drop to the ground rather than skilfully alighting on a branch. The alula prevents this from happening. By raising the first finger, and so raising the alula at the same time, the bird opens up a slot between the main part of the wing and the alula on the front edge of the wing. Air comes through the slot and glides smoothly over the surface of the wing without causing turbulence; stalling is prevented. *Archaeopteryx* did not have an alula and this may be further evidence that it was not capable of powered flight—landing would have been a matter of hitting the ground while running. It is clear that *Archaeopteryx* could not have landed on a branch.

Towards the end of the Cretaceous period (see Figure 2.1) most birds still had teeth, a reflection of their origins in meat-eating theropods, and many had become partially adapted to aquatic life. Then, at the end of the Cretaceous period, there was a massive extinction of species—this was when the dinosaurs became extinct. Although most mammals and birds did not survive this period, some did: the question is, how many? According to Alan Feduccia only a small group of shorebirds survived,[28] deduced from evidence in the fossil records. The new technique of determining the evolution of species using analysis of the genetic material

(DNA) inside cells of living species[29] reveals that as many as 22 lineages of modern birds survived the period of mass extinctions to enter the Tertiary period.[30] These included parrots, wrens and penguins, as well as the water-birds, shearwaters and loons. They also included chickens, guinea fowls, emus and rheas. The ratite (rhea, ostrich and moa) and galliform (chicken) lineages branched off from the main line very early. Next the parrots branched off.[31] There is still much debate about the accuracy of these claims, but another molecular study has revealed that chickens and emus diverged from each other 80 million years ago.[32] This divergence took place before the mass extinction and so suggests that the ancestors of these birds survived that period.

Many of the species that survived the Cretaceous–Tertiary boundary may have done so on the continents of the Southern Hemisphere, those continents that had once formed the great southern continent of Gondwana. It was thought that the landmass that became Europe was the site of evolution of most modern birds and mammals but now the focus is shifting towards Gondwana. The earliest fossil records of ratites, galliformes, parrots, pigeons, loons, penguins and passerines all come from Gondwana.

Birds were certainly well established in the Southern Hemisphere by the end of the Cretaceous.[33] As Alan Cooper and David Penny have reasoned, perhaps it was in Gondwana that many species of birds survived the time of mass extinctions. In their opinion, the extinctions were not quite as massive as once thought, at least in some parts of the earth.[34]

Birds of the Tertiary period

The Tertiary period extends from the time of the so-called mass extinctions 65 million years ago to just over 2 million years ago (Figure 2.1). During this period enormous radiations of avian species took place. Radiation means the process of spreading geographically over increasingly wider areas and the evolution of many species. The Tertiary period has been referred to as a time of explosive evolution for birds.[35] Quite how explosive it actually was depends on how many lineages of birds survived from the Cretaceous to the Tertiary period but, certainly, a great many new species did evolve. First the Coraciiformes (kingfishers, bee-eaters and allies) evolved, then the passerines (perching birds, including songbirds), beginning at about 56 million years ago. The passerines now common in Europe are believed to have evolved 23 million years ago.

Thus, after the extinctions marking the end of the Cretaceous period and the beginning of the Tertiary period, many recent lineages of birds arose in a second, explosive radiation that went on for 10 million years of the early Tertiary period.[36] Most of the categories (orders) of present-day birds, except the passerines, appeared during this period. Passerines (including true songbirds) may have begun to evolve during the late Oligocene (starting at about 35 million years ago) and radiated during the Miocene epoch (starting about 23 million years ago and ending about 5 million years ago). But some evidence suggests that the first song-birds evolved in the Southern Hemisphere even earlier than this, in the early Eocene epoch (around 50 million years ago), and migrated later to the Northern Hemisphere. Walter Boles has identified the fossil bones of a songbird found in south-eastern Queensland and dated to 54 million years old.[37] This discovery represents the oldest songbird known so far.

Evidence of feathers from Cretaceous deposits in southern Victoria shows that ancient birds were present on that part of the Gondwanan landmass that was to become Australia.[38] The other early record of modern birds on the Australian continent is that of penguins (Spheni-sciformes) found in late Eocene (that is, roughly 40 million years ago) marine sediments in south-eastern Australia.[39] It seems possible, therefore, that songbirds arose on the landmass of Australia, rather than being migrants from the Northern Hemisphere. Other species did migrate from the north but at a much later time. The Corvidae also originated in Australia, where they radiated in the Tertiary period and much later dispersed to the Northern Hemisphere as the Australian landmass drifted northwards.[40]

Passerines now make up 60 per cent of the world's species of birds (more than 5000 species), reflecting the most recent explosive radiation of bird species. This took place particularly in the Miocene period. Almost half of the passerines are oscines, the term used for songbirds.[41] With their evolution and migration, the music of birdsong must have filled the forests and savannas of the earth.

Evolution of the avian brain

Almost all the dinosaurs had very small brains relative to their body weight. Some had a special collection of nerve cells, like a 'second brain', in the sacral region of the spinal cord to control movement of the massive hind limbs. This 'sacral brain' was often larger than the brain in the dinosaur's head. Larger-brained dinosaurs were present in the late Cretaceous period but even these had brains much smaller than birds.[42]

We can obtain some idea of the main structure of the brain of different dinosaurs by making a rubber mould inside the fossil skulls and then pulling it out to examine the shape. From these endocranial moulds we can see that the dinosaurs had large olfactory lobes for smelling, but small optic lobes for vision and a small cerebellum, used for balance and control of the limbs when moving. This brain construction is similar to that of present-day reptiles. Compared with their equivalent in a modern bird (see Figure 2.2), the optic lobes and the cerebellum of the dinosaur were very small. Of course, the 'sacral brain' of the dinosaur may have done some of the work of the avian cerebellum, explaining, in part, why the cerebellum is relatively smaller in dinosaurs than in birds.

The need for balance and wing control when flying is likely to be another important reason for the larger cerebellum in birds. One function of the cerebellum is the learning of different patterns of movement.[43] Since birds have to learn many complex movements in take-off, flying and landing as well as in walking, running or hopping, this too might explain why they have a larger cerebellum than their reptilian ancestors. *Archaeopteryx* fossils show that this species had a much more bird-like brain than its ancestors; its forebrain was larger than that of the dinosaurs and so was its cerebellum.[44]

Vision is also highly specialised and complex in birds and it must have far exceeded that of their flightless ancestors. Vision plays a key role in navigating flight and in many other functions. The large eyes of birds and the large optic lobes of their brain reflect this superior vision. Other regions of the brain process visual information but the optic lobes are very important for vision and they are the only visual regions that can be seen clearly on the surface of the brain. Another prime visual area, called the Wulst, can be seen as a slight bump on the top of the forebrain in some species

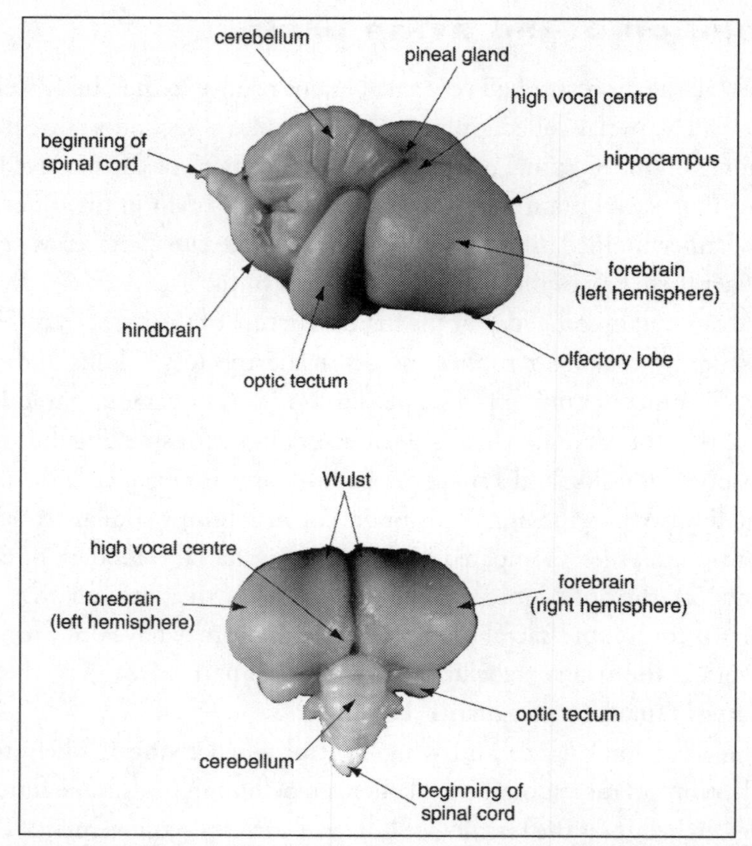

Figure 2.2 The brain of the Australian magpie: top, a side view (bird's head would be facing the right side of the page); bottom, a view from the back of the brain.

but it is hidden inside the brain in other species. The Wulst is the region of the brain where the higher processing of visual information takes place, and auditory and touch information is also processed there. It can be seen quite clearly in the Australian magpie (Figure 2.2).

Dinosaurs also had a forebrain, the part of the brain where the higher processing of information takes place and decisions are made, but it was usually much smaller than the forebrain of birds, relative to body size. With the evolution of birds, the forebrain also evolved and became more complex. In fact, it is in the forebrain that we see a clear difference between birds and mammals. Birds evolved a more complex forebrain by elaborating on an ancient part of the brain called the paleocortex (meaning 'old cortex'), whereas mammals achieved a similar result by adding a whole new structure called the neostriatum.[45] The modern avian brain is very different from the mammalian brain but it is by no means inferior to it.

Every time a species has a particular need that will enhance its survival, a special area of the brain can be found for controlling that function. One example is the hippocampal region of the forebrain (Figure 2.2). The hippocampus is unusually large in birds that store their food and retrieve it later for eating and this is, perhaps, not surprising because the ability to learn and remember the spatial position of things resides in the hippocampus. Food-storing is typical of nutcrackers, crows, jays, marsh tits and several other species.[46] Relatives of these species that do not store food have much smaller hippocampal regions. Clark's nutcracker has an extraordinary ability to remember where it has stored its food and it also has the largest hippocampus seen so far.[47] This species lives at high altitudes and stores food for the season when it is scarce. One bird will store about 30 000 seeds in a year at over 6000 locations and manage to retrieve them quite accurately.[48]

Another new structure evolved in songbirds—it was actually a set of connected new structures, called nuclei, used both to process and produce song. The high vocal centre is at the top of the forebrain (indicated for the magpie in Figure 2.2) while the other song nuclei are deeper within the forebrain.[49] Without these nuclei, birds cannot sing; naturally, they are not present in the brains of non-oscines (species that do not sing). The specialised brain nuclei for singing evolved in oscines together with the vocal apparatus for singing (the syrinx, located where the two trachea from the lungs meet). The size of the song nuclei varies between species and tends to be larger in those species that have more complex songs.[50]

Comparing the brains of modern reptiles (lizards and snakes), amphibians (toads, frogs and salamanders) and birds shows us that reptiles and amphibians have brains very similar to the dinosaurs. One special characteristic that emerges is that amphibians have larger, but fewer, nerve cells than birds or mammals.[51] By having fewer and larger cells the brains of amphibians have severe limits on how much information they can process. Birds and mammals made an evolutionary step forward by having smaller and more numerous nerve cells—it meant they could pack more capacity for information processing and storing into the same sized brain.

The brain is the heaviest tissue in the body, so birds have to keep their brains as small as possible in order to remain aerodynamically streamlined. They have a larger brain, relative to their body size, than their dinosaur ancestors. They need a complex brain to be able to carry out complex behaviour, including flight. To overcome the problem of weight, they evolved a special way of making new nerve cells in the brain when they are needed, an ability that is unique to birds among vertebrates and one that was not maintained in the evolution of mammals. Once mammals reach adulthood, they have a very limited capacity for making new nerve cells—as they age, they lose nerve cells without replacing them. Birds, on the other hand, can generate new nerve cells in adulthood[52] and this means they can increase the number of nerve cells in the brain when they are needed and decrease them when they are not needed. In Northern Hemisphere species that sing only in spring, the breeding season, the song nuclei are larger and have more nerve cells than during winter when they do not sing. They shrink in size when not needed and perhaps another area expands to take the place of the song nuclei. This time-sharing of brain capacity means a bird can keep the overall size and weight of its brain to a minimum. Seasonal increases and decreases in the number of nerve cells have also been seen in the hippocampal regions of food-storing birds,[53] where the size of the hippocampus changes with the season.[54] These changes are associated with peak times when it is necessary for the birds to remember where they stored their food.

Another important characteristic of the avian brain is the fact that the left and right hemispheres process information differently and also control a different set of behavioural responses. This characteristic is referred to as lateralisation, once thought to be present only in the human brain. Research on the domestic chicken has shown that many brain functions are lateralised.[55] For example, the left hemisphere is used by the chicken when it discriminates grains of food from similar, but inedible, small objects and the right hemisphere is used when the chicken is distracted by an unfamiliar stimulus. The right hemisphere is also used to control attack and copulation responses.

These differences between the left and right hemispheres can be seen in the way the bird uses its eyes to attend to different stimuli. This lateralisation of eye use comes about because most of the visual information from the bird's left eye goes to the right hemisphere, and from the right eye to the left hemisphere. The chicken tilts its head to look up with its left eye when scanning overhead for an aerial predator[56] and it examines a novel stimulus by looking with its left eye.[57] It can discriminate food grains from inedible objects when using the right eye but not the left eye, and it will attack when using its left eye but not its right eye.[58] The same lateralisation, at least for pecking at grain, has been shown in the pigeon.[59]

Lateralisation of the brain is also seen in songbirds and seems to be an essential part of their ability to recognise familiar songs sung by other birds and to produce their own songs. Although the same set of song nuclei is present in both hemispheres of the songbird's brain, only the set of song nuclei in the left hemisphere controls singing.[60] This dominance of the left hemisphere for song control has been found in all species of songbirds studied so far, except the zebra finch. In this species the right hemisphere plays a greater role in the production of song, although the left hemisphere still has some role.[61] The song nuclei are used not only to produce song but also to perceive song, and this perception of song is different in the left and right hemispheres.[62] Zebra finches use the right hemisphere to process information about the harmonics in individual syllables of songs to which the bird is listening, and the left hemisphere to process information about the whole song.[63] In other words, the right hemisphere attends to the details of a song, whereas the left hemisphere listens to the entire song and so is used to discriminate between familiar and unfamiliar songs.

The reason a brain is lateralised is not yet known, but we think it may increase the brain's capacity to process information.[64] In fact, lateralisation of the brain seems to have evolved very early in the vertebrate ancestors of birds—we know that reptiles, amphibians and even fish have lateralisation of the brain.[65] It is, thus, likely that the dinosaurs had brains that were lateralised to carry out different functions, even though each side of the brain may have looked the same. Of course, the exact functions that were lateralised in the ancestral birds may have been different from at least some of the lateralised functions of present-day birds—lateralised control of song was not present in the early birds—but some functions would have been the same. For instance, present-day fish, toads, lizards, birds and even some primates are more likely to attack a member of their own species (conspecific) seen on their left side than on their right side.[66] Toads are more likely to strike at prey on their right than on their left[67] and this is similar to the bird's use of the right eye for pecking at food, as shown in the chicken and the pigeon. Thus it seems that lateralisation of the brain is characteristic of vertebrates, including birds. As a generalisation, the left hemisphere is used for processing information that needs to be weighed up and considered in some detail before a response is given while the right hemisphere is used for rapid and immediate responses, as in attack.

Birds have retained this early evolving division of functions between the hemispheres. It would have been an advantage for them to do so because a brain that carries out different functions in each hemisphere would be lighter than one that is just as complex but does the same in both hemispheres that is, duplicates the activity. To have a light but 'intelligent' brain would be advantageous for flying.

Flightless again

Most modern birds can fly but in some habitats flight is not necessary for survival. In such habitats birds soon lose the capacity to fly, either completely or partially. The physical and energy demands of flight are a considerable biological investment and this explains why flightlessness evolves whenever these demands are relaxed. All flightless birds have evolved from ancestors that were able to fly.

Flightlessness evolves when too main conditions are met. First, there must be no need for the species to migrate to find food and warmer climatic conditions in order to survive and reproduce. Second, there must be no need to fly in order to escape a predator. Hence, flightlessness is more common in species living in warmer climates and in isolation from predators, particularly larger mammals that hunt them on the ground. These conditions occur most often on islands. New Zealand, for example, has a number of flightless species, all quite unrelated. The now extinct New Zealand owlet-nightjar was almost completely flightless. It was similar to the existing owlet-nightjars of Australia and New Guinea but had larger legs, adapted to living continuously on the ground. New Zealand also has a ground parrot, called the kakapo, which is largely nocturnal and runs with its wings outstretched to provide balance. In addition, New Zealand has the flightless weka, the takahe and the kiwi and, in the not-so-distant past, it had the large moas (several species including *Dinoris maximus* and *Euryapteryx* spp.) that evolved one to two million years ago. All these species evolved because New Zealand had no mammalian predators.

An earlier evolution of flightless birds occurred in South America 50 to 60 million years ago. Throughout the Tertiary period South America had no advanced predators. The carnivorous dinosaurs had become extinct and the mammalian carnivores had not yet reached South America. This allowed the evolution of a diverse group of birds, the *Phorusrhacos*. They were flightless and tall (up to 3 metres in height) but rather slightly built. Another ancient flightless bird was the giant *Diatryma* which inhabited the landmasses in the Northern Hemisphere not long after the dinosaurs became extinct. Some think it was a carnivore, stepping into the niche vacated by the extinct carnivorous dinosaurs, while others believe it was a herbivore.[68]

Becoming flightless has certain advantages. Flightless birds can afford to be larger than birds that fly and they can lay larger eggs. The moas stood 3 to 4 metres tall. They fed exclusively on plants, another adaptation made possible by being flightless. Digesting the leaves of plants requires a large appendage of the gut, called the caecum, containing bacteria that digest the cellulose in the plant material. The weight of this caecum would hinder flying and so it may have evolved only after the ancestors of moas became flightless. Only then could they use leaves as a source of food. Keeping the weight of the digestive system to a minimum may be one reason why plant eating is rare in birds that fly.[69]

Flightless birds can also afford to lay very large eggs; not only are the birds large themselves but their eggs can be large relative to their body size. Moas laid eggs about one hundred times larger than the egg of the domestic hen. The kiwi is not a large bird but it lays a very large egg relative to its body size. The egg takes as long as 30 days to form inside the bird's body and by that time it almost fills the abdominal cavity. The kiwi's egg size relative to its body size is much greater than that of the domestic hen, even though the hen can fly for only short distances (Figure 2.3). A kiwi could not possibly fly with the weight of its egg inside, even if it had wings. Laying a large egg passes on an advantage to the bird's offspring because the embryo obtains all its nutrients from the yolk inside the egg. So the hatchling is

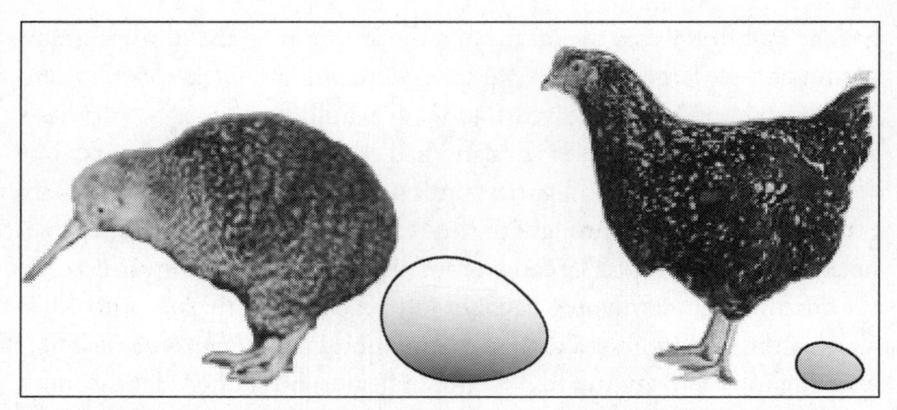

Figure 2.3 Egg size relative to adult body size. The egg of the kiwi (left) is much larger, relative to body size, than that of the domestic hen (right).

better nourished and larger, and its survival increased (see Chapter 5). This is another advantage of not having to fly.

With some clear advantages of flightlessness, it is not difficult to see why birds forfeit flying whenever and wherever they can. Their wings become small and vestigial. It is interesting to speculate why flightless birds did not evolve arms, hands and fingers in place of their wings; after all, their ancestors, the frogs, toads and reptiles, had well developed hands and fingers. Perhaps this re-evolution of the forelimbs was not required of birds because the beak had taken over the role of manipulating objects. The size and shape of the beaks of ancient birds varied greatly but all could be used to manipulate objects during feeding and other activities. Nevertheless, the equivalent hands may have evolved in some of the flightless birds; the large flightless *Titanus walleri*, for example, may have had claws that functioned as a hand to hold down struggling prey.

The extinct elephant birds (*Aepyornis maximus* and another six species) were even heavier than the moas, although not as tall. They evolved about the same time as the moas but on the island of Madagascar. Like moas, they ate the leaves of trees and laid huge eggs. Their ancestors, it is thought, flew to Madagascar and then evolved into flightless birds. Without major predators they were able to survive until humans arrived on the island and brought about their demise in the tenth century.[70]

The elephant bird laid enormous eggs, of about 8 to 9 litres capacity. But both its egg size and body size were rivalled by the thunderbirds (family Dromornithidae) which inhabited Australia from 25 million years ago to about 26 000 years ago. One member of this family (*Dromornis stirtoni*) is the largest bird ever known to have existed. It stood 3 metres high and weighed 500 kilograms. The origin and date of the Dromornithidae are uncertain. They may be related to the anseriformes, the geese, ducks and waterfowl.[71] Their gigantic beaks were used to crack open nuts or devour animal prey. We are not certain whether they were herbivores or carnivores. Stephen Wroe argues that their beaks were probably too large to serve only as nutcrackers and would have been better adapted for eating flesh.[72]

Another famous but extinct flightless bird is the dodo of Mauritius, to the east of Madagascar. Its extinction was caused by humans in the 17th century. Dodos, of turkey size, made an ideal meal for sailors. Hunting reduced their numbers and then pigs introduced to the island ate their eggs. Dodos derived from pigeons and doves (the Columbiformes). Their immediate ancestor is thought to have been a pigeon similar to the tooth-billed pigeon of Samoa, which spends much of its time on the ground although it can still fly. Pigeons, it seems, have a tendency to become flightless whenever possible, and the same is true of parrots.[73] This similarity between pigeons and parrots may not be accidental because, it is thought now that pigeons and parrots are quite closely related. Mauritius was also the home of a large, nocturnal, broad-billed parrot (*Lophopsittacus mauritianus*) which is now extinct. We have mentioned the flightless parrot of New Zealand and here we note that Australia too has a ground-living parrot (*Pezoporus wallicus*).

Rails have even more tendency than pigeons and parrots to become flightless. Numerous fossil records testify to this. More than half the various species of rails have evolved flightlessness and most have become waterbirds. Living in and on water leads to the adaptation, for swimming, of structures that were once used for flight. Penguins, for example, even swim underwater. There were ancient birds of the Cretaceous period that swam underwater in a similar manner. This change to life in and on water occurred in conjunction with many evolutionary changes in bone and muscle structure and in wing and feather construction.

We should not leave the topic of flightlessness without mentioning the largest flightless birds living today—the ratites. They include the ostrich of Africa, the rheas of South America, the emu of Australia, the cassowaries of Australia and New Guinea and the kiwi. All the ratites evolved strong legs for running to escape predators in open flat terrains. The evolution of these species is still a mystery but some scientists think they might all have evolved from a single, flightless species living on the landmass of Gondwana during the Cretaceous period.[74] As the continents of Africa, South America and Australia broke off from Gondwana and drifted apart, each population of ratite may have followed its own evolutionary course to give rise to the various ratites of today.[75] Other scientists believe that the present-day ratites all evolved from an ancestor that could fly which arrived at the various continents by air and evolved flightlessness in each locality. This hypothesis is supported, to some extent, by fossil ratites found in the Northern Hemisphere.

Broadly speaking, birds appear to take the opportunity to give up their ability to fly whenever possible. When they do, they lose some of their special adaptations for flight and acquire new functions to exploit new sources of food and to give their offspring a better start in life. At the same time, they become highly vulnerable to new predators entering their environment and so, as they become extinct one by one, they have come to symbolise the disastrous impact of humans on birds.[76] Theirs is, or was, a very special adaptation to a stable environment. Their disappearance carries a warning for all avian species. Survival and reproduction are very precarious in many bird species.

part II

THE LIFE CYCLE

chapter 3

CHOOSING A MATE

Two main ingredients for survival are distribution and adaptation. Spreading as far and wide as possible and adapting as well as possible to changes in the environment increases the chances of living a long time and producing many offspring. A bird that travels far afield but then finds no mate or not enough food to reproduce will not radiate—this means that it will not produce offspring to establish a viable population further afield than it had been before. To achieve wide distribution, successful reproduction must occur, not only during the lifetime of this one bird but among its offspring and their offspring as well. Successful reproduction is by no means easy or automatic.

It is one of the longest held myths about birds, and animals in general, that the life cycle always includes reproduction. In fact, a large number of individual birds never achieve reproductive status. They never mate, never have a brood of young to rear, never own a territory or defend a nest site. They are either not successful or die well before these processes come into play. Thus, the minority of birds that are successful raises a multitude of questions. Why do they succeed? What are the processes by which successful breeders raise offspring that will also generate one or more breeders? What is special about individuals or pairs that succeed not just in raising one brood, but a series of broods over a lifetime? Finding a suitable territory with adequate food supply and suitable nesting habitat is just one condition for success.[1] Another is choice of the right mate. Darwin

Figure 3.1 Found in Australia, black swans mate for life.

argued that mate choice was the second most important influence on survival. Choice of mate is very important in avian species. A good mate, one that is healthy, alert, assertive, resourceful and, where applicable, a good provider and tutor, will contribute significantly to a good outcome.

Why is mate choice of particular interest in avian species? Birds are unusual for two reasons. First, in birds we find examples of extensive parental care: some birds not only choose an appropriate location for the nest and build a structure that will control the temperature of the egg and the offspring, but they also care for the young long after hatching. Birds also frequently form long-lasting pair bonds[2] which is a very special behaviour in the animal kingdom (Figure 3.1). A few invertebrates and lower vertebrates have evolved some degree of care of a nest site and of their own offspring but these species rarely know joint parental care.[3] Even among mammals, pair bonds and joint parental care are relative oddities. According to Timothy Clutton-Brock,[4] only about 5 per cent of mammals, including gibbons, jackals, marmosets and certain mice species, form lifelong pair bonds or even short-term pair bonds, while nearly all avian species (more than 9000 species) pair-bond with a mate! That is, most bird species have a mate at one time or another, forming a relationship that goes beyond courtship and copulation. Choice of mate is thus an extensive topic in avian ethology.

While pair bonding is common in birds, there is enormous variation across species in the durability of pairs. Australian ravens and the albatross (*Diomedea* spp. and *Phoebetria* spp.) may well rank first among the most faithful of all species, by forming stable lifelong relationships that are broken only by the death of a partner. Both species are long-lived. The Eurasian eagle owl and the American bald eagle usually also pair for life. There are other known cases, such as tundra swans which almost never separate, and parrots, especially galahs and sulphur-crested cockatoos, which tend to pair-bond permanently. Other pair bonds may be fleeting or extend over several mating seasons. There are also those pairs that set up for a long duration but then separate. In the 1960s, J.C. Coulson developed the so-called incompatibility hypothesis.[5] The hypothesis argues that some bird pairs are incompatible and reproduce poorly when together even though they may both do well with a different mate. More recently, Paulo Catry and Robert Furness have provided examples that contradict Coulson's hypothesis. They observed great skuas and found that the abandoned males were simply poor providers for any partner. The female had found a better option for partnership, referred to as the 'better option hypothesis'.[6] Strategies for 'divorce' vary widely among species but presumably the ideal is to benefit the partners' overall reproductive success.[7]

It is possible that there are many more lifelong bonds in birds than we know at present. Longitudinal studies (research that follows individuals over a long period of time) are not yet available for a large range of species. One of the authors recently discovered that pair bonding in tawny frogmouths can occur over several seasons: a hand-raised couple bonded in the first year of life, produced an offspring and has been together now for five years since release.[8]

The newly available technique of DNA fingerprinting has made it possible to isolate the DNA and establish paternity reliably. Very simple methods of collecting a sample have made it also very attractive. Just a small speck of blood or a tiny strand of hair, skin or feather is needed for the analysis. This modern technique has revolutionised the entire field of reproductive biology.[9] Until such tests were used, it was often merely assumed that the bonded pair were the true biological parents of the brood they had raised. We now know that this is not so.

Both male and female birds are known to indulge in copulation outside their pair bond (extra-pair coition) producing fertile offspring for which the pre-established pair then cares. Extra-pair coition may be socially foisted on females or solicited by females.[10] Thus, true paternity can be relatively uncertain in a wide variety of species, including passerines, raptors, waterfowl and seabirds. Even among socially monogamous species, such as the short-tailed shearwater, extra-pair fertilisations do happen, although at a relatively low frequency.[11] Pied and collared flycatchers and starlings are known for their high rate of cuckoldry.[12] Sperm competition has also been shown in the zebra finch, the cattle egret, the bobolink and in swallows.[13] Sperm competition occurs after the female has mated with two males in quick succession and any one suitor's sperm could fertilise the egg. Bluetit males that indulge in extra-pair copulations have been shown to produce more fledglings than monogamous males in the same number of seasons.[14] Paired black-capped chickadee females visit other males despite having nest-mates. Their affairs 'on the side' with higher-ranking males produce offspring that are cared for by the female's partner.[15]

Superb fairy wrens, known cooperative breeders (see Chapter 4), have one of the highest known frequencies of extra-group matings. Peter Dunn and Andrew Cockburn have shown that females prefer males that have moulted and taken on their breeding plumage earlier than others. In fairy wrens, this time advantage of the early moulter has turned into a reproductive strategy. The longer the male keeps the breeding plumage the more matings he secures. Male superb fairy wrens that acquire early breeding plumage also begin to display earlier than others, in some cases several months before the onset of the breeding season.[16] In summary, females and males may initiate extra-pair copulations and may produce offspring in the nest cared for by a male or female that is not the biological parent.

Sexual dimorphism and mate choice

One of the enduring questions in avian ethology is how a partner is actually chosen. Research interest in mate choice has tended to focus on two variables—song and plumage. It is assumed that these contain special attributes that occur only in males during the breeding season and are thus specifically related to mate choice and reproduction. While this may be correct for many species, especially for those in the Northern Hemisphere, it is certainly not true for all. In a sense, the concentration on these two aspects is limiting because these special attributes are found only in species that are sexually dimorphic. Species that show little difference in appearance between the sexes (at least, as far as human eyes and our current state of knowledge can tell) presumably have to choose their partner by other means. Much of this is still unknown.

Sexual dimorphism refers to differences in appearance by sex—the size or coloration of the body may differ between the sexes. The capacity to sing may also be a trait of sexual dimorphism. There are species in which only the male sings and he does so only in the breeding season. The assumption is that this dimorphism is important in mate choice. There may be a number of reasons for sexual dimorphism: it may suggest a segregation of tasks in raising offspring or defending a territory, or it may be related to the fact that one sex is dominant in the process of selecting a mate. The most exaggerated sexual dimorphism occurs in those species in which several males compete to attract a female. The peacock's tail is an example of this: females choose the males with most eye-spots on the tail (see Plate 1).[17]

Sexual dimorphism is widespread among invertebrates, amphibians and many other genera. It may not be as widespread among birds as once thought although it is still proclaimed in a surprising number of books and articles. Most texts still suggest or imply that avian males, in general, are more beautiful, more active, more accomplished (in song for instance), stronger or bigger and more aggressive than females. They also say that males are not usually involved in incubating eggs or raising the young.[18]

Generalisations of this kind (often resulting from human attitudes to gender) are rather unhelpful. Although these views hold true for some species, there are countless examples that disprove them. Great skuas, for instance, are fighting birds in which the female, rather than the male, will attack and even kill another bird to take over its territory and partner. The female budgerigar, although the same size as the male, is the more aggressive of the two. She will maim and kill a female competitor for a breeding site or will chastise or kill an unruly male who makes advances when she does not desire it.[19] Spotted sandpipers have organised life around a dominant female who keeps several males around her. The female will not hesitate to fight for her 'harem' and site even if this means serious injury to herself or to the other female bird.

Females are not always smaller either. In many species, males and females are of equal size. In some cases, female birds are larger than their male counterparts. Among most birds of prey (eagles, falcons, hawks, kites and owls) the female is larger and heavier than the male. In the Australian wedge-tailed eagle, the female may weigh nearly twice as much as the male (some small adult males may weigh about 3 kilograms while the largest female that Kaplan has had in rehabilitation weighed just over 5.6 kilograms). The same is true of the martial eagle, the largest of Africa's many raptor species. The male would lose a fight with a female.

This sexual dimorphism in favour of the female among most birds of prey in the world may have developed for several reasons. First, the female would be better able to protect the young from the male by being larger. Second, it may be connected with the male giving up food for his offspring when he takes a catch to the nest. The female takes the prey from the male and tears off small pieces for the chick. The male may not give up his prey voluntarily if she is not able to assert her prowess over him. We have seen eagle females raise their neck feathers in a low-level and potentially aggressive posture when the male brings food. He is being warned in advance that not giving it up will result in conflict. Third, there are examples across a range of vertebrate species of carnivorous males that consume their own offspring or those of a competitor. The protective role of the female may not be obvious in their behaviour today but it could have been important in the past, and so be a reason for the evolution of the size difference. In the magnificent frigatebird too, females are larger and heavier than the males and the same function of protecting the brood might well be attributed to female frigatebirds. So, the female being larger than the male is not a unique feature of birds of prey.

There may be other reasons why, in some species, the female is larger. The male might abscond if given half a chance. Pairing with females in those cases may be based on the male meeting several criteria: providing evidence of good health and of well developed skills in securing food, and offering evidence that he will feed the female. We have also noted that plumage differences between males and females are minimal, if there are any at all, when the size difference between the sexes is large.

Females do not always incubate the eggs. The emu male incubates the eggs, usually of several females, and then guards his chicks until they are seven months old. In another flightless bird, the New Zealand kiwi, incubation takes eleven weeks (the longest of any bird) and is done by the male. In quite a number of species, other variations occur. For instance, in the black-winged stilt, the female initiates breeding by invading the male's feeding territory, but she incubates alone; with the vulturine guinea fowl, the female incubates the eggs but the male broods and feeds the young for the first few days.

There are many other examples of bird species where male and female share the roles of incubation and parenting equally. In these cases, there are fewer or no differences in plumage between male and female and also their size and weight are about equal.

When males are more colourful than females—and this actually applies only to a small range of avian species—two conditions usually apply: the nest is built in relatively exposed terrain and the female alone incubates the eggs. Mostly, the two conditions function together and it is of great advantage for the female to be camouflaged from predators by being small or inconspicuous. In species in which the nest is concealed, either because it is in a cavity (tree or dirt hollow) or disguised (perhaps among dense foliage or by the elaborate design and fabric of the nest), the male and female plumage is usually identical (independent of whether parenting is shared). In those cases, both male and female can afford to be brightly coloured (for example, rainbow bee-eaters, toucans, parakeets). In nocturnal species, on the other hand, both male and female are usually drab-coloured, as in nightjars (including tawny frogmouths), owls and the three nocturnal parrots of the world.

Brilliantly coloured males usually have the singular distinction of doing little if anything for their offspring. Once such a male has fertilised the female he plays no further part in reproduction. There are degrees of social uselessness. In some avian species the males will attempt to mate with as many other females as possible. Such a male will leave all the work

Figure 3.2 The peacock male does not just display the front of his feathers to draw attention to his body, but the rear as well.

of nest building, incubation and rearing of the young to the female and take no interest in his offspring at all. The highly prized male birds of paradise with their extravagant plumage and courtship displays are typical of this form of mating. These males work very hard and practise for years before they perfect their display and are able to allure the females into a trance-like state. They dazzle them with their plumage and with a light show reflected from their irridescent feathers. But once they have mated, they drop the female entirely and turn their attention to the next possible conquest. The much shyer male bowerbirds spend all their energy building bowers that serve no purpose in raising the young. The bower is used for displaying and mating only.[20] There are a few exceptions. Some males of other species will protect a female during incubation and then disappear once the young have hatched. This is true of the black-winged stilt and the woodcock.

Plumage colour may signal individual identification, dominance status or mating readiness. However, in the species where plumage colouration differs between male and female, males tend to use their plumage to attract a mate. Indeed, the brightly coloured plumage of males and/or their elaborate song during the breeding season is said to have evolved as a result of competition between males for female favours. This is called the female choice hypothesis.

The female choice hypothesis argues that females will respond more to a male if he is brightly coloured, or builds the best bower, performs the best dance or sings the best song. This selection process fosters greater and greater exaggeration of those features to which females seemed particularly attracted, whether it be colour, a particular display performance or a song, thus increasing the sexual dimorphism over time (Figure 3.2). Sometimes the male features are so exaggerated that they become a handicap, as in the case of the peacock's train.[21] Exaggerated sexual differences are found more often in species of the Northern Hemisphere, in temperate zones, and also in subtropical and forested regions.

The differences between success or failure of a male in attracting a female may be very specific. In canaries, for instance, the distinct canary whistles have been shown to be of no great importance to females. Instead there is a particular trill which females prefer and, apparently, the winning competitor is the one with most two-note trills and the fastest runs. The two-note trill can be produced sixteen to twenty times within a single second.[22] Thus, auditory cues can also be very important in some species as a way of selecting a mate. Generally, it seems that female mate choice is one of the few counterbalances for a female in a very unequal contest. After mating, she will usually build a nest alone, incubate alone and raise the brood alone. Given that she has all these daunting tasks before her, she may as well 'shop for the best'.

In some cases, it seems that plumage colour becomes more important than song as a determinant for female choice.[23] This may be true of the vermilion flycatchers, a species in which both male and female sing but their plumage is very dissimilar. Recognition of sex, in some species, may occur exclusively by visual cues—plumage colour or eye colour. For instance, the red breast alone of the male European robin functions as a signal. Even a model placed on a branch will provoke an attack when the breast is red, but not if the red colour is missing.[24] In experiments with caged pied flycatchers, it was found that sex recognition was based purely on colour. When a pied flycatcher female was painted in the colours of a male, all other males treated the bird as if it were male. When a male was painted as a female, all others treated him as a female.[25] This identification was maintained even when the song of the male was played in conjunction with the male bird painted as a female.[26] It is worth noting here that some male pied flycatchers naturally have plumage coloration that is quite close to that of the female. In free-ranging birds, males will treat such birds as if they were female and may even engage in courtship rituals towards them. Males equipped with a plumage colour that mimics that of a female can accrue territorial advantages. They may invade a territory without encountering the aggression of a competing male and may succeed in staying.[27]

An unusual twist to the female choice hypothesis has been given by J. Briskie and R. Montgomerie, who reported on sexual selection in birds based on the absence or presence of a penis (called the 'intromittent organ' in birds).[28] In about 97 per cent of bird species, males do not have a penis. It is thought that all avian males probably had a penis once but, over evolutionary time, gradually lost the organ. Today, only about 246 species of modern birds sport a penis. Among them are all waterfowl, screamers, cracids and flightless birds such as kiwis, ostriches, emus, rheas and cassowaries. The remainder (about 9000 avian species) have lost it.

Briskie and Montgomerie proposed that a penis is a tool to force copulation onto an unwilling female. Forced copulations have been observed in waterfowl.[29] If the reason for forced copulation is to have more offspring, male birds have a disadvantage.[30] Because female birds ovulate and fertilise just one egg at a time, they have the ability to abort an embryo without having invested much energy in it. An egg may take a day or two to develop and its abortion is a minor physiological stress, as compared to mammals with their long gestation periods or reptiles with their simultaneous fertilisation of many eggs. Hence, male birds gain little advantage by forced insemination since the female can desert an unwanted egg within a matter of days.

If all a penis is good for is to force insemination, then the penis must be useless if such a strategy does not work. Sperm can be transferred simply by the joining of the vents (cloaca) of both birds. Those species that have retained a penis, so Briskie argues, are ones in which the female investment in producing an egg, relative to body size, is very great, as in emus, ostriches or kiwis.[31] While interesting, this hypothesis is not entirely convincing in our opinion, because so far we do not know whether it can be upheld for all 246 species with intromittent organs.

Without doubt, birds have developed some of the most elaborate courtship rituals among vertebrates. One of the reasons for this may well be that copulation based on a cloacal meeting (called a cloacal kiss) requires collaboration because the cloaca is located below the tail feathers in both sexes. The male, sitting on the female's back, must bring his cloaca half-way round to meet with hers. This is possible only if she raises her cloaca sideways to align it with his. The female of most avian species may be considered highly successful in keeping a good measure of control of her own fertility if it is her collaboration that leads to successful fertilisation.

Hidden sexual dimorphism also exists, meaning that some dimorphism is hidden from human eyes. Birds with little evidence of sexual dimorphism may still make decisions about mate choice on visual cues. The starling is a case in point. Males and females look alike but there are cues in the refraction of light on the feathers that are revealed only under ultraviolet light. While we are unable to see ultraviolet light and cannot really imagine what its influence may do to the avian female's perception of the male's feathers, it is conceivable that the irridescence of his feathers is enhanced. In budgerigars, the patches on the side of the head reflect ultraviolet light and the female can see it. It could well be that we make some incorrect assumptions (though at times only in degree), about the visual signalling that occurs in mate choice because we read colour only from the perception of human eyes and thus not in the ultraviolet range.[32] Staffan Andersson called ultraviolet differences in plumage the first, but probably not the last, example of hidden sexual dimorphism in birds. He and his colleagues found that blue tits in the wild prefer mates with high ultraviolet-reflecting plumage.[33] Recent laboratory studies on ultraviolet vision have confirmed this role independently. Andrew Bennett and his colleagues conducted a series of experiments with zebra finches allowing the female to see the male through a series of filters of two types—ultraviolet-blocking filters and ultraviolet-transmitting filters. The female strongly preferred viewing the male through the ultraviolet-transmitting filters.[34] For the first time there is also evidence that some males may choose females solely on the radiance provided under ultraviolet light, as is the case of the blue tit. The blue tit male showed clear preference for a female with brighter ultraviolet reflectance.[35] Choice of partner may be guided by criteria that we may not see or have not yet discovered.

Even if there are forms of hidden sexual dimorphism that require further exploration, it can be hypothesised that sexual dimorphism disappears almost entirely in species where rearing the young is a shared role or in species where the male does most of the work. Sexual dimorphism is not limited to avian species but, phylogenetically, is a very old form of fostering recognition of potential mating partners. What is new in birds is the shared parenting role of the majority of species and the *lack* of sexual dimorphism in a large number of species.

Putting on a show

Plumage colour is often not enough to impress a female and the male interested in enticing as many females as possible may need to advertise his presence and his qualities by a range of activities, vying with other males for female privileges. There are exceptions, however, where females do the displaying and the males the choosing—for example, the red-necked phalarope.[36] Courtship displays are thought to have evolved as a set of social and cultural rules to help in selecting a mate and in cementing pair bonds. Courtship rituals may determine the partner, regulate the timing of sexual readiness and also strengthen the bond of a bonded pair.[37] Courtship displays are often carried out by a single male. Courtship dances are always carried out by a pair. The difference between the two forms of display is enormous. In the former (male only) the male will usually take little interest in his offspring and be polygamous. In courtship dances, male and female cement a strong pair bond and, often, a lifelong commitment to each other.

Location

Courtship rituals, whether solo or couples, may take place in the air, on water, on tree branches in the forest or on the ground.

Many birds of prey have evolved elaborate courtship displays in the air. Sometimes these are solo, as in the snowy owl, which is one of the largest and most powerful owls in the world, with a wingspan of about 1.5 metres. The courtship flight, by the male only, involves a dangerous endurance feat of holding the wings upright in a V-shape during fast flight, causing undulating movements and demanding great muscular control. Osprey males also perform an aerial daredevil feat. First the male flies rapidly upwards displaying a captured food item (such as a fish) and then plunges some 300 metres downwards with wings folded. Males in species as different as roadrunners, dollarbirds and woodcock perform aerial displays. The courtship flight of male dollarbirds is a distinct rolling flight accompanied by shrill screeches. Roadrunner males make flight patrols over and over. In addition to the aerial display, the roadrunner will also come to the ground and continue by raising his crest and flicking his tail while cackling and pattering his feet on the ground, alternating this with bowing his head and cooing. The male fairy wren may need to fight over his territory but, when successful, the victorious bird will perform a victory display flight, puffing itself up and returning straight to the nest. The woodcock is one of very few species that restricts its courtship flight to twilight periods. It has a flight pattern called roding which is conspicuous and unique among birds in Britain but similar to the display of the roadrunner. This involves a sustained and exaggerated flight above the tree canopy, with the altitude of flight decreasing as the light fades, accompanied by growling, sneezing and croaking sounds. A polygynous or promiscuous female may reply from the forest floor by making odd sounds, called sneeze notes, or she may fly up to him and travel alongside him before they land together and then mate. Flights may last up to twenty minutes but, on average, are six minutes long. This is unlike the Eurasian woodcock's American cousin (*Scolopax minor*) which displays largely on the ground in woodland clearings or woodland edges (much like the lyrebird), and only then it flies up vertically, delivers a song and performs a circular display flight.[38]

The blue-footed booby (Plate 5) also has an aerial display although it consists of little more than flying over his territory and, before landing near the female, displaying his bright blue feet. This display is a little odd because there is no sexual dimorphism in blue-footed boobies. The sexes look quite similar and the female also has blue feet. We can only surmise that the feet are important to the display. The feet are endowed with plenty of blood vessels to maintain a high temperature and the webbing between the toes is used by either parent during incubation of the eggs. The chicks, once hatched, then sit for an entire month on their parents' feet before their own temperature control develops and they can step off.

Some species display on the ground, where the individual male usually has a particular place for display. The display area goes under a number of different names—'booming field', 'drumming ground', 'hill', 'strutting ground' or 'lek'. They all signify the same area, a posturing scene where the bird's trysts and tourneys are performed. This dancing place is kept free of debris and usually remains occupied and defended by the individual for the entire period of the breeding season.

Among the solo ground-performers, the bowerbird males build seemingly useless bowers and decorate them with coloured objects, often with one colour dominating, to attract the females. The bower of the tooth-billed bowerbird is particularly elaborate in size and number of objects displayed.[39] The actual display by bowerbird males begins only once a female has come near the bower. The male's rhythmic opening and closing of one wing after the other, stretching each wing over its head and bobbing the head as it does so, attracts the female. This visual display is accompanied by shot-like sounds and the combined auditory and visual performance makes the female sexually receptive. Lyrebirds are famous for their dancing displays (Figure 3.3) as well as their versatile vocal displays. These vocalisations contain beautiful musical sequences as well as exquisitely mimicked sequences of other bird sounds and even car horns, chainsaws, horses, dogs and many other animate and inanimate objects, all strung together to make a statement and attract a female.[40] The chaffinch male also displays on his own, showing a series of lopsided crouches, singing and other antics. The male magnificent frigatebird extends his red throat sac accompanied by rattles of the feathers and the beak. Perhaps the most spectacular use of feathers in display is that of the peacock with its tail feathers fanned out like a wheel, shimmering with each new turn of the body. Apart from its irridescent green and blue colours, the peacock's tail has hundreds of eye-spots, patterns that mimic eyes (ocelli), all appearing to be looking towards the centre, the body of the peacock. When the peacock shakes his tail feathers the ocelli vibrate and move, dazzling the female (Plate 1).

Most display grounds are circular and less than a metre across but there are substantial variations, especially in species that display communally such as the frigatebird and the sage grouse. Sage grouse may occupy an arena up to 200 metres wide and three-quarters of a kilometre long, containing as many as 400 to 500 resident cocks.[41] The arena is so large not only because of the number of occupants but also because, within this space, each cock has his own private area. The spacing between the male birds may be as great as 10 metres or as small as 5 metres. And this organisation is not random. There are master cocks and sub-cocks, and even

Figure 3.3 The lyrebird's wings, spread in this spectacular shape, gave the bird its name—they resemble a lyre, a musical instrument of ancient Greece.

guard-cocks. The master cock gets most of the mating privileges but there is a limit to how many matings he can have in a day, so some matings are passed on to sub-cocks.

Finally, some birds display exclusively in trees. Among the most spectacular solo performances are the displays of the riflebird, one of 43 species of the birds of paradise. The male Victoria's riflebird will choose a sunny, exposed part of the rainforest and rhythmically display his tail or wing feathers, performing an intricate set of body movements, feet firmly on the branch, with plumage flashing in the sun, that will attract a female to come close for inspection. When she does so, he proceeds with his display by half folding his wings around her (without touching her) in rapid succession of left and then right wing in such a way that the female becomes quite engulfed in the courtship ritual. The raggiana bird of paradise with its striking head colouration of yellow and irridescent green displays by fanning out his dazzling long maroon feathers and allowing them to stream down. The much smaller superb bird of paradise is largely black but at the time of his courtship performance displays a throat shield of metallic green-blue feathers by moving his upper body from side to side in a sunny display spot in a tree. The male palm cockatoo, found only at the very tip of Australia's tropical north and in New Guinea, also displays in a tree. His display is perhaps one of the most unusual because it involves tool use—he advertises himself by drumming a stick on the tree (see also Chapter 10). The village weaver male uses a wing and head-pointing display to attract a female's attention to himself and to the nest he has built.

Some species develop fixed places that may well be ancestral. For instance, sage grouse continue to use the same strutting ground even if a road is built through it. The displays of the birds of paradise also have a fixed address so it has been easy for the Papuans to continually replenish their supply of the spectacular feathers of the birds. While the greater birds of paradise have dancing trees rather than ground leks, they return to the same branches every year and hence make it easy for the locals to find and kill them.

Courtship dances and pair rituals

Many performances are not solo but in unison with the female. These are the famous courtship dance displays. It would seem more appropriate to speak of mutual mate choice in the case of such pair performances.

The dances are performed with little variation between individual performers and involve patterns of behaviour that are quite distinctive. Many of them present elaborate choreography performed in a highly stylised or stereotyped manner. Usually there are several phases to a dance. In 1914 Julian Huxley first described the extraordinary and complex mating display of the great crested grebe. It involves the courting pair in a complex ritual of precision swimming. It begins with synchronised skimming across the surface of a lake, diving at the same time and then rising together with weeds in their beaks and assuming an upright posture by treading water while they face each other.[42] The courtship choreography of the western grebe also includes a 'weed dance' in which the partners give weeds to each other and both may hold a weed in the beak simultaneously.[43] Many other waterbirds boast complex courtship displays on water, such as the great northern diver, a most spectacular-looking duck with its bold black and white patterning in stripes, pearls and dots. Its appearance is, perhaps, surpassed only by its very haunting call. It is at home in North America and Scandinavia. Norse legend has it that, when a flock was calling overhead, it was following souls to heaven.

Dance types vary from one species to another but, overall, they are very similar to those that have evolved in human societies. There are static forms of dance involving only the upper part of the body, as in the solo posturing of gannets, including bobbing and swaying of the head and the 'pumping' up and down of the belly used by many species of pigeons and doves. Then there are circular dances, thought to be the oldest human dance style. Here a bird may take the lead to run around a tree in a follow-the-leader style, going faster and faster until the female, following the male, finally stops and consents to mate. In rose-coloured starlings, the male circles the female in crouching position with short, quick steps until she joins in and they mate. Albatross females may be ringed by several males. Then there are elaborate line dances that involve a number of dancers, as in shelducks.[44] Finally, a series of place-changing dances have been described for partridges and razorbills. These are so complex that their performance would require extensive memorising.[45]

Courtship displays in trees are not just the province of the male riflebirds and other male birds of paradise. The topknot pigeon is an Australian rainforest species that is a little larger than a domestic pigeon but of very different appearance; it rarely if ever comes to the ground so the courtship display takes place in a tree. The male lands on a branch near the female, half spreads his wings and tail and holds his body erect, approaching the female. With crests fully erect, the birds intertwine their necks. There is also a bowing action that is unique to the display of the topknot pigeon.

Some of the most acrobatic and breathtaking pair displays are those that take place in the air. Flight shows are a feast to the eye and acrobatic in the sense that they could be dangerous to birds executing a particular figure. Birds of prey are the true masters of aerial displays. The courtship flight by Bateleur eagles involves locking claws in flight and rolling like a windmill while hurtling at back-breaking speed towards the ground. This has also been observed in sea eagles, in the peregrine and the brown falcon. But not only birds of prey give aerial displays: raven pairs perform aerial displays together, interlocking their feet.

Courtship displays are by no means limited to a dance but may involve elaborate displays or actions of the bill. Ravens hold each other's bills in a lengthy 'kiss'. Courtship displays may resemble the behaviour of nestlings begging for food or that of parents providing food for nestlings. It has been suggested that this is the source of some ceremonies and rituals, such as wing quivering in currawongs, bill fencing in albatrosses, or movements as if to regurgitate food in doves and pigeons.[46] Herring gull courtship involves mock feeding. In laughing gulls, food begging is a prelude to copulation and here feeding and copulation are very obviously associated.

There is also a set of displays and ceremonies referred to as 'ceremonial gaping'. Ceremonial gaping of the beak occupies an interesting and even ambiguous position because gaping is also found in plumage display, dancing, food begging and threat. Gaping is related to plumage displays by its display of colours. The interior of a bird's beak may be very colourful or striking and so contribute to the dazzling courtship display. Red-breasted mergansers gape in courtship displays revealing the brilliant red interior of the bill.[47]

Ceremonial gaping is more common among birds that live near water than among land birds. Seabirds are not brightly coloured and it is thought that visual displays of colour may at times be limited to revealing the inside of the beak. Yet visual displays may be more effective than vocal displays because of the ongoing high background noise of the surf. Shag and cormorants gape revealing a bright gamboge yellow. In kittiwakes, the gape is a lurid orange-red. North Atlantic cormorants and southern cormorants exhibit the brilliant yellow interior of their mouth, but they emit few vocal signals, as if to suggest that the pounding of the surf would make this ineffective. This form of gaping is sometimes considered a muted vocalisation.

Gaping may also serve as an identification of sex and dominance. It is used in courtship displays, as if showing a membership card. It seems to be important in sex identification in the rhinoceros hornbill, where the male mouth is black and the female's flesh-coloured, as Darwin noted.[48] Ravens gape in courtship displays and threat displays. The dominance of a raven is revealed by the colour of the interior of the beak. The gape is pink in young males and black or maroon-coloured in adult and

Figure 3.4 The beginning of a threat display of a tawny frogmouth. The beak is half-open and the bird watches intently, pupils dilated.

dominant males in the group. A black gape shows credentials of seniority. These markings are secondary sex markers but they may develop before full sexual maturity. Bernd Heinrich described the case of a tamed male raven that grew up in captivity and tended to rule the house. This bird apparently developed the black interior of his beak well before sexual maturity. Both in behaviour and gape colouration, he was very clearly a male who, for lack of opposition, was the ruler of the roost.[49]

There are also gaping or yawn-displays that have been observed in Japanese swamp warblers, blackbirds, tree sparrows and others. While the phylogenetic roots of this behaviour are not always clear, there is a threat component in some species. For instance, barn owl males gape in mutual courtship displays but also use gaping, usually combined with hissing, as threat displays. Similarly, gaping has been observed in Australian tawny frogmouths (Figure 3.4), in dollarbirds and kookaburras, and most birds of prey.[50] Gaping is often a sign of the dual flight/fight response that is also found in snakes, such as the pink-mouthed green tree snake of India, in lizards (such as the frilled-necked lizard of Australia) and in monitors. The mouth is opened wide as a menace enhanced by brilliant colouration. The wide-open menace display of the mouth is a phylogenetically very old expression.

The involvement of the beak in courtship can be seen in the elaborate gift-giving ceremonies developed by some species. The male European robin brings titbits for the female which she then consumes. The kookaburra male also has to present an edible gift to his potential partner but he will not give it up until she has emitted a specific call of approval.

Perhaps the most dramatic exchange of gifts is that of peregrine falcons. Here too the male has to provide food but, instead of landing and handing the food to the female, he takes it high up into the air. The peregrine female's task is then to take the prey from the male in mid-flight. The only way she can achieve this is by rolling over and flying on her back, with feet outstretched upwards, at which point he drops the prey into her talons and she then rights herself and flies off with the gift. This is quite a dangerous procedure and puzzling in so far as it seems that the female's fitness is tested here more than the male's willingness to part with food.

The meanest and most cautious of these gift-giving ceremonies is probably that exercised by the roadrunner. Here the male also obtains food for the female he wants to attract and proceeds to display it. However, he is cautious: she has to mate with him first and only then, after mating, is he willing to relinquish the gift to her! Courtship feeding may chiefly serve to strengthen and maintain pair bonds but, as in the case of roadrunners, may also maintain dominance patterns.

The sheer range, complexity and diversity of rituals suggest that many species are governed by strict rules of social conduct that have become ritualised and species-specific. Displays may have the function of ensuring adherence to same-species pairing and making individual recognition easier. Birds need to pass on their genes. They also need to ensure they have the maximum safety and food supply for their own survival, as well as that of their offspring. For these reasons, the choice of a mate is of great importance.

chapter 4

REPRODUCTION

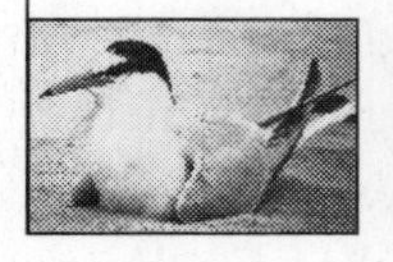

Reproduction in birds is not simple. The life of birds, especially small birds, is fraught with dangers and potential mishaps. We need to understand why particular individuals (and species) survive better than others, why some reproduce and not others. In some cases, this knowledge is needed urgently since it has become apparent that many formerly abundant species are declining in numbers. Many bird species are on the brink of extinction, or soon will be. Much of this chapter is based on what we know of birds living in a world that is largely intact ecologically. However, the reality is that humans have intercepted almost all stages of the life cycle in birds and they have often altered conditions to the extent that they are no longer optimal or natural for birds.

We have little evidence as to what might influence breeding success and the survival of offspring. In great tits, life in general and breeding success in particular seems largely due to chance.[1] Climatic conditions alone can be responsible for levels of breeding activity and survival of the young in any particular season. However, simple one-to-one relationships between breeding and climatic conditions can be difficult to establish. In great tits, for example, it could not be established that breeding success was related to any single specific factor of the environment.

For many species, surviving to the age of sexual maturity and breeding readiness is already the exception rather than the rule, no matter how healthy the birds may be at the time of fledging. Collared flycatchers and pied flycatchers have a staggering annual death rate (attrition rate) of nearly 78 per cent. The majority do not reach breeding age. Of those that remain alive, only a portion will engage in pairing and reproducing. Indeed, less than one-quarter of any generation contributes fledglings for the next generation. In addition, humans have made it increasingly hard for a vast range of species to find appropriate breeding places. From one year to the next, a specific plot of wood may simply disappear and the number of applicants for nest sites outstrip the availability of suitable housing. Birds that could be breeding might not get a chance to do so. They might not even find a partner.

Despite the low number of active breeders in any given generation, the few birds that do breed may produce enough young to replace not only themselves but all the other non-reproducing individuals.[2] Breeding is thus not the rule but the exception. This in itself does not tell us whether numbers of birds of one generation are replenished in the next. Remarkably, in pied flycatchers, fewer than 25 per cent of breeding birds are capable of replenishing the entire population for the next generation.[3] There may also be an element of chance determining which birds breed.

Environmental conditions aside, among the few real indicators of breeding success is longevity. In Eurasian magpies longevity is apparently an important factor influencing reproductive success because a long life may provide more opportunities to reproduce. Although this may seem obvious, the important point is that longevity itself is not simply due to chance. It tells us something about the individual bird, its health, skills, experience and even habitat.[4]

Choosing a nesting site

Birds are very special when it comes to rearing their chicks. Unlike the majority of mammals, most avian species provide a real home for their young. If we think of herd animals, such as ungulates or elephants, the young are dropped to the ground and have to stand up and walk with the mother usually within hours of birth. There is not much room for quiet and protected development. Some precocial species (i.e. birds that are born already covered with down and able to move about), such as ducks, chickens, turkeys and other fowl, share the fate of the newly born elephant but the majority of avian species do not. Rodents, rabbits and canine species may develop burrows and dens but there are relatively few examples in the world of mammals that rival the elaborate strategies of birds to accommodate their brood.

Finding a place to rear offspring is subject to rules and regulations, and depends on suitable habitat and the right seasonal conditions. For sedentary species (that is, those that do not migrate) the very idea of breeding depends on having a secure territory that fulfils four equally important criteria. First, at the time of planned nesting, the territory must be free of competing other members of the species and other closely related competing species. Species segregation was discovered by David Lack in the 1940s. The theory argues that closely related species segregate in their habitat to ensure a greater chance of reproductive success by reducing the need to compete.[5] Second, the territory should be large enough to provide sufficient food for the brood. Third, the area for nesting should not be infested with predators. The presence of too many potential predators risks nesting failure. We call this 'predatory balance', meaning the relative number of predators that can forage in the same territory and still meet their food requirements: the requirements of the predators must not exceed the available prey.

Finally, the microhabitat that the bird selects must suit the physiological endurance range of the parent birds, eggs and nestlings. Physiological ecology is the study of a bird's interaction with its environment and looks at humidity, air temperature, exposure to the sun (radiation), air quality (gaseous composition) and wind.[6] A wrong choice by the bird or changing weather conditions can dehydrate the egg. An increase in humidity or lack of humidity may affect the osmosis and respiration of the embryo. The wrong concentration of oxygen and carbon dioxide in an enclosed nest can lead to stress and the death of the nestlings, as can exposure to heat and cold beyond the tolerance of the species. These are all important factors in breeding success. They may influence a bird's choice of site for a nest, the nest construction type and parental behaviour during incubation.[7]

Parasitism

Some avian species have found it beneficial to give up the idea of raising young themselves and instead deposit their eggs in someone else's nest (this is called 'interspecific brood parasitism').[8] These are the cuckoos, the honeyguides and the cowbirds of the world. The cuckoos are a relatively large family of 136 species which have somewhat unjustly been thought of as bird parasites *par excellence*. In fact, less than 40 per cent of them (53 species) actually do so. The majority of cuckoos, such as the American greater road-runner and the Australian pheasant coucal, rear their own chicks. By contrast, all eighteen species of honeyguides, all five cowbird species and a variety of other birds, such as the whydah, are always parasitisers.[9]

The hosts are often relatively small passerine birds whose own clutch of eggs may be removed by the invading bird. Or, if the hosts do not notice the substitute or additional egg, the bigger 'guest' chick, when hatched, will heave the competing host chicks from the nest and to their death. Fairy wrens, for instance, regularly accept parasitism by Horsefield's bronze-cuckoo.[10] Some cuckoos (such as the Horsefield's bronze-cuckoo) are specialists in that they choose only a discrete group of possible hosts, but others are generalists—the brown-headed cowbird regularly parasitises 50 host species and may at times make use of up to 200 different avian host species.[11]

Although cuckoo chicks are often larger than the host chicks, there is usually some correlation of size between parasite and host. Cowbirds, for instance, are successful generalists because they are relatively small birds and thus have a wide variety of host species from which to choose. The brown-headed cowbird is only 18 centimetres in size. The Horsefield's bronze-cuckoo is 17 centimetres. For them, to parasitise birds such as fairy wrens, which vary in size from 11 to 20 centimetres, is therefore logical. Relatively few cuckoo species parasitise the nests of large birds. One of the exceptions is the channel-billed cuckoo which occurs in Indonesia, New Guinea and Australia. It parasitises large species such as currawongs which are 40 to 50 centimetres in length. The channel-billed cuckoo is about 60 centimetres in size.

Why would birds allow their nests to be parasitised? Earlier theories have suggested that the host birds simply do not notice—that cuckoos have exploited an evolutionary niche by adapting to hosts in such a manner that the hosts have not caught up. This is called the 'evolutionary lag hypothesis'. There are good reasons why a host would not notice that the nest has been parasitised, even after only brief absences from the nest when feeding. Cuckoos have developed specialised egg-laying behaviour.[12] A cuckoo may remove a host's egg from the nest and then deposit her own so that the number of eggs remains the same. And the eggs of many cuckoo species look so much like those of their hosts that detection of the exchange is difficult if not impossible, although this is not true of all host–parasite relationships. Some cuckoos do not mimic the host eggs very well. Third, a cuckoo has potential host nests under constant surveillance during the breeding season and the female cuckoo lays her egg when her host lays hers. It is timed very precisely. In fact, some female cuckoos need no more than 10–40 seconds to remove a host egg and lay their own in its place.[13] The time period during which the host female could detect the foreign egg being laid in her nest is thus extremely small.

Other theories propose a kind of pay-off for the host species by allowing a few nests to be parasitised, leaving the remaining conspecific nests alone.[14] Yet another argues that the costs of acceptance and rejection have to be weighed against each other.[15] For instance, in cases where the hosts have resisted being parasitised, the adult cuckoos have returned and retaliated by destroying the nest of the ungracious hosts. This has been observed in the parasitic relationship between the Eurasian magpie as host, and the great spotted cuckoo.[16] Retaliative behaviour by parasites could ensure that the host populations do not become fixed in a strategy of always rejecting the intruders.[17]

The destruction of nests and broods

Parasites such as cowbirds sometimes choose not to parasitise a specific host nest but merely to prevent the host brood from surviving. To do this, both male and female cowbirds will at times go to the nests of their potential hosts and puncture the eggs with their beaks[18] or they will actually eat the eggs of their hosts. It is thought that this behaviour limits food competition between species and thus gives their own offspring in the same territory a better chance of survival. In other words, parasitising birds may at times cull reproduction in their host species as an additional insurance for the survival of their own offspring.[19]

Another strategy that, presumably, also maximises breeding success by a species is to ensure that competitors with similar feeding requirements are not encouraged or permitted to set up nests in their nesting territory. We have seen pied currawongs that are intolerant of magpie-larks in their nesting territory. Australian magpie-larks build their nests with mud, the pair usually acting swiftly to ensure its completion before it sets hard or cracks. One particular pair of currawongs waited until the magpie-larks had nearly completed the nest and then moved in and, with their strong beaks, managed to destroy the nest completely before the pair of magpie-larks returned. The magpie-larks were incensed and gave incessant alarm calls. Although they are prone to chase any similar species off their breeding area, they were powerless against the currawongs because they had to leave the nest in order to finish it, and that is when the currawongs attacked it. The magpie-larks rebuilt the same nest three times, finding it destroyed each time, before they gave up.

Then there are the nest raiders that time the arrival of their own offspring to coincide precisely with the availability of eggs and nestlings of other avian species to feed their own young. Among them are the species belonging to the family of Artamidae, subfamily of the cracticids, such as butcherbirds and currawongs. The four species of butcherbird in particular include small birds in their diet, not only nestlings.[20] Currawongs, although largely frugivorous (fruit-eating), make a substantial dietary shift to high-protein foods, including eggs and nestlings, after their own nestlings have hatched.[21] When their nestlings have fledged, but are then fed for at least another two months post-fledging, the adults gradually switch the feeding of their young to fruit and berries.[22] Ravens and birds of prey also feed on the nestlings of other species. In all these cases, however, it is not clear whether the eating of nestlings simply provides another food source or, instead, a means of reducing interspecific competition for resources. There is no proof that the destruction of the brood of others is, in fact, a competitive strategy.

Leaving aside the constant vigilance necessary to protect eggs from other birds, even birds of the same species (conspecifics), there is also the constant risk of eggs or nestlings falling victims to other species. Eggs are a prized food for many species, including amphibians, reptiles and larger mammals such as cats, dogs and primates. Nests are often invaded, raided or destroyed and the young stolen and consumed.

To build a nest or not

There are other species that build no nests at all. For instance, we find many birds that nest in colonies making do with just a depression in the ground, such as the gannet, the blue-footed booby (Plate 5) and the little tern (Figure 4.1). Some penguins do not build nests and the parents of the wonderful and unusual emperor penguin will not even entrust the one egg in their care to the ground because of the forbidding temperatures in the Antarctic winter. The single egg is carried on the parents' feet and covered with a fur-sack of their skin. But not only seabirds make do without a nest. European nightjars find a sheltered spot on the ground and rely on their own plumage to camouflage and incubate the eggs. The grass owl and the short-eared owl choose a spot in trampled vegetation to lay their eggs. Even more precarious, some species lay their eggs on depressions in the branches and bare top of tree trunks. The white tern, for example, places its one egg in a depression on a horizontal branch. Presumably, in some seasons its egg may be blown off in a storm. Only a little safer is the choice made by the South American great potoo which, similar to Australian nightjars,[23] places its egg on the upper jagged platform of a broken off tree trunk. Ostriches and emus do not build nests either.[24]

Some ground-laying species, including occasionally ostriches and emus, do not incubate their eggs.[25] They leave the work to the sun. Mallee fowl and brush turkeys leave the incubation to take place in a burial chamber, building a mound into which their eggs will be placed. They are continually busy maintaining the temperature of the mound at a constant incubation level (about 34°C for brush turkeys) because fermentation inside the mound may raise the temperature too much or the heat of the sun may overheat the incubation chamber. So they have to either add a layer or remove soil to bring the temperature up or down. It is believed that this extraordinarily complex behaviour is partly a consequence of substantial temperature variations in the arid areas of inland Australia (see also Chapter 5).

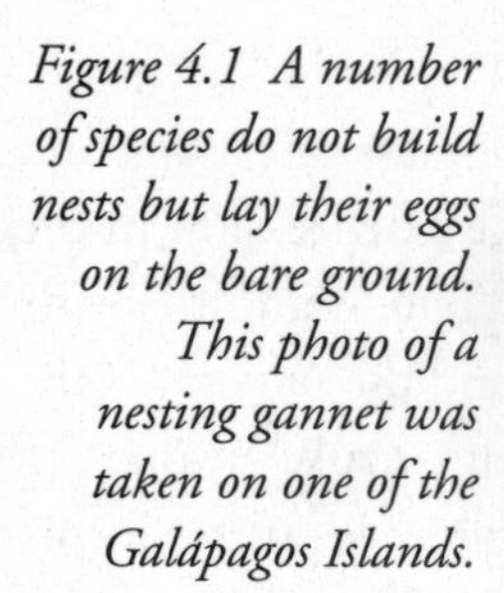

Figure 4.1 A number of species do not build nests but lay their eggs on the bare ground. This photo of a nesting gannet was taken on one of the Galápagos Islands.

Species in one distinct group are called 'primitive' nest builders. Among these are species that make do with very little as a home but, according to P. Goodfellow, any form of work carried out at the site of the eggs being deposited qualifies as a nest.[26] The greater flamingo might qualify, scraping together sand to form a mound with a depression in the middle where the single egg is laid. Peregrine falcons do no more than assemble a few twigs. The same can be said of crested pigeons, which place a few sprigs of pine branches across a horizontal branch structure, or the tawny frogmouth, which adds a few leaves and twigs to the natural centre of the fork of a tree. As these two species lay their eggs high up in trees, the accident rate of losing nestlings from the nest is relatively high; without tying down or weaving together any of the twigs, these primitive nest structures can degenerate very readily.[27] There are several species that appreciate a proper nest but tend not to build one themselves. The wood sandpiper finds discarded nests in trees in which to lay its eggs. Brown falcons, which pair for life, need a nest but do not build one; instead they take over the empty nests of other species.

Some species do not nest in trees or on cliffs or on the ground but, instead, dig a hole underground usually with a nest chamber at the end. For example, the small spotted pardalote digs a burrow parallel to the ground. The end of the tunnel widens out into a nest chamber and is lined with a few twigs and grasses. Similar burrows, only wider and higher at the end, are dug by kingfishers which tend to choose entrance sites higher off the ground than pardalotes, preferably on a river bank or the embankment of a dam or lake.

The nest building of the rainbow bee-eaters is of particular interest. They too dig tunnels by loosening the ground with their long, strong beak. They then do something extraordinary in the bird world. They arrange their body in a tripod shape, using the wings and beak as a stand in order to free their legs for digging. Like riding a bicycle, the legs go back and forth, scratching the loosened soil and throwing it behind the bird. In this fashion, even in difficult soils such as hardened clay, digging is effective and preparation time is short. Their burrows, like those of the European bee-eater, can be quite long and are dug precisely to the size of the bird's body. One reason for this tight fit may well be to secure a supply of fresh air to the nest site. The bird's body functions like a suction pump and draws in the air as it moves through the tunnel.[28] Maintaining an adequate oxygen supply is an issue in enclosed nests.

The reputation of birds as superb architects and builders, however, stems from the nests they build above ground that we are able to see. There is a large variety of shapes and sizes, and many different materials are used for nest building. There are the dainty cup-shaped nests of small songbirds, the hanging baskets of the various species of weaverbird, the skilfully crafted mudnests of barn swallows and the nesting colonies in trees of the social weaver. This weaver species of south-west Africa lives in flocks and builds gigantic compound nests in which each individual pair has its own nest-chamber. These rather ungainly looking nests hang off trees in large clumps. Inside the nest, it is all very ordered but, because new nest-chambers are added each season, the structure may extend to more than 7 metres in length and 5 metres in height. Eventually it may break and dismantle under its own weight.

The inventive use of materials ensures that the nests will last and also fulfil thermal and humidity requirements to prevent dehydration of the eggs.[29] The challenge is not only to fashion a nest that will keep its shape and ventilate and protect the eggs but to attach it firmly to the branch, house beam or other chosen surface. Australian magpies, crows and many other Corvidae integrate wire and other human materials into the nest structure. Willie wagtails use spiders' webs to bind their nests and make them watertight. Skill in combining and interweaving these various materials is not enough—the bird must also be able to transport the materials. Wagtails will hover in front of a spider's web and then fly backwards in a jerky way, tilting their head sideways. In this way the very fine, sticky strands do not get entangled in the bird's feathers. Even more elaborate is the stitching and suspension method of nest building used by the long-tailed tailorbird of India which manages to make a cradle by sewing leaves together with cobwebs or silk. But the most intriguing nests are built by the nearly 100 species of weavers—their name is deserved for they weave their nests in the most complicated patterns and shapes.

The largest individual nests of all are built by the hammerkop, at home in Africa, and the bald eagle, the national emblem of the United States since 1782. Hammerkops build a nest in a tree fork that can grow to weigh several 100 kilograms. It is roofed with grass and mud to make it watertight and has a smooth V-shaped entrance. Sometimes the structure has several internal 'rooms', including a nest-chamber that is especially carefully woven.[30] Bald eagles build the heaviest and most massive structures of any bird. Called eyries, they may weigh up to 2000 kilograms. They are erected either in large trees or on the ledge of a cliff. The nest has to support at least two adults and one offspring with a combined weight of more than 10 kilograms. But even such a weight, it seems, does not really require a nest of this size.

Not every bird builds a noteworthy nest but some are outstanding architects,[31] far surpassing the abilities of any mammal. While tool use in mammals is regarded as a problem-solving activity and generally related to a higher level of intelligence, the same admiration is not often accorded to the builders of nests. There is still a misapprehension sometimes that nest building involves no learning at all. But a good deal of learning and trial-and-error is necessary for a young bird to achieve the kind of perfection that will serve the purpose of incubating eggs and impress a female sufficiently to mate with him. The village weaver male, for instance, displays not only to attract attention to himself but to the nest that he has built.[32] In this competition with other males, he has to learn to perfect his art before a female will even deign to give his construction an inspection. In other species, such as Australian magpies and many of the species with polygamous males (such as bowerbirds), the female builds the nest on her own. There are, after all, female architects in nature.

Cooperative breeding

Cooperative behaviour in birds is very widespread and occurs across a large variety of species and social contexts. There are bird species that live communally, as do many shorebirds and also ostriches[33] and a significant number of passerines. Even nomadic and semi-nomadic species, such as budgerigars, many parrots and some corvids, may live, feed and breed in groups or even large flocks. Many sedentary species actively collaborate in territorial defence, hunting, food location and in the maintenance of effective warning systems (see also Chapter 8). This can take the form of mutual defence in the case of a threat to a territory—for example, noisy miners and Australian magpies unite to ward off an intruder.[34] Cooperative breeding is thus just one of the areas of cooperative behaviour among birds. It was first discovered by F.F. Darling in 1938 in a study of gulls. He found that large colonies began laying eggs earlier and needed a shorter incubation period than small colonies.[35] These communal activities are measurably advantageous—the co-timing of incubation throughout the colony reduces the incident of predation overall by creating a glut and so larger numbers of eggs survive.[36] Also, some older birds begin breeding earlier in the season than birds nesting for the first time, as is known to be the case in herons.[37] Here, cooperation consists of nothing more than timing the event of incubation to coincide with others in the colony. This is the most passive way of cooperating.

Various kinds of active cooperation have also been observed. One form of cooperation is to build nests together. Grey-crowned babblers and the apostlebirds of eastern Australia cooperate in building a nest. Ten or twelve babblers will combine to build half a dozen nests. The monk parakeets of southern South America choose not only communal living but communal nesting. The nests can be as much as 3 metres in length, providing each pair with its own high-rise apartment. The nest-chambers are also used for overwintering with the new offspring, raising the number of occupants per compartment from two to five or six birds. Cooperation can also entail more than building a nest—many birds cooperate to raise their young. The stripe-backed wren breeds cooperatively in groups of up to fourteen. Only the principal female of a group lays eggs but all help to build the nest, defend boundaries and collect food for the offspring.

There are also cases in which birds that are not generally cooperative breeders become so when the season is good enough to allow for a second clutch to be reared. It has been observed in swallows how the first brood will help to raise the second.[38] Not all species that live cooperatively necessarily breed cooperatively. Australian magpies will defend their territory cooperatively and bachelors and couples may live in groups but, usually, raising the young is undertaken by the parent magpies alone.[39] The jury is still out on this. We have seen a pair of Australian magpies with a helper at the nest in inland northern New South Wales. There may be local and regional variations that account for the different findings. Quite a number of species have been identified as choosing to breed cooperatively. It is possible that this strategy of contributing to the well-being of the next generation is more widespread than we know.

Cooperative breeding is a subject of enduring interest in avian studies because it raises the puzzling question why any bird would volunteer to raise young that are not its own.[40] The underlying assumption here is that survival is a selfish matter. Therefore altruistic acts that are seemingly of no immediate benefit to the borrowed parent are an anomaly requiring explanation.

Another puzzling fact is that, while not even 2 per cent of all birds worldwide are estimated to breed cooperatively, there is a marked skewing of the number of cooperative breeders in the tropics and in Australia. Of the 222 species that J.L. Brown listed, 67 occur in Australia, a remarkable accumulation of one specific reproductive strategy in one geographical region.[41] This finding suggests that more than altruism may be involved in cooperative breeding—certain ecological factors may play a part in explaining this behaviour.[42] Birds may not just be overwhelmingly sociable, but communal breeding practices may confer clear survival advantages.[43] Raising young together may improve the health of chicks and also be related to predator reduction.[44]

Clutch size

Once the nest is established, the size of the clutch is determined. The females of a large number of species may actually decide on the size of the clutch at the time of laying. The decision is related to nest predation (the chance that the nest will be raided) and to the ability to feed a new brood.[45] The 'food limitation hypothesis' predicts that the abundance of food during the breeding season will determine clutch size because the energy provided by the parents is determined by the amount of food in the environment.[46] A small clutch may be favoured when food is not abundant but available over a good period of time. Also, low efficiency in foraging will result in small clutch size, but can lead to multiple attempts of breeding, as in tropical birds.[47] Again, the amount of food determines how many offspring can be raised at one time. Alternatively, there is the predation hypothesis,[48] which predicts that a higher chance of predation will result in a smaller clutch size with multiple attempts. Here the explanation is not concerned with food but with the risk that is reduced by raising fewer offspring at one time.

These hypotheses may not be sufficient to explain why a clutch of eggs is small or large. The small clutch size may have evolved because of the higher risk of an overload of external parasites in large clutches.[49] This is so because nest environments can get contaminated, given unfavourable conditions of temperature or humidity, and highly infested nestlings are sapped of energy and require more food to cope with the overload. Hence a small clutch size will make it possible for the parents to raise the young despite their high-energy demands. A small clutch size can also make it easier to re-nest after failure because the bird's own physical resources have not been depleted. As well, some species have the habit of returning to the same site, a behaviour referred to as 'site faithfulness' or 'site fidelity',[50] and this may determine clutch size in a given year. Knowing the site may enable the birds to breed early by better exploitation of the food supply, as do many experienced breeders, and thus support a larger brood, or several small consecutive clutches.

Once the eggs have been laid, the nest becomes the most precious and important aspect of the bird's life. Vigilance is necessary at all times. Danger is everywhere and a number of rituals and behaviours have evolved to ensure that this nest is protected.

Reinforcing the pair bond

One of the first and perhaps most important aspects of rearing young is that the parents reinforce their bond and reassure each other that they both have the best interests of the brood at heart. For those that share incubation and feeding, each time a partner returns to the nest there has to be some form of statement that the incoming partner arrives with good intentions. A large number of species employs some kind of greeting at the nest (see Plate 2). In addition, when one partner comes to relieve the other on the nest, there may be a changeover ceremony, presumably because it is important to make decisions about any admission to the nesting territory or the nest itself. Ceremonies related to a changeover at the nest site were described in detail by Niko Tinbergen.[51] Such ceremonies or displays are thought to have evolved as recognition and reconciliation signals.

These displays may be purely greetings or connubial posturings. Gannets return to their mates with 'billing' or 'bowing'. Some billing and swaying of the head and neck also occurs in albatrosses (see Plate 2). Mutual ceremonies of the nesting pair (both perform similar rituals) often resemble the courtship dance and these displays may well have evolved from them. For instance, the ceremony of nest relief in grey herons is similar to courtship pairing. Gentoo penguins include in their ritual the viewing of the eggs together once the incubating partner has been persuaded to rise from the nest. Examination of the eggs is also found in many other species, such as the common screamer, as if to suggest that the health and number of the eggs need constant reappraisal.

The evolution of the nest changeover display may be related not just to the courtship dance but to conflict and threat displays.[52] Alighting from the nest is a tense moment and disagreement is a possible response. Conflict can be deduced from certain elements in the display—departing or arriving birds may cast behind them fragments of material (herbage, pebbles) before entering the nest. Peacocks scratch the ground and collect straws between bouts of displaying. And grey peacock pheasants will throw a seed or pebble at the female. The female skua drops grass before the male and the female ruffed grouse throws leaves over her shoulder.[53] Some bird species use the throwing of grass, herbage and pebbles exclusively in ritualised threat displays.[54] For instance, when avocets are angry they throw straws and shells about.[55] Niko Tinbergen described herring gulls tearing up grass in rage.[56] Gulls pluck herbage in a symbolic form of threat fighting. Marsh tits pluck moss from trees during courtship and disputes with other marsh tits.[57]

These rituals raise the question of recognition. Do birds recognise each other by sight and sound alone? Or do they employ extensive rituals at their nest sites because they need to engage in a series of recognition rituals before they can be absolutely sure there is no imposter? We still have only patchy information on the recognition of individuals among birds and even among mammals. Highly social species, such as gannets and Galápagos albatrosses, tend to extend their greeting ceremonies to unrelated individuals with whom they do not share a sexual bond.[58] In a large social organisation of birds with a complex social structure involving a dominance hierarchy (as in all species of cockatoo), the entire system would be likely to fail were there not certainty in identifying individuals. However, in socially less complex situations and individual pair groups, even within colonies, the situation of partner recognition is not always clear.

Some pair-bonded birds do not just engage in visual ceremonies. Instead, or in addition, some species have evolved a specific form of song, called 'duetting'. Duetting occurs in a wide range of avian species and it is now recognised that it plays an important role in the vocal communication system, especially of birds in the tropics.[59] It is a specific form of communication in which one bird of a pair initiates a call and the other one answers, usually involving sequential calling rather than singing together, as used in human song. Duets may overlap but usually the calls of the two birds follow each other so closely and so precisely that they sound like the vocalisations of one bird. This is referred to as 'antiphonal song'. Although duetting may play a part in synchronising the gonadal state of the pair (inducing readiness for breeding), its functions also include communication when visual contact is lost, or at risk of being lost, and as a warning. This is particularly true in wooded areas and dense rainforest (hence the prevalence of duetting in tropical regions) or during winter flocking and migration.

Duetting may also be used to synchronise defence of a territory or, more commonly, to reinforce a pair bond.[60] Duetting seems to occur more frequently in pairs with a prolonged monogamous bond. Australian magpie-larks duet regularly, as do Australian magpies, the black-faced cuckoo shrike and the bar-headed goose. Wood rails and the barred owl of Texas sing duets. Cardinal males sing antiphonally with females.[61] The duets are not necessarily initiated by the male. In the bar-headed goose and the bay wren, for instance, it is the female who calls first, answered by the male. These birds do not choose a partner by song. The context of the duetting situations is different each time but it is noteworthy that duetting occurs across a wide variety of species.

Strategies to minimise egg loss

Many strategies have evolved among birds to minimise the possible loss of eggs or nestlings to predators.

Camouflage

One obvious strategy is to reduce visibility. Nesting in burrows and tree holes avoids direct exposure to predators. As a choice against detection, nest holes in trees generally offer superb protection from many predators, as well as from adverse weather conditions. Unluckily, the species that opted for tree holes as a measure of safety have been hit by the worst predator of all—humans. The evolutionary script clearly did not allow for the removal of entire trees, including nest holes.

Those species that nest in open spaces have often developed the very specific strategy of camouflage, both in the plumage of the incubating birds and in the colouration and patterns of the eggs and nestlings (see Plate 3 and Figure 4.2). Other species have acquired the skill of adopting camouflaging postures. Tawny frogmouths stretch to take on the appearance of a gnarled tree branch. Some species cover their clutch with leaves, branches or feathers. Blue tits and black-capped chickadees pull some of the nest lining over the clutch when they go off to feed. Honey buzzards place branches over their eggs.[62] Some duck species denude their breasts of down to make a concealing blanket for their eggs. The down also helps to keep the eggs warm. And many nestlings develop down feathers that help them to blend in with their environment.

Figure 4.2 A kestrel chick camouflaged by its plumage. The downy plumage blurs the features of the bird and breaks up the overall form; thus the chick blends in well with the colours and structures of tree bark and leaves.

Many bird species that build nests in trees take additional precautions once the eggs are hatched. They will remove the faeces of their young. Indeed, many species have developed signals that encourage the nestlings to defecate only when a parent is in attendance at the nest. Very young nestlings produce faeces in a sack so that it will not fall apart when the parent collects it. The parent will then fly some distance and drop the faeces well away from the nest. Presumably this is a useful strategy when ground-dwelling (but tree-climbing) predators are about. The smell of faeces in the nest would attract any predator with a well-developed sense of smell (e.g. snakes, lizards or small rodents).

Attack

If all attempts to remain unnoticed fail and a predator is on its way to steal eggs or nestlings, there are ultimately only two further strategies available to avoid the loss of the brood. One mode is attack. Cooperative breeding clearly confers an advantage by enabling the group to defend its broods better than if they nested separately. Mobbing is an adaptive behaviour of smaller passerines that has paid off by aiding the survival of offspring and by actually shaping the behaviour of predators. We have seen these scenes countless times in the Australian bush: a pair or group of magpies mobbing a wedge-tailed eagle, or a group of kookaburras attacking a goanna, their fiercest enemy. The mobbing bird is not even the size of a morsel in the talons of the bird of prey or in the jaws of a 2-metre-long goanna (a lizard). The mobbers have to take care not to be caught because most birds of prey can turn in flight and grasp an object in mid-air, even if upside down or on their side. Hence, the mobbing birds tend to fly next to the head of the intruder. Perching predators are mobbed about the head and can actually sustain injury. Konrad Lorenz described corporate defence reactions in jackdaws, a species with closely knit social systems.[63] Mobbing behaviour usually achieves the desired goal and the intruder leaves.

There are some birds that act in interspecies cooperation to ward off a dangerous predator. This is usually termed the 'dear enemy' effect. They may be neighbours in fierce competition for boundaries but both species may have common enemies and, in such situations, will cooperate to attack the intruder, even in the neighbour's territory.[64] Some species co-exist in the same territory and may go to the aid of a nesting pair. Usually, these combined defence activities are preceded by warning and mobbing calls and birds rally round to follow them (see also Chapter 8).

Attacking an intruder is often not possible, however, especially when the birds are small and the intruder very large. There may also be the problem that, while warding off one intruder, another waiting in the wings will use the opportunity to raid the nest (as ravens do).

Threat and decoy

Finally, to defend the nest and brood, breeding birds may have to resort to tricks and decoys if the nestlings are to have a chance of survival. There is, of course, the possibility of threatening an intruder. Some species have the capacity to make themselves look larger and more ominous when faced with danger. But this is relatively rare and not always effective. Perhaps the most unusual ways of protecting the nest are the various distraction displays.

Although their origin may be fear and flight responses, distraction displays have become an effective diversionary tactic to protect the young from predators and are given exclusively by nesting birds. By distraction displays we refer to activities of the adult bird designed to lure a potential predator away from the nest. One of the most practised forms of distraction is for the parent bird to draw attention to herself (it is usually the female who carries out these behaviours). There are several kinds of display: feigning injury, performing impeded flight motions, feigning lameness or playing dead. Sometimes, a combination of these activities is used. Golden plovers feign injury. As the predator approaches the plover moves away from the nest in a manner that signals she has a broken wing and, as if to extenuate the performance, she then plays dead. This is a dramatic form of interspecies signalling. Adult black skimmers give a striking injury-feigning display that takes them away from the nest, fluttering and stumbling. Black-throated divers, when flushed from the nest, pretend to have broken wings. Skylarks may become totally inert as if dead. Pratincoles feign lameness and so do American long-eared owls and buff-breasted sandpipers. Oystercatchers use 'impeded flight', hopping along with futile wing flutters or very slow flight. A number of waders alternate injury feigning with squatting, as if sitting on or laying eggs. Injury feigning by ducks, as ground nesters, is often successful in luring foxes and dogs away from the nest. There are several examples where birds resort to communal action to achieve a distraction. Some species even mimic dying in groups, such as stilts (e.g. the pied stilt of New Zealand). Australian white-fronted chats when performing 'disablement displays' usually get their neighbours to come and join in.[65]

When distraction strategies do not work, some species will defend their young physically. The corn crake will even attack dogs and rats and may die in the process. Woodcocks are among the very few birds that carry their young in flight away from danger. Some waterbirds hide their young in their own plumage and run with them.

Yet the rules for raising a brood are not uniformly in favour of the nestlings. In some birds of prey and a number of other species, such as kookaburras, eggs are laid a few days apart and the first-born may be so savage to the later-hatched sibling that the older will eventually kill the younger.[66] Many eagles have two eggs initially but will usually raise only one.[67] Siblicide is a widespread occurrence in avian species (more of this later). Likewise, infanticide occurs in some avian species, such as noisy miners, for reasons that are not entirely clear.[68] We do know that sudden variations in food supply can change the behaviour of some avian species dramatically—they become aggressive.[69] It is conceivable that infanticide could function as a form of self-culling when food supplies dwindle.

Parents will stop feeding offspring that have fallen from the nest, developed a disease or are injured. Such nestlings are doomed and the parents will abandon them.

It is a complicated and precarious endeavour for birds to create the right environment for their eggs and nestlings and to fulfil the needs of growing chicks. The variety of strategies and skills that avian species have developed to cope with the demands of successful reproduction is impressive. Yet all these activities just set the scene for the development of the chicks.

chapter 5

DEVELOPMENT

The development of avian embryos begins as soon as the parents start to incubate their eggs. During the incubation period the embryo goes through a series of stages that unfold according to a precise plan. Hatching marks the end of the embryonic period and occurs at different stages of development in different species. Many birds hatch in a very immature state, before they open their eyes and without any feathers (Figure 5.1). The young of these species usually stay in the nest and are dependent on care from their parents for all their needs. That time of total dependence on parental care may be as short as a week but usually it lasts much longer. They are called 'nidicolous' species, meaning 'nest-dwelling', and the pattern of their development is described as 'altricial'. All the passerines, including the small songbirds, fit into this category and so do owls, eagles and hawks. The young of other avian species hatch at quite an advanced stage of development and are referred to as 'precocious'. They have their eyes open and are able to walk, and in some cases swim, very shortly after hatching. These species require some parental care but far less than the nidicolous species. Even though their eggs might have been incubated in a nest, the hatched young soon leave it and are referred to as 'nidifugous', meaning 'nest-fleeing'. Many domestic birds, including chickens, ducks, quails and turkeys, are nidifugous.

The chicks of the megapodes are the most extreme examples of a nidifugous species, being hatched at an advanced stage of development

Figure 5.1 Kookaburras (left) are an altricial species. Their chicks hatch at an earlier stage of development than do precocial megapodes, such as the orange-footed scrubfowl (right). The kookaburra on the left is completely naked on day 1 post hatching. The second kookaburra shows the first pin feathers on wings and head because it is about two days older than the other. Kookaburras are completely helpless after hatching and for months thereafter, but this orange-footed scrubfowl is ready to go out into the world alone on the first day after hatching.

(Figure 5.1). The megapodes include the Australian brush turkey and the malleefowl, as well as the yellow-legged brush turkey and the scrub fowl of New Guinea, and several more species. Brush turkeys and malleefowl lay their eggs in a huge mound of leaves, sand and decomposing organic material, which they build themselves.[1] Although brush turkey males and the malleefowl uncover the eggs and check the temperature of the nest from time to time, no other care is given to the eggs or the hatched chicks.[2] After hatching underground, each chick digs its way to the surface, sits with its head out of the mound, looks around for a short time and then takes off alone into the forest. Since each one hatches at a slightly different time, the chicks do not even have each other as companions. Some megapodes of New Guinea and the Philippines do not even prepare a mound but simply burrow and deposit their eggs under the sand on a beach or in warm volcanic sand. After that they leave them to incubate in the warmth of the sun or sand and then to hatch alone.[3]

The next major step in the development of most birds is the period of fledging—of course, this does not apply to those species that do not fly or fly to only a limited extent—followed by puberty and reaching sexual maturity.

Egg size

The size of the egg determines the size of the nutrient store available for the developing embryo. So it is not surprising that the larger the offspring at hatching the larger the egg from which it hatched. Egg size (and weight) also depends on the size of the female who laid it. When a graph is plotted of the average egg weight in various species belonging to the same order against the average weight of the females of those same species, a clear mathematical relationship is found between increasing egg weight and increasing body size.[4] Put simply, large females lay large eggs and small females lay small eggs and, as adult female weight doubles, egg weight increases by about 70 per cent.[5]

Egg size becomes important when we compare precocial and altricial species. As the embryos of precocial species undergo more development in the egg (i.e. before they hatch) than those of altricial species, they require more energy supplies and so larger eggs. In fact, the egg weight of precocial species is on average ten times that of altricial species.[6] The adult birds of precocial species are also larger than altricial species, ostriches and emus being the most obvious living examples of this phenomenon. The evolution of altricial development, in which the embryos hatch at an earlier stage of development, meant that eggs could be smaller and adults could be smaller. This factor was important in the adaptive radiation that occurred once small passerines evolved; there was greater flexibility of habitat choice and survival. Of course, smaller adult size is also essential for flying, an ability soon lost in favour of larger size if there is no longer any pressure to fly.

The eggs of precocial species also have more solid material and less water than those of altricial species, as well as more energy content per unit volume. They have more yolk and proportionately less albumin (the white of the egg); the egg of a megapode, for example, has an extremely large yolk and very little albumin.[7] Nevertheless, this tighter packaging of supplies is not as important as egg weight in determining how much development can occur before the embryo hatches. Within a species, irrespective of whether the development of the embryo's species is precocial or altricial, egg weight determines the weight and survival of the hatchlings.[8] The heavier the egg, the more nutrient reserves are available and the heavier the chick at hatching.

Although the genetic characteristics of a species are important in determining egg size, environmental conditions can also have an effect on egg size. The size of eggs laid by the pied flycatcher depends on the body condition of the female at the time of laying; females in a better condition lay larger eggs.[9] These larger eggs are more likely to hatch than smaller ones and offspring hatched from larger eggs are more likely to survive to breed.[10] The condition of the adult female at the time of laying depends partly on the amount of food available at the time but also on the size that she was at hatching. A flycatcher that is small at hatching never entirely catches up with one larger at hatching. The contents of the egg are the legacy passed on from the adult female to her offspring. It can have long-lasting consequences for development and even adult condition and survival, although there are bound to be species differences in exactly how long the effects last after hatching.[11]

Egg size may also depend on the male partner. For instance, female mallards lay larger eggs after they have mated with a male they prefer than they do after mating with a less preferred male.[12] Female mallards are very choosy about mating. Some males are much more attractive to them than others, and mating with these males leads to better survival of the offspring to adulthood. This was thought to result because the preferred males passed on superior genes to their offspring. Instead it seems to be caused by the female laying larger eggs. Mallards do not feed their offspring but the males do defend feeding areas from other ducks. A preferred male may be one holding a larger or better territory, providing his female with better nutrition during the breeding season. Therefore, preferred males may, indirectly, increase egg size and survival of the offspring.

The time for which the eggs are incubated varies greatly among the different species of birds. The shortest periods of incubation are found in altricial species, which have the smallest eggs, but many altricial species have very long incubation periods, such as the parrots.[13] The megapodes and the kiwi have long incubation periods and large eggs. Other precocial species have incubation periods of differing duration but again those with smaller eggs tend to have shorter incubation periods. As a general rule, within the taxonomic group of an order, the duration of incubation of the eggs before hatching is related directly to egg size.[14]

Inside the egg

At first the embryo is a small body of tissues on the surface of the egg yolk. It is not long before a brain, heart blood vessels and other tissues begin to form. The embryo obtains from the egg yolk the nutrients it needs for growing and forming its various specialised tissues. All its life processes occur within the egg. Vital supplies of oxygen enter the egg through its porous shell and the outside humidity is crucial, especially close to the time of hatching. Otherwise, the embryo must make do with the supply of nutrients and other materials encapsulated inside the egg, put there when the egg formed inside the hen's body.[15] The female even deposits a certain amount of her hormones in the egg and these can affect the development of the embryo and the behaviour of the young after hatching. As the canary hen lays each egg in her clutch, her body deposits increasing amounts of the sex hormone, testosterone, in the egg. This hormone is known to elevate the level of aggressive behaviour in birds and, in line with this, the canaries that hatched from eggs laid later in the clutch were more assertive and, possibly, more aggressive than those hatched from eggs laid earlier in the clutch.[16] The measure of their assertiveness, or dominance, was their supplanting other young canaries at the food dish. This relationship between order of laying of the eggs, testosterone level in the eggs and dominance behaviour occurs for both male and female young. The young canaries hatched from eggs with more testosterone also grow at a faster rate and beg for food more persistently than those from lower testosterone eggs.[17] This means that those hatching later in the clutch might be able to compensate by begging for food more and growing faster than their older siblings.

Although eggs laid later have more testosterone in the case of the canary, the order of laying and level of testosterone in the egg is reversed in some other species. The amount of testosterone in zebra finch eggs decreases with each egg laid.[18] This means that there is likely to be a strong hierarchy among the young in competition for food. Possibly, this is an adaptation to survival in environments where the food supply is poor or unpredictable since the competition would lead to the death of later-hatched offspring. In cattle egrets too, earlier-laid eggs have more testosterone than those laid later in the same clutch. This may be related to the fact that the first egret chicks to hatch often kill those that hatch later.[19] Social conditions can also influence the amount of testosterone deposited in the eggs—housing several female canaries together resulted in higher levels of testosterone in the eggs than housing females alone with their mates.[20]

As the embryo develops it starts to move inside the egg. At first its movements are uncoordinated and sporadic. They gradually become more coordinated, reaching a maximum about half-way through the incubation period.[21] The wings, legs, head and beak all move and sometimes the whole body is moved and turned. This activity is essential for the developing nerves and muscles. In the last few days before hatching the embryo will move in response to being stimulated by sound, touch or light. The embryo is already reacting to the world outside the egg.

Each sensory system develops at a different time during incubation and we know from detailed studies of the developing chick embryo that the sense of touch develops first at about a quarter of the way through incubation.[22] We can tell when tactile sensitivity first develops by opening up the egg to expose embryos at different stages of development, and touching the embryo gently with a hair. A response to sound develops next, about half-way through incubation, and the embryo moves when it hears sounds of certain pitches. It does not have full hearing capacity yet but it is starting to respond to some sounds. Sensitivity to taste may develop at about the same time as hearing first appears but this is not known definitely and it could be much later. Just two or three days before hatching, the chick embryo begins to respond to stimulation by light. This is the stage of development when the nerves from the eyes to higher parts of the brain become functional. At this stage the chick embryo can even learn and remember particular colours of light.

Finally, the sense of olfaction (smell) develops at the stage when the embryo pushes its beak and nostrils through the membrane around the air sac in the egg and starts to breathe air. Tissue blocking the embryo's nostrils is resorbed (disappears). At this stage the embryo will move when exposed to different odours and can even learn by being exposed to particular odours.[23] The eggs of megapodes, buried in mounds or under warm beach sand, have only a very small air sac or none at all and the embryos of these species breathe air only after they have broken the shell.[24] It is probable, therefore, that olfaction is impossible until after hatching in these species. Whether or not olfactory ability develops just before or just after hatching, as far as we know it is the last sensory system to become functional in birds.

The ordered sequence of development of the sensory systems from tactile first to olfaction last is very important. It allows the earlier systems to become functional without interference from later ones. For example, the embryo can hear before it can see and that appears to be essential in determining how the young bird will integrate what it hears and sees after hatching. Changing the order of sensory experience experimentally alters the behaviour of the chick after hatching.[25] If the air sac end of the bobwhite quail egg is opened and the chick is prematurely exposed to patterned light instead of the usual blurred, unpatterned light seen through the shell, the hatched quail chick will not recognise the sound of the mother's call heard on its own. Before it will approach her, the chick must see her at the same time as hearing her. After normal hatching, chicks of this species approach just the call of the mother.

Stimulation from the environment around the egg is important for the embryo's development. Just before hatching, domestic chicks not only respond to hearing the hen vocalise but they can also vocalise themselves and the hen responds.[26] If the embryos are cold, they peep, and the hen responds by moving them into a position where she can incubate them better. Added to this, some embryos communicate with each other. Domestic chicks and quails make clicking sounds inside the egg. These sound ensure that all the eggs hatch at about the same time even though they may have been laid over a period of several days and the incubation of some began well before others. The clicking of eggs laid earlier speeds up the development of those laid later.[27] In the same way the later-laid eggs of mallards and black kites appear to have shortened developmental periods and so hatching time is similar for all eggs in the clutch.[28]

Hatching

Hatching is a remarkable event involving special biological problems. It requires a large amount of energy and coordinated movements by the embryo. The embryo prepares for hatching by tucking itself into the correct position for hatching, folding its legs with toes near the head and ankles at the other end of the egg, the pointed end. The head is next to

Figure 5.2 A chick embryo in the tucking position that is adopted four days before hatching. The air sac end of the egg has been removed and the chick's beak has penetrated the membrane of the air sac.

the air sac at the blunt end of the egg and the head is turned so that the beak points towards the air sac (Figure 5.2). The beak penetrates the membranes of the air sac and the embryo begins to breathe air (not in megapodes, as mentioned before). At the same time as the embryo is preparing to hatch, the shell becomes thinner because calcium is being resorbed from it. Just before hatching, the embryo starts to move its head more than before and to clap its beak more often. This activity is triggered by the bending of the embryo's neck to one side, which occurs as the embryo grows bigger—if the neck is straightened, hatching does not occur.[29]

Eventually these movements cause a small break in the shell—the egg has been pipped. This action is assisted by the egg tooth, projecting as a sharp point from the tip of the upper mandible of the chick's beak. The embryo then rests and some time later begins the climax of hatching. The hatching embryo enlarges the break in the shell with the beak as it moves its head up and down and in so doing strikes the egg tooth against the shell. At the same time, it uses its feet to rotate itself inside the egg. This entire process demands the expenditure of much energy.[30] Eventually the end of the egg is opened and the chick completes the hatching process by pushing with its feet and body until it is free from the eggshell.

This is the usual hatching procedure but there are some minor variations. Megapodes, for example, break out of their shells feet first after the shell has cracked in several places.[31] Woodcocks and sandpipers push the beak through the hole pipped in the shell and split the shell along the longer axis of the egg, instead of chipping around the egg near the air sac. We have observed that the tawny frogmouth hatches in a similar way. The embryo first pips the eggshell in two spots, one above the other, on the longer axis of the egg, and then it splits the shell open along the long axis (Figure 5.3).

In some species the hatching of each egg in the clutch occurs at about the same time (e.g. domestic fowls and quails, as mentioned above). In other species each egg in the clutch hatches at a different time and hatching may occur over a period of as much as ten days (e.g. the blue-throated bee-eater).[32] Hatching asynchrony occurs more commonly in species that start to incubate their eggs before the whole clutch has been laid. This happens more often in climates that would reduce the viability of the eggs if they were left exposed for too long before incubation commenced (e.g. climates that are either too hot or too cold for the eggs to survive for long).[33] Hatching asynchrony is also more characteristic of altricial than precocial species. It is less characteristic of species that eat both animals and plants (omnivorous species) than of species that specialise in feeding on only plants or only animals.[34] When asynchronous hatching has taken place, the offspring in the nest may vary considerably in size and stage of development, a fact that only some species take into account when they are feeding

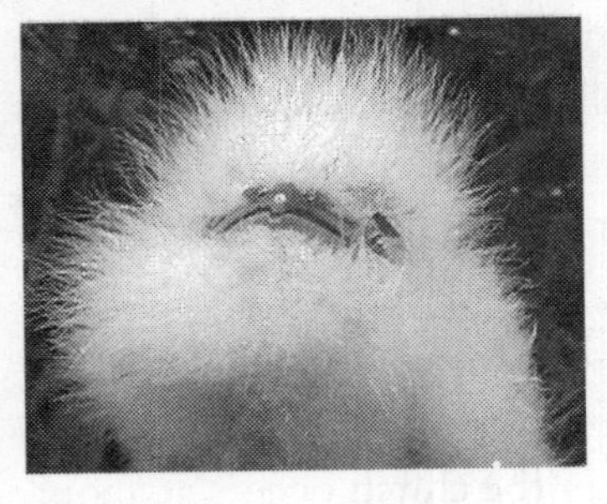

Figure 5.3 A rare pictorial record of the stages of development of a tawny frogmouth. Note that the egg is pipped and then split lengthwise on the side (rather than around the end, as is more common). With this strategy, the hatchling manages to split the egg in half. Once dried it shows a thick, white, downy cover. Note the 'egg-tooth', the white shiny protrusion on top of the beak—this is a strengthened part of the beak that allows the bird to chisel the egg from the inside. Within a day, the hatchling adopts the typical frogmouth posture, head up and eyes half-closed.

the nestlings.[35] In some cases the variation in hatchling strength and size reduces aggression between siblings and in other cases it increases it. Increased aggression may result in siblicide. The offspring that hatches first pushes its unhatched sibling or siblings out of the nest or, after all eggs have hatched, the strongest nestling pushes the weaker ones out.

Struggle for survival

Development may be thwarted completely for a number of eggs or newly hatched young. The new brood may be culled by one of the hatchlings. Occurring in a number of species, this may be a way of dealing with insufficient food supplies for all hatched offspring to be fed adequately. In some species hunger drives the stronger nestlings to get rid of the weaker ones (siblicide), thus allowing at least some of the clutch to survive, but in other species siblicide is not related to food supply. Great egrets do not become more aggressive to each other if they are fed less and this may be an adaptation of this species to cope with the fact that the parents normally supply fish after varying periods of time spent catching it.[36] Space in the nest appears to be a factor causing siblicide in egrets; fighting is less frequent in smaller clutches than in larger ones even though the parents feed the same amount per chick.

The blue-throated bee-eater hatchling has a sharp hook at the end of its beak, used by the stronger, first-hatched young to inflict wounds on its siblings. These wounds are often severe enough for the wounded chick to die.[37] After the nestling stage, the beak hook is lost or worn away, so it appears to develop only to inflict wounds on siblings or to ward off this aggression. Other species may not inflict wounds but still cause the certain death of their sibling by heaving it out of the nest. As well as in great egrets and bee-eaters, the practice of siblicide has been reported among cattle egrets, blue-footed boobies (Plate 5), jackdaws, the American white pelican and many other species.

Competition between siblings for food can also be seen in the begging responses of the offspring. Larger and stronger nestlings can beg for longer than weaker ones and can beg more effectively by holding their gaping beak higher. In some species, the parents respond preferentially to the most effective begging and so create a feeding hierarchy that favours the stronger nestlings.[38] In fact, this seems to be a common form of parenting.

Selective and more equal feeding of weak as well as strong nestlings has been observed in only relatively few species, and then usually when food for the nestlings is abundant. These include budgerigars, white-winged choughs, tree swallows, pied flycatchers, Australian magpies and crimson rosellas. In the crimson rosella, an Australian parrot, the female feeds all her offspring equally by regurgitating food into the nestling's beak, despite the fact that hatching occurs asynchronously and the offspring are at very different stages of development and of different sizes.[39] Male crimson rosellas, on the other hand, feed the first-hatched offspring more than the last-hatched. In addition, all the female nestlings were fed the same amount, whereas large male nestlings were fed more than the smaller males.[40] These findings show that very complex factors can be operating in the feeding behaviour of parents. The patterns of feeding behaviour, of course, determine the rate of growth of the nestlings. The reasons why a particular pattern of feeding should exist for some species and not others, and for one sex and not the other, have yet to be determined. The crimson rosella appears to be making sure that more female than male nestlings will fledge and this might be balanced by greater mortality of females in later life.[41]

Altricial young undergo very rapid growth after hatching. This places enormous demands on the parents, particularly if food is difficult to obtain. Their absences from the nest expose the young nestlings to predators and many nestlings are lost in this way. Absences must also be balanced against loss of body heat by the nestlings. Birds are unable to maintain their own body temperature (i.e. thermoregulate) in the early period after hatching. Once they develop this ability, the parents can leave the nest for longer and travel further in search of food. The growth of the downy feathers also helps the young to stay warm, as does huddling together with siblings and shivering.[42]

Keeping the body temperature of the hatchlings within the correct range is a great challenge to most avian parents, particularly those living in either very hot or very cold climates.[43] Antarctic petrels and king penguins are exposed to temperatures well below freezing point during the breeding season. King penguins have no nest but they keep the newly hatched young away from the snow and ice by resting it on their feet and surrounding it with a fold of their abdominal skin. At the other extreme, species that breed in the desert may experience temperatures well above body temperature. Not surprisingly, therefore, shielding their young from cold or heat is one of the main roles of parenthood in birds, as in many other species.

Precocial young are well developed at hatching but they develop more slowly than most altricial young and they cannot thermoregulate at first. When they get cold the hatchlings either crawl under the hen or they make special calls that elicit brooding by the hen (i.e. she fluffs her feathers and sits on her hatchlings). Domestic chicks, for example, peep when cold, as they also do just before hatching. They are able to follow the parent birds soon after hatching and may soon learn to find their own food, but they must stay near the hen and frequently seek cover under her body for warmth.

Keeping the nestlings at the right temperature in very hot environments is, perhaps, a greater challenge. Dehydration of the hatchlings is a serious problem. The cactus wren solves this problem by leaving the nestlings' faeces in the nest. They contain water that cools as it evaporates in the heat.[44] In other species, nest cleanliness is of high priority and the parents remove faeces as soon as they are deposited, often assisted by the faecal waste being inside a gelatinous sac. The Australian magpie parent is ready to collect this sac as soon as the nestling expels it, even before it touches the nest.

The birds' early life is a time when learning is very important. There are sensitive periods during which certain types of learning occur and, as each of these stages of learning leads on to the next, their unfolding is an integral part of the process of development (see Chapter 9). Domestic chicks and ducklings, for example, must imprint on the hen about a day after hatching. Once they have done this, they move on to the next stage of learning.

Food for the young birds

Precocial young are not fed by their parents. Immediately after hatching they have enough nutrients from the yolk sac left in their body to sustain them without feeding for a couple of days. By then they are able to walk and peck at grain or insects and so will find their own food.[45] They learn what to peck at by observing their parents as they feed. By contrast, altricial young must be fed entirely by their parents, often for several weeks, or even months. The diet of young birds is specific to each species but is very diverse between species. The method of feeding also varies. A classic study by Niko Tinbergen showed that the parent herring gulls are stimulated to regurgitate their catch when their chick pecks at the red spot on the parent's beak.[46]

Some young obtain their food from the crop by actively searching in the parent's beak, others have to take the food from the beak, while yet other species just open their beak and have the food placed inside it. Grain-feeding parents, such as parrots and pigeons, feed their young by regurgitating food from their crop. The pigeon forms what is known as crop milk and regurgitates that to feed the young. Crop milk may also transfer antibodies to the young which would assist them to develop immunity to infection and parasites.[47] This would be a very important contribution to the survival of the young. The parents of other species have been seen to feed saliva to their offspring and this is very likely a means of building up the immune system of their offspring. Such behaviour has been observed in vultures and by us in the tawny frogmouth.

Begging is the most noticeable behaviour of nestlings. They stretch the neck, gape the beak and make begging calls. This response is often triggered by the arrival of the parent at the nest, either when the nestling sees the parent perched on the edge of the nest or when the landing parent causes the nest to move abruptly. Simply vibrating the nest triggers the behaviour in some species—starlings, for example—and seeing a cardboard model of the parent is sufficient for other species, as in the case of nestling blackbirds.

Fledging

The timing of the first flight varies between species and so too does the type of flying that occurs. Domestic fowl and ptarmigan are not birds that fly a great deal but they develop the wing feathers necessary for flying (i.e. the primary and secondary feathers) quite soon after hatching and this allows them to flutter above ground level early in life. Ducklings, on the other hand, develop strong feet and legs for swimming but do not acquire the feathers and wing strength needed for flying until they are much older. There is apparently no survival need for young ducklings to fly since they dive for cover from overhead predators, whereas domestic fowl chicks may need to fly to escape predators approaching them on the ground.[48]

Fledging is a stressful time for parents and offspring. It is a stage when many new patterns of behaviour must emerge in addition to flying, which is the most important step at this stage of development. Fledging is more dramatic in those species that fly expertly as adults and in species that nest in high, inaccessible places. A seabird leaving its nest on a high cliff may need to glide and have expertise in flying on its maiden flight. Other birds fledging from nest holes in trees may fly to nearby branches and make shorter trial flights as they perfect their skills.

Fowl chicks may fly in a limited way from very early in life but they pass through other stages of development that may be as stressful as leaving the nest. Their problem is to stay next to their parents, particularly when roosting at night. Glen McBride and colleagues conducted a comprehensive study of the behaviour of feral fowl on North West Island, off the coast of Queensland.[49] They described a stage of development when the chicks attempted to follow the hen to roost on higher and safer branches above ground level but were not very successful in doing so. This transition in the hen's behaviour took place when the chicks were about four weeks of age. It was a stressful period for the chicks, as is any separation from parents. In this case, the adult takes the active role by temporarily leaving her offspring, whereas in fledging the young leave the parents who must follow. Fledged young still need to be fed and they ensure that this happens by making begging vocalisations and often adopting begging postures to attract their parents.

After fledging has taken place, most young are fed by their parents and stay in the vicinity of the nest site or territory. Some of them have not fully mastered flight yet. This is a vulnerable period because they are out of the nest but not yet able to fly off if danger threatens. They are sometimes referred to as 'branchlings' at this stage of development, hopping from one branch to another, slowly increasing their flight distance. Some species, such as Australian magpies, remain in this branchling state for up to two weeks, until they have fully mastered flight and, equally important, landing.

Young birds may join other young of the same age and so form a nursery flock, or crèche. Galahs fledge in about the seventh week of life and then join a crèche. While in the crèche, they continue to be fed by their parents for several weeks, as shown by Ian Rowley.[50] Since galahs hatch asynchronously and also fledge asynchronously, the parents always face a week or so when they must feed their first-fledged young in the crèche as well as their young still in the nest. To do this they must ration their time precisely to cover the distance between the food source, the nest and the crèche. Soon after all the young have fledged, the family reassembles and flies off as a unit to a site close to food. The time spent by each individual in the nursery flock is not very long but the crèche itself persists for several weeks during the breeding season. When in the crèche flock, the fledglings practise flying and perfect the complex techniques that they need, including landing, gliding and soaring.[51] Although the onset of flying in birds is due to developmental changes that take place as the muscles and nerves mature, perfecting the art of flying requires practice and almost certainly involves learning.

Juvenile canaries fledge in their third week of life and the level of the stress hormone, corticosterone, circulating in the bloodstream increases at about this time. This indicates that it is indeed a time of physiological stress. Hubert Schwabl has found that at this age there is a relationship between corticosterone levels and order of hatching: the levels of corticosterone are higher in first-hatched canaries than in later-hatched ones.[52] This effect was not related to the growth rate of the birds, measured as body mass. The birth-order effect on corticosterone levels may, therefore, have come about because first-hatched chicks experience more social stress than later-hatched ones or that deposits of this hormone in the egg, made by the maternal bird before laying, have a delayed effect. The answer to this is not yet known.

Some time after fledging has occurred and the juvenile birds have reached a stage of development that allows them to survive alone, a new set of rules comes into play. It depends whether a species lives in communities, in which case the young may stay and become helpers, or in semi-nomadic groups, in which case they may either leave or stay. Migratory species often disperse and migrate as soon as they have left the nest. Starlings can form enormously large flocks of juveniles, all taking to the air at once. In territorial species, departures are sometimes not required until the new generation itself comes of breeding age. In kookaburras, this can take five years and parents are often willing to let last year's offspring stay if this helps to secure their territory against another strong group of kookaburras.

In many avian species the juveniles must disperse from their parents' territory. Exactly when this takes place may depend, at least in some species, on competition between the siblings or on size and stage of development. Juvenile western screech-owls of the Rocky Mountains in North America leave the nest in an order based on their social position with respect to each other.[53] The more dominant nestlings move away from the nest first, perhaps to find the best territories, and the least dominant ones leave last. They leave to find an area where they can settle for the winter. It is interesting that the level of corticosterone increases in the bloodstream of juvenile screech-owls at about the time they disperse.[54] This suggests that social stress may increase corticosterone secretion from the birds' adrenal glands and this, in turn, may lead to dispersal and foraging for food away from the nesting site.

Reaching maturity

As birds grow and reach sexual maturity, their feather colours may change radically. In some species adulthood is marked by the development of magnificent colours and patterns. Tails may grow, as in the peacock, or the beak may change colour—from grey to orange in the dollarbird. Even the skin of the legs and feet may change colour; the blue-footed booby develops its blue feet as its mark of adulthood. These changes in appearance are used in social communication, particularly in the performance of mating displays. The peacock raises and spreads its spectacular tail and the blue-footed booby dances with foot treading to display its 'blue boots'.

The plumage of the currawong does not change markedly as the juvenile becomes adult but the brown colour of the iris pales to a lime green or yellow. The iris colour also changes with sexual maturity in galahs, turning pink in the female and a dark brown in the male.

These changes are associated with rising levels of the sex hormones. The comb of the domestic fowl grows large and turns bright red in colour as the level of the hormone testosterone rises. If testosterone is injected into young domestic chicks the comb will grow and turn red. The same takes place if the adult female is injected with testosterone. At the same time, changes in behaviour occur. For example, young domestic chicks will copulate and attack after they have been injected with testosterone.[55] Vocalisations change also. The cock begins to crow and songbirds begin to sing.

Development is a complex process involving both genetic influences and experience. It is characterised by constant change and passage through different stages, some taking place in sequence and others all at the same time. There are also key aspects of development that require learning (Chapter 9). But first, we look at the sensory system of birds to establish what it is and how much a bird might need to learn in order to digest and process experiences adequately.

part III
THE SENSES

chapter 6

VISION

Birds have excellent sight. It is one of their most important senses and in many ways they can see better than we can. They have wide fields of vision and the ability to see different hues and colours, as well as to detect movement and differences in texture. They are able to process visual information rapidly enough to guide their flight through forests of branches or to capture an insect as it flies away or runs for cover. Eagles have such superior powers of visual acuity that they can detect their prey from hundreds of metres above ground level. The pigeon pecking at grains scattered on the ground can, at the same time, focus clearly on distant objects on its right and left sides and so is always ready to avoid an approaching predator. The palm cockatoo can even see behind its head and the mallard can see extremely well above its head, as well as in front and to the sides. The heron walking in shallow water has excellent vision below its beak and can capture a fish darting away in one rapid strike. In these and many other ways the visual world of birds is very different from our own.

Panoramic vision

Most species of birds have their eyes on the side of the head and so have full view to the front, sides and overhead. A bird can, of course, move its head to allow it to scan visually all the surrounding region but, even with its head held stationary, it can see in almost all directions. This enables the bird to watch out for predators that approach from the side or above at the same time as it attends to catching prey or finding grains using the frontal field of its vision. In flight the bird's wide field of vision allows it to navigate with great accuracy while at the same time attending to the position of other birds in the flock, watching out for aerial predators and monitoring the ground for sources of food or landmarks on its flight path.

The visual world seen by the left and right eyes is completely different, apart from a relatively small area where the fields of the left and right eyes overlap. The overlapping area is referred to as the 'binocular' field of vision, and the areas of the visual field seen by only one eye are referred to as the 'monocular' fields. The monocular fields look widely to the left and right sides of the bird. Many species of birds have a binocular field in front around the beak, and often slightly below and above the beak. The binocular field of vision is specialised for comprehensive and detailed vision, allowing the bird to see clearly what it is doing with its beak as it searches for food or manipulates objects or live prey.

In the binocular field, the bird can make accurate assessments of the distance of objects, known as 'depth perception', but we are not certain whether birds are better at judging depth in the binocular or monocular fields of vision.[1] There are three ways in which depth can be determined and one of these is possible only in the binocular field. It is called 'stereopsis'. Pigeons are able to use stereopsis and it is likely that many other species of birds, but not all, can do so too.[2] Stereopsis relies on the fact that the visual image seen by each eye in the binocular field is slightly different and this difference (discrepancy) is used by the brain to calculate depth since, for any one position of the eyes, the amount of discrepancy varies. We humans are familiar with stereopsis in three-dimensional movies that require us to wear special lenses. The images received by one eye differ slightly from those seen by the other eye, and three dimensions emerge because our brain interprets these discrepancies in the two-dimensional images as depth. Stereopsis is carried out by higher and more complex regions of the brain.

A second way of seeing depth relies on the degree to which the optical system of each eye must be adjusted to focus on an object, or the degree to which both eyes must be converged (turned inwards towards each other) to focus on an object. The third way of determining depth relies on motion parallax, which uses the differences in the amount of movement of images of objects relative to each other—for example, when we are in a moving vehicle, distant objects appear to remain almost stationary whereas those nearby speed past us. There is a graded range of movement between these two extremes and the brain uses this to determine depth.[3] Enough movement to see depth can be achieved simply by moving the head back and forth or by moving it around in a circle. Some birds do exactly this. Tawny frogmouths frequently move their heads through one or more full circles to see depth, especially before they strike at prey. They do this while keeping their eyes looking forward, and always in the horizontal plane. The use of parallax to determine depth does not require two eyes and can be done using the monocular fields of vision. Depth can, therefore, be seen in the monocular fields, but the binocular field of vision has more ways of determining depth.

Visual fields vary among species of birds. Mallards and woodcocks have a narrow binocular field extending in a strip from the region in front of the beak to directly overhead and continuing down behind the head.[4] This means that a predator swooping down from above and behind can be clearly seen and its distance estimated accurately. The rest of the bird's wide visual field is monocular and, in the horizontal plane around the head, vision is almost panoramic, meaning that the bird can see almost all the way around through 360°.

The size of the monocular and binocular fields of vision depends on the position of the bird's eyes in its skull and this varies from species to species, according to ecological requirements such as feeding strategies. Even though most avian species have only small binocular fields, the location of the binocular areas in a bird's visual space offers the greatest advantage in finding food and detecting predators. A heron standing with its beak horizontal can view its own feet binocularly, as in the case of the cattle egret in Figure 6.1.[5] This means it has excellent vision at the spot where it is likely to disturb its prey as it wades through the water. Typically a heron searches for prey by walking slowly with its beak held horizontally so that its binocular field is directed below its beak and in front of its feet. Once prey is detected, the heron is usually able to catch it with a single strike of the beak.

Mallards and woodcocks cannot see under their bills. In fact, they cannot see at all in a small area under the bill (Figure 6.1). This is only an apparent disadvantage since they do not use vision but touch to find food. Ducks, for example, dabble their bills at the bottom of ponds. The duck makes up for not having vision under the bill by having better overhead vision than the heron—its binocular area extends well overhead. As Graham Martin has suggested, comprehensive vision overhead may be possible only in those species that do not depend primarily on vision for finding their food.[6] Those species that are highly dependent on vision to find food have binocular vision below and around the beak and monocular vision overhead. The monocular vision overhead of the heron and the cattle egret, is a case in point—the binocular field of the cattle egret is a narrow strip from below to above the beak (Figure 6.1).

Some bird species have even wider fields of vision and can switch between a focused view for foraging and a wider view for scanning. Herons have almost panoramic vision in the vertical plane, extending from under the beak to above and behind the head. However, in the horizontal plane, they have a blind area of about 40° directly behind the head (Figure 6.1). To minimise this problem, they can turn their eyes outwards (diverge them) so that this blind area is reduced to only 10° to 20°. This diverging, however, is at the expense of the binocular field in front, which is reduced to half its size.[7] Herons probably use this ability to diverge their eyes when they are on the alert for approaching predators or even conspecifics (members of their own species). This ability to switch between visual modes is highly developed in starlings. Starlings can swing their eyes downward and forward to achieve a wide binocular field around the bill, used when foraging for food, and they can also swivel them backward and upward to look overhead for intruders. They may look up from feeding momentarily by flicking their eyes back and up from time to time.

Ostriches have a large blind area above and behind the head, which might result from the need to have eyelids and feathers to shade their eyes from the glaring African sun.[8] In front, they have a surprisingly narrow binocular field centred around the beak, as do chickens, pigeons and other birds that peck at grain. In fact, all these species have a blind area just in front of the tip of the beak, but at greater distances from the beak tip they can see binocularly. This means that they can see grain when their head is

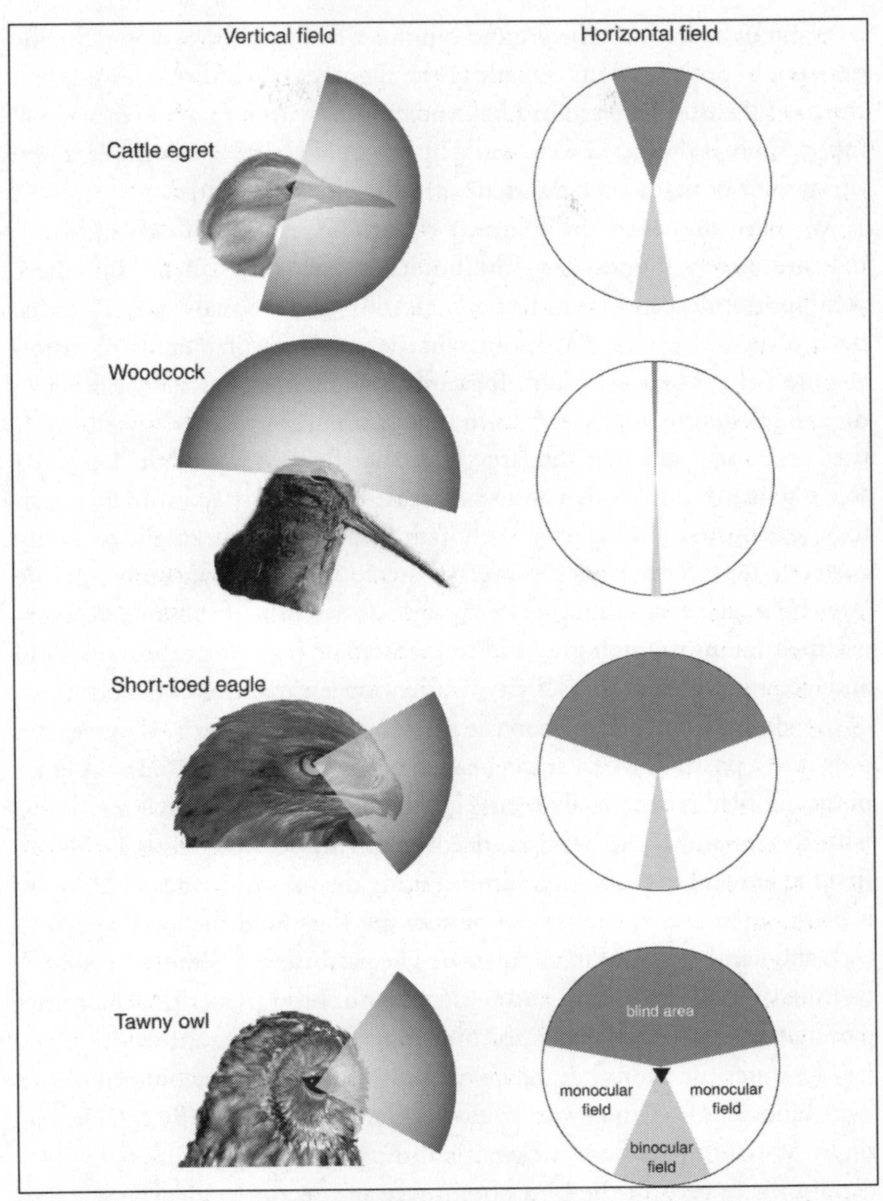

Figure 6.1 Visual fields vary for different species of birds. The diagrams on the left-hand side show the different locations and extents of the binocular field in different species. The diagrams on the right-hand side, drawn as if the viewer is looking down at the bird from above, illustrate the extent of the monocular field (white), binocular field (dark grey) and blind area behind the head (light grey). In each example, the bird's beak faces towards the bottom of the page.

a certain distance from the ground but not when they move closer. So, the decision to peck at grains is made at the slightly greater distance and then the head is thrust forward in a ballistic motion without any further visual input. Only if their eyes were wider apart could ostriches see closer to the tip of their beak, but their eyes are already widely separated.

We have discussed the frequent occurrence of wide fields of vision that are largely monocular—the binocular fields are small—but there are important exceptions to this organisation of the visual fields. Raptors, both owls and eagles, have somewhat larger binocular fields of vision (Figure 6.1). Their eyes look forwards and their monocular, sideways-directed fields are not as large as in birds with eyes in a lateral position. It used to be thought that the large binocular field in raptors had evolved solely to achieve stereopsis and so increase their ability to estimate depth for the capture of living prey. Although this explanation might be partly correct—raptors have good powers of stereopsis[9]—it now seems that the large binocular fields of raptors serve at least two other functions. Raptors use their talons to catch prey and to manipulate it during capture, killing and feeding. Much of this activity requires fine estimations of the positions of the toes and limbs relative to the prey and, typically, the bird moves the prey into a position where it can be seen binocularly (Figure 6.2).[10] A large binocular field is beneficial because it allows the bird to see what it is doing with its feet and talons without needing to turn its head sideways to see first the left and then the right limb. Tilting the head sideways to see what is being eaten is characteristic of parrots but they hold the food with one claw and use the beak to manipulate it. The parrots have no need for skilled coordination of both limbs and so they do not need to sacrifice their near panoramic vision for an enlarged binocular field, as the raptors do.

The other function that may have contributed to the evolution of the large binocular field in raptors could be related to precision flying. During flight, visual images flow backwards through the bird's visual fields and certain nerve cells in the bird's brain respond to the 'optical flow'. The central point from which the optical flow pattern radiates out is located directly in front of the flying bird. By having the eyes directed forward so that the binocular overlap is large, the optical flow seen by each eye is more symmetrical than in species with eyes positioned laterally, and both eyes see almost the same flow field.[11] As two eyes are better than one, this

Figure 6.2 The feeding posture of the wedge-tailed eagle. Note the direction of the bird's gaze—this provides excellent binocular vision when the bird is manipulating food between its beak and talons.

might be an advantage for judging rapid adjustments in flight speed and direction when swooping on prey. This argument applies to eagles and it might also be especially important to owls—their binocular field is twice the size of other species. It is unlikely that owls evolved their large binocular field solely for stereopsis because they hunt at night and mostly locate their prey using sound. Having two eyes seeing almost the same optical flow might be important in owls because at night the symmetrical optical flow seen by each eye may aid stealthy flight in search of prey.

Each species strikes a balance between the need to find its food and the need to detect predators and other forms of danger. If vision is not very important for finding food, the visual fields will optimise predator detection, and vice versa. Use of vision in social communication might also determine the relative sizes of the binocular and monocular fields of vision.

Structure of the avian eye

As in other vertebrate species, the avian eye performs the function of projecting an image onto the retina, which is a layer of nerve cells on the inside surface at the back of the eye (Figure 6.3). Before reaching the retina,

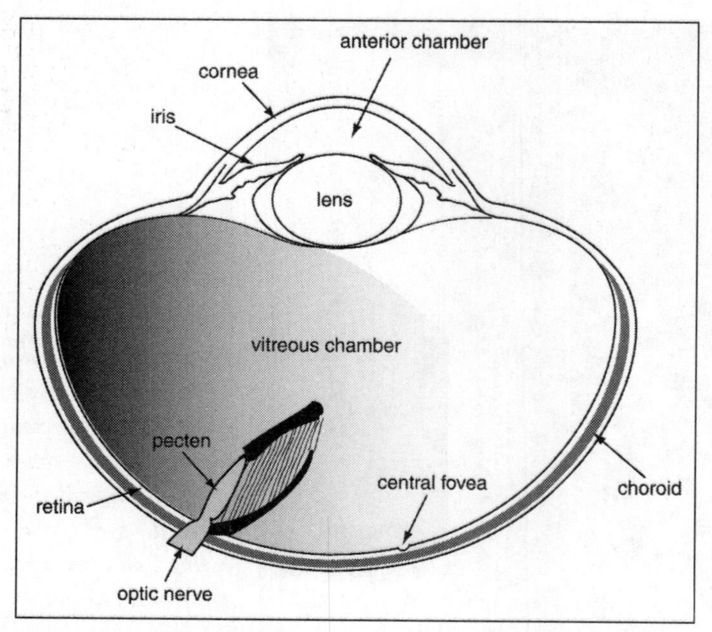

Figure 6.3 Anatomy of a chicken's eye. The diagram shows the eye opened through the middle. Light enters from above and passes through the cornea, lens and vitreous chamber to reach the retina. The shape of the eye differs from this in some species of birds but the principles of vision remain the same.

the light passes through the cornea of the eye and then the lens. Both the cornea and the lens focus the rays of light onto the retina, in the same way that the lens of a camera focuses the image onto the film at the back of the camera. Special nerve cells in the retina, called photoreceptors, absorb the light energy and transform it into electrical energy that is transmitted first to other nerve cells in the retina and then along the optic nerve to the brain, where the visual information is processed and interpreted.

The avian eye has some unique structures. First, the eyes of birds are large compared with the eyes of mammals, taking into account brain and body size. The size of birds' eyes is not usually obvious because the skin and feathers cover most of the eyeball, leaving only the iris and pupil exposed. Feeling the top of a bird's head, the size of the eyeballs will be apparent as two large bulges, depending on the species. Or the size of the eyes can be seen by examining the optic orbits (cavities) in a bird's skull. Having a larger eye means that the image formed in the eye is larger and

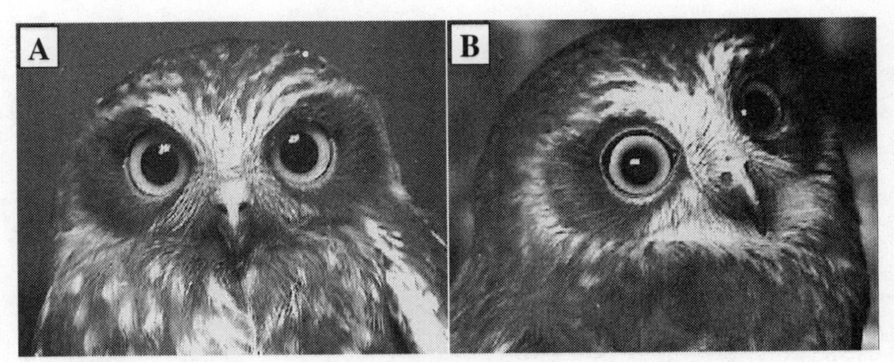

Figure 6.4 A boobook owl with its eyes converged (turned inwards) (A), and diverged (turned outwards) (B). Note the position of the pupils.

the bird is able to see fine detail.[12] Birds with larger eyes can, therefore, see more detail than those with small eyes.

Large eyes cannot be moved as easily as the smaller eyes of mammals and so birds are more likely to turn their head to see something. Even so, this does not rule out some very important eye movements—those that birds make to change their fields of vision are an example. In addition, with the exception of owls and eagles, birds are able to move each eye independently. Tawny frogmouths, for example, can move their eyes in opposite directions and most of their rapid eye movements (known as saccades) are like this.[13] Most owls, eagles and mammals with large binocular fields cannot do this. Tawny frogmouths also make frequent convergent saccades that turn their eyes inwards to look in front and, in fact, boobook owls can do this too (Figure 6.4).

The eyes of species active at night (nocturnal species) are larger than those of species that are active during the day (diurnal species). Owls are characterised by their large eyes and so are frogmouths (see Figure 3.4). Diurnal species can see only during the day and must roost before the light levels fall too low in the evening. Nocturnal species can see at very low light levels and most of them can see in the day as well, although they are unable to obtain as sharp an image as can diurnal birds. This is because their photoreceptor cells are spaced widely apart in order to collect as much light as possible in dim light. The image seen by a nocturnal bird is 'grainy' like the photographic prints obtained by using very fast film, whereas the image seen by a diurnal bird is sharper.

Figure 6.5 Constriction of one pupil as seen in a goshawk. The bird's left pupil is larger than the right—light input on the right side of the head has constricted the right pupil independently of the other eye.

The pupil adjusts the amount of light entering the eye. It dilates in dim light and constricts to a pinhole in bright light. In fact, birds can control the size of each pupil separately, a skill that mammals do not have. If the light of the setting sun is striking at an angle on one side of the roosting bird, the pupil on that side will constrict while the other pupil may remain dilated (Figure 6.5).

The second unique feature of the avian eye is the presence of a structure called the 'pecten'. This lies inside the eyeball and projects into the large internal part that is filled with a clear viscous fluid (called the vitreous humour) (see Figure 6.3). Using an ophthalmoscope to look into the eye of the bird, it is possible to see the pecten as a dark, pleated structure lying along the bottom of the inner side of the eyeball. The pecten has a network of blood vessels that supply nutrients to the retina. Each time the bird moves its eye in what is called a saccadic oscillation, nutrients leak out of the pecten and move across to the retina.[14] In birds, there are no blood vessels in the retina itself and this is beneficial since they cause some obstruction to vision. The mammalian eye does not have a pecten but it does have blood vessels in the retina. Both birds and mammals have further blood vessels in a network behind the retina and these too supply nutrients to the retina.

The third unique feature of the avian eye is the presence of oil droplets in the retina.[15] These sit next to the photoreceptors (the cone cells) that are used in seeing colour.[16] Light has to pass through these oil droplets before it can reach the cone cells. Oil droplets vary in colour from pink, in chickens, to yellow, red, orange or green in other species. The pigments in the oil droplets are carotenoids that come from carotene in the diet of birds. By feeding quails a diet free of carotene, and so ensuring that the oil droplets would lack their usual pigmentation, it was possible to show that the oil droplets play a role in colour vision. The quails fed on the carotene-free diet had impaired colour vision.

The oil droplets act as little filters in the eye and another important function they may have is to protect the photoreceptors from harmful ultraviolet rays. In our eyes the lens and the vitreous humour (inside the vitreous chamber) filter out much of the ultraviolet radiation so that it does not reach the sensitive cells of the retina, but in birds the vitreous humour does not do this. The oil droplets next to some cells in the retina may, therefore, act to filter out the ultraviolet rays.

Other photoreceptor cells in the retina are not so protected—they are exposed to the ultraviolet rays. This is a special adaptation of the avian retina that allows some species to see into the ultraviolet region of the visual spectrum, whereas mammals are unable to do this. At least some of the photoreceptors of the avian retina must be exposed to ultraviolet light if the bird is to see this kind of light. Hence the vitreous humour does not filter out the ultraviolet rays—but this causes a problem for the photoreceptor cells, which will be destroyed. The solution is to protect some photoreceptors with the oil droplets and leave others exposed. The exposed cells succumb to the damaging effects of the ultraviolet rays and have to be replaced frequently.

Another specialised characteristic of the eyes of some birds is the ability to see in fine detail in two directions at once.[17] Our eyes are designed so that we can see best directly in front. Here we see colour best and we have the best visual acuity (i.e. we can see fine detail). That is why we read by holding the book in front of us and not to the side while we look ahead. By holding the book in front of our eyes we make sure that the image of it falls on a specialised part of the retina where cone cells are concentrated. These particular photoreceptors are the best ones for seeing detail and colour. The specialised part of the retina is called the fovea. Birds like the pigeon can see well in front and to the side at the same time. This is because each eye of the pigeon has two foveae. One fovea is used to see in front and the other to see to the side. Humans have only one fovea in the middle of the retina of each eye.

Let us imagine a pigeon pecking at grain on the ground. The bird positions its head so that the grain is in the binocular field and the image of the grain is focused on the fovea located to the back and side of each eye. The cornea and the lens function together to focus the image and the focal point is about 10 centimetres in front of the bird's beak (it is myopic). At the same time, images of more distant objects in the left and right monocular visual fields are focused on the other fovea, located in the middle of the retina. The bird's eye is constructed so that the focal point for this sideways vision is several metres away from the bird. It is designed to allow the bird to see what is going on at a distance while it is feeding. It is perfectly arranged to allow the bird to detect intruders while feeding. The sideways-directed fovea is also used to look at large objects at a distance. The bird sees distant objects better with this fovea than with the short-sighted (myopic) one that looks straight ahead.

Chickens have a similar ability to see up close in front and at the same time to see further away at the sides but, instead of two foveae, they have an elongated, horizontal strip of retina in which the cone cells are packed more densely. As in the pigeon, the frontal field is focused for close up and the lateral field for further away, and this is possible because the cornea is curved more in front than to the sides. The lens, of course, works together with the cornea to focus the light rays and each eye can be focused independently of the other.[18] Therefore, not only can each eye be moved independently of the other but also each eye can be focused at a different distance. This is in addition to the fact that, in birds with eyes on the side of the head, each eye supplies entirely different information to the brain.

Birds are also focused for near vision (i.e. myopic) in the lower field of vision.[19] When the bird stands normally with its head up, it can see its feet and the surrounding ground in focus at the same time that more distant objects are in focus in the horizontal plane. This allows the bird to monitor what is at and around its feet at the same time as looking out to the horizon for predators or other intruders—similar to wearing glasses with bifocal or graded lenses. The shorter focal distance needed for the visual area around the feet varies with the bird's height and always matches it. It varies from one species to another, short and tall, and changes as the bird actually grows taller. The wading heron mentioned above makes

Plate 1 The colour gradients and shapes in a peacock's train are beguiling, even to human eyes. When the male rattles the extended wheel of his tail feathers, the turquoise shimmers and flashes. This is still one of the most dramatic visual displays for courtship among birds.

Plate 2 Albatrosses form lifelong bonds and this is partly responsible for the elaborate set of rituals they have developed as a pair. Here is the nest-greeting ceremony, a lengthy process of swaying and bill fencing, which we were able to watch on the Galàpagos islands.

Plate 3 A young albatross can wait for up to two days before a parent returns to feed it. The large and somewhat ungainly bird is entirely defenceless and its only safety is in hiding. Its camouflage works surprisingly well from a distance.

Plate 4 Birds' eyes come in a variety of colours. From top to bottom: crowned crane, lorikeet, boobook owl, common koel (female or juvenile), goshawk and heron.

Plate 5 The feet of the blue-footed booby attain their distinctive colouring in adulthood—note that the youngster behind the parent has pale feet. The adult's feet, as for penguins, function to keep the body of the nestling warm.

Plate 6 An egret devouring its prey.

Plate 7 A male tawny frogmouth, not usually as clearly visible during the day as in this photo. However, this bird had been hand-raised and was therefore content to be seen in daylight and often roosted near the house. Tawny frogmouths are frequently heard at night. Indeed, the hooting of this species is an intricate part of the soundscape of the Australian bush.

Plate 8 An Australian magpie carolling, a vocal activity to affirm ownership of territory. The male usually begins and one or two others then enter into the music, forming a loud and unmistakable chorus.

Plate 9 Hidden in the reeds, there are always alert eyes watching for any intruders.

Plate 10 In the Galápagos islands. Pair-bonding can last a year to many years among species of gannets and boobies.

Plate 11 The photo of this bird was taken in northern Italy. It is a rehabilitating griffon vulture and part of the griffon vulture reintroduction program (Progetto Grifone) in the Riserva Naturale del Lago di Cornino. Vulture 'restaurants' have been established in the mountainous parts of this region (Regione Autonomica Friuli-Venezia Giulia) to help increase the numbers to a viable level. This region was once part of their natural territory.

Plate 12 The author, Gisela Kaplan, with an Australian wedge-tailed eagle which she rehabilitated.

Plate 13 A young eastern rosella growing its first pin feathers.

good use of this focusing ability as it searches for its prey and so do many other species in their feeding activities.

Birds that peck grains do not keep their eyes open when they thrust the head downwards in a ballistic motion. They do not use their normal eyelid for this but a so-called third eyelid, the nictitating membrane. Since the bird cannot see well close to its beak, the nictitating membrane closes in a reflex to protect the eye from any particles. This membrane folds up into the nasal corner of the eye (next to the beak) and moves across from there. In some species it is transparent, whereas in others it is partly opaque and so the bird cannot see through it clearly. When the bird has made a decision to peck, clear vision is no longer necessary, the nictitating membrane is closed and the eye is protected from injury.

Pupil and iris

Two further features are noticeable when observing a bird's eye, the pupil and the iris. Both vary greatly among species. Birds that have to forage for their food in darkness are able to dilate their pupils wide in order to collect as much light into the eye as possible. This dilation is seen in nocturnal species such as owls and nightjars and also in species that must enter dark environments to search for prey. King penguins, for example, dive down to ocean depths where little light penetrates and there they rely on detecting prey that emits light from photophores. The penguins can dilate fully the pupils of their large eyes so that they can see these dim lights. On land their pupils close down to a square-shaped pinhole against the blinding glare of the snow and direct sunlight in the summer months.[20] The constriction and dilation of the pupil come about as a result of changing the tension in the muscles of the iris. Thus a large pupil means that the iris is barely visible while a small pupil reveals more of the iris. Most birds have spherical pupils but some have an ellipsoid shape and others can close the pupil down to a small slit or square.

The iris varies in colour enormously among avian species due to the presence of different pigment cells. Brown, yellow, red, blue and green irises of different shades and hues are found. Some birds have irises with reflective cells that make them gleam. In many birds the iris is a light colour clearly visible against the pupil and surrounding feathers. In other species it is a dark brown colour not easily distinguished from the pupil.

In some species, the iris may be used in social communication because it changes size in different states of emotional arousal[21] and it may be a different colour according to age and sex. The galah male has a dark brown iris and the female has a pink iris. In addition, we have observed that the tawny frogmouth can change the colour of its iris from a greenish-yellow colour, when it is in a relaxed state, to a reddish colour when the bird is aroused or distressed. The red colour is strongest around the edges of the iris and may be caused by dilating the artery known as the *circulus arteriosus iridicus*, which circles the iris in this outer region.[22]

Movements of head and eyes

When on the ground or perched on a branch, a bird tends to hold its head stable in one position in space for as long as possible, and when it does move its head it often does so very quickly. By these means, the bird ensures that the visual images on its retina remain stationary for as long as possible.[23] This is what is happening when a pigeon apparently bobs its head back and forth as it walks along. If we take a videotape of a pigeon walking and play it back in slow motion, we can see that the pigeon's legs move its body forward at a steady rate but the head remains stationary in space as long as possible. When the head does move forward to catch up with the body, indeed to overshoot the body, it does so very rapidly (Figure 6.6). This makes it appear as if the head is bobbing (or hitching) back and forth, whereas the head is actually stopping and then moving forward rapidly. Another example of head stabilisation is seen in a bird sitting on a moving branch on a breezy day. The branch may sway around, and the bird's crouched body goes with it, but its head stays almost stationary in space.

Head stability is often seen in birds looking for prey while hovering. A kingfisher, for example, is able to hold its head stationary in space even though its wings are flapping and its body is moving as it hovers in search of prey.[24] To show how important it is for the bird to maintain a stable visual image one researcher designed an apparatus that moved the surrounding visual scene along with a pigeon as it walked along.[25] This meant that the image of the surroundings remained stable on the pigeon's retina. The pigeon no longer performed head bobbing. The same researcher sat the bird on a stationary perch and then moved the whole

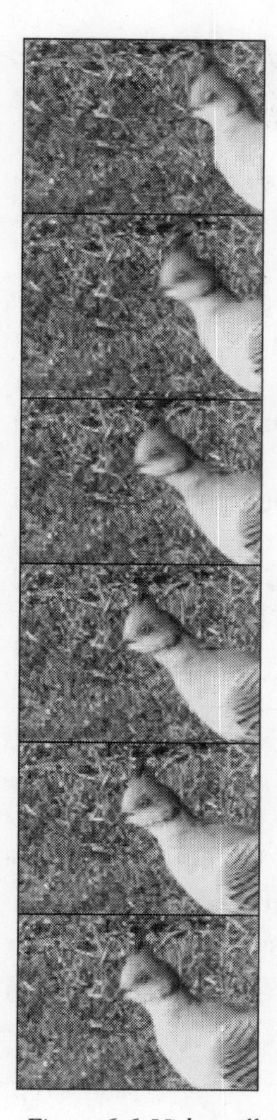
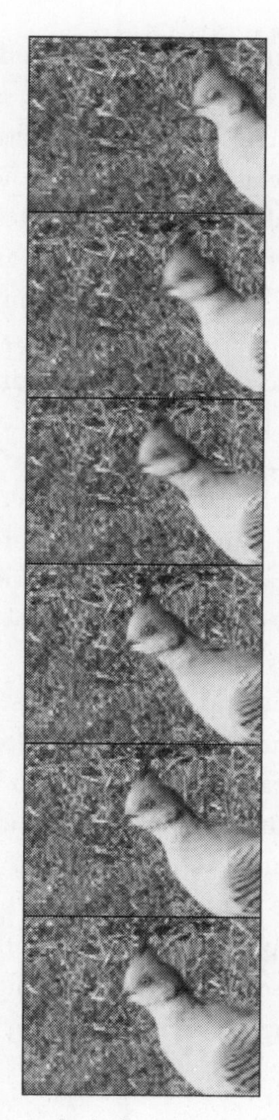

Figure 6.6 Video stills of a walking pigeon which show how the head remains stationary for as long as possible and then bobs forward rapidly. The frames are arranged in sequence starting from the top left-hand side and running down the page. The sequence begins with rapid forward movement of the head (frames 1–2) and then the head remains stationary (frames 3–7) to allow the body to catch up. Then the head moves forward rapidly again.

visual scene gently back and forth and up and down around it. In this case, the bird moved its head with the moving visual world while its body remained crouched on the perch without moving.

Having a long and flexible neck helps a bird to achieve stability of the head, and hence stability of the visual image. Mammals have short necks to hold up their much heavier skulls and jaws and thus they have less ability to stabilise the head in space and must deal with seeing the visual image as it flows past them. They are, however, able to move their eyes much more than birds can. A pigeon walking along may see the world in a series of still images, particularly since vision is often suppressed (or turned off) as the head is moved rapidly forward. The main reason for seeing the world in a series of 'stills', or fixed gazes, is to avoid blurring of the image caused when the head is moved. The photoreceptors cannot respond fast enough to cope with rapid movement.[26] Another reason is to allow the bird to tell its own movement from that of the world around it. These reasons are also true for species other than birds.

Head bobbing up and down is used by many birds that search for food in shallow water. It is commonly seen in shorebirds such as sandpipers, oystercatchers and plovers, and also in dippers and kingfishers, as well as many other waterbirds. Head bobbing helps the birds to locate their prey beneath the surface of the water.[27] By up-and-down head bobbing, a bird can gain more accurate information about where its prey is underwater using motion parallax. The head bobbing may also overcome some of the problems caused by reflection of light from the water's surface and by refraction of light at the interface between air and water.

Colour vision

The abundance of brightly coloured feathers in birds is matched by a superior ability to see colour. Birds can see a greater range of colours than humans can. The key to seeing colour is to have pigments in the cone photoreceptor cells in the retina. These trap different wavelengths of light (i.e. different colours of light) and communicate information to the brain. Humans have three different pigments in the cone cells, or two in people who are colour-blind. It is the mixing of stimulation of cone cells with the different pigments that allows us to see the full rainbow of colours.

Many bird species have four different pigments and so are likely to be able to see a greater range of colours than we can.[28] Some birds even have five different pigments. There is still much to be learned about colour vision in all species, and we need to have more behavioural tests of colour vision in birds, but we can say that almost certainly birds have the most elaborate and complex colour vision of all animals. The variously coloured oil droplets also have a role to play in the bird's ability to see colour and they are an additional reason why the colour vision of birds is more elaborate than that of humans.

Colour vision is better in diurnal birds than in nocturnal ones. Nocturnal species make use of photoreceptor cells (rod cells) that are more responsive to dim light. Rod cells have a pigment that traps light but they do not have the range of pigments that allow cone cells to see colour. All birds have both rods and cones, as do other mammals, but nocturnal species have more rods and fewer cones than diurnal species. For example, the American white ibis, a species that feeds only during the day, has three times more cones than rods, and the black skimmer, a species that feeds mostly at night, has five times more rods than cones.[29] Owls have even more rods relative to cones than the skimmer. These nocturnal species sacrifice colour vision for superior ability to see in low intensities of light.

Each species has its own special ways of seeing, designed to fit its requirements for finding food, detecting predators, recognising individuals and communicating using visual displays. Some of the elaborate visual displays used by birds to attract a sexual partner or to signal the intention to take flight may exploit visual abilities that have evolved, in the first instance, for finding food and detecting predators. The ability to see colour might be such a characteristic. Colour vision is essential for birds that feed on fruits that change colour as they ripen or for those that must recognise the patterned colours of flowers to obtain nectar. It is also important in species that must distinguish one coloured insect from another to ensure that toxic insects are not eaten. There were very good reasons for birds to retain the colour vision of their reptilian ancestors and to elaborate on it.

During evolution, colour vision disappeared in nocturnal species or species living in very dark places. In fact, colour vision has evolved and disappeared several times in the different branches of the evolutionary tree.[30] The early primates were, for example, nocturnal and unable to see colour. They lost the colour vision that was present in their non-primate ancestors. Only later, when primates became diurnal, did colour vision evolve again.[31] This rather recent appearance, in the evolutionary time scale, of colour vision in primates may partly explain why humans have less detailed colour vision than birds.

Birds have often exploited their ability for colour vision to its full advantage, resulting in the wonderful range of plumage colours in avian species. Insects and flowers also exploit the colour vision of birds either to attract their attention, as in the case of many flowers, or to warn the birds off, as in the case of some insects.

Visual displays are often modified to meet the visual characteristics of the birds' surrounding environment. Plumage colours and patterns vary with the light levels in the bird's habitat and the colour of the surrounding vegetation. The variations in the number of white patches in the plumage of the eight species of warblers illustrate this well. All the warbler species are yellow-green in colour but they may have from zero to five white patches depending on the species and the habitat in which it lives. The species living in dense, dark forests have more patches than the species living in more open forest, and these in turn have more patches than the species living in the bright environment of open scrub.[32] These patches of white feathers enable the warblers' displays to be seen by conspecifics and they are most valuable in the darker environments. Thus we see an interaction between the bird's visual abilities and its habitat.

Even within its own habitat a bird may perform some of its visual displays only in places where lighting conditions maximise their colours and contrast, for example in open parts of the forest.[33] A bird may also display only at times of the day when the lighting conditions are best for showing its patterns of colour. At other times of the day, or in other parts of its habitat, the same bird may use colour to conceal itself from both avian and non-avian predators.

Seeing in the ultraviolet

Some species of birds can see the very short wavelengths of light (ultraviolet) because one of the four or five visual pigments in their cone cells is specifically designed to trap ultraviolet light.[34] Sensitivity to ultraviolet light has been shown in the pigeon, hummingbird, kestrel, thirteen species of passerines, two species of boobies, the zebra finch, blue tit and starling.[35]

Although the capacity of birds to see ultraviolet light was discovered nearly three decades ago, exactly what they use it for is still not known.[36] Birds may use this sensitivity to ultraviolet light in detecting ripe fruits. Many flowers and leaves have patterns that can be seen only in ultraviolet light and they may be used to guide birds (e.g. hummingbirds) to their food source. Also, many fruits that are spread by birds carrying the seeds from one place to another, often after first eating them, are coloured red or black and their waxy bloom reflects ultraviolet light.[37]

Even hunting birds may use ultraviolet light to find their food and in this case it is to detect the urine trails laid by their prey. This was shown in the kestrel. Voles are hunted by kestrels and the vole's urine absorbs ultraviolet light very strongly, leaving a visible trail (as a dark area) to the eyes of those capable of ultraviolet vision.[38]

Reflection of ultraviolet light by the plumage of birds may be important in social communication. To our eyes male and female blue tits appear identical but the patch of feathers on the crown of the head is different in the ultraviolet region of the light spectrum.[39] It is therefore likely that blue tits can perceive this sexual difference. Another study has shown too that the irridescent plumage of starlings reflects ultraviolet light and that a clear difference between males and females, not seen by the human eye, emerges in the ultraviolet range of the spectrum.[40] Males and females have different patterns of ultraviolet reflection from different parts of their bodies. The same is true for budgerigars and zebra finches.[41] These results, together with others showing that blocking out the ultraviolet light alters the bird's choice of partner,[42] indicate a wide potential for use of ultraviolet wavelengths in the display signals that birds send to each other. So far, there has not been a great deal of research in this area.[43]

Ultraviolet vision helps to assess the colour gradients in the sky, which birds might use when navigating their flight paths. Birds might even use their ability to detect ultraviolet light as a light-dependent magnetic compass.[44] This would allow them to orient themselves using the earth's magnetic field and would be useful on long migration flights. The ultraviolet wavelengths of light would be more effective than blue light in enabling the bird to secure correct magnetic orientation. It is possible to test the magnetic orientation of birds in the laboratory and to do so under different wavelengths of light. Under white and blue light silvereyes and European robins can orient their flight direction according to the magnetic compass but they cannot do so under red light.[45] The same birds were not tested under ultraviolet light but current knowledge suggests that this might be even better than blue light. More research will be needed before this important aspect of vision is understood in any detail.

Seeing polarised light

Birds can make use of the polarisation of light to determine their direction of flight during migration. This is particularly so at sunset when scattering of the light by the earth's atmosphere makes the rays partly polarised. The directions of polarisation form a regular pattern across the sky. Birds taking to the air at sunset to begin their nocturnal migration flights can see the pattern of polarised light.[46] They use these cues to orient their direction of flying.[47] They also take into account the direction of the earth's magnetic field, and it appears that this magnetic information can be used together with the information on light polarisation to navigate during migration. For example, if either the pattern of polarised light or the direction of the magnetic field changes, they become somewhat disoriented.[48]

In summary, we have seen that many of the behaviours that birds perform depend on their specialised visual abilities and requirements. It is difficult for us to imagine exactly what a bird sees with its wide visual fields, superior colour vision and ability to see ultraviolet light. Added to this, birds have the unique ability to focus close up for feeding and at the same time see far away to their left and right side. They can also focus and move their left and right eyes independently of the other. These abilities require different kinds of processing in the brain. The processing of visual information is also integrated with auditory, tactile, olfactory and taste information. What other sensory information will be processed together with the visual information depends on what the bird is doing at the time, as well as what information is available. Information on the earth's magnetic field may, for example, be used in association with information on light polarisation only during migration and not at other times.

chapter 7

HEARING, SMELL, TASTE AND TOUCH

Birds rely on visual and auditory cues to communicate with each other, often over some distance. Vocalisations and hearing are very important to birds and songbirds have the most complex auditory signals among vertebrates.[1]

We, as a species, like listening to birdsong because birds' tunes usually sound pleasant and melodious to our ears. The reason for our partiality is that most bird sounds fall into the range of human hearing and sound musical to us. The human ear hears across about ten octaves of sonic frequencies. The frequencies detected by birds fall almost entirely within the upper four octaves of this audible range, between 0.5 (an octave above middle C on the piano) and 8.0 kHz.[2] It was discovered only last century that there are also birds that hear and emit sounds above the range of human perception, particularly above 8 to 10 kHz.

Structure of the ear

If humans can hear many of the same sounds that birds hear we might assume that there are similarities in the structure of the ear of humans and birds. There are some. The avian ear, like the mammalian ear, consists of three interrelated structures: the external, middle and inner ear. Unlike humans, however, birds have no external trumpet (or pinna) to collect sound and to assist in locating the source of the sound. External sound-collecting structures have not evolved in birds, presumably to avoid friction in air or water. Large flightless birds have a very large naked ear opening, whereas, for most other species, the entrance to the ear is covered by feathers. Birds, like all vertebrates, have two ears (i.e. they have what is called a 'binaural receiver system'). Each ear is set apart from the other being located to the left and right of the head, and usually each ear faces in a different direction. The general design of the external ear is similar in most birds, although there are large variations in details.

Differences in the ear opening may be related to methods of foraging. Birds that forage under water tend to have very small ear openings, especially small in diving birds such as cormorants and smallest in the Guanay cormorant. In some diving birds, such as auks, the external opening can be actively closed off when the bird is diving.

The external ear

Differences in the size of the ear opening may also be related to the bird's relative need for acuteness of hearing. The largest and geometrically most complicated external ear is found in some owl species. Acoustically, owls are also the most sensitive birds, matching the hearing ability of a cat.[3] In the barn owl, the ear opening is almost square and relatively small; in other owl species it is often a vertical slit, situated near the top of the skull, as in Tengmalm's owl and the long-eared owl. A number of owl species, such as the eagle owl, have skin flaps next to their ears. Some birds have full muscular control over their flaps allowing part or complete covering of their ear slits, as in the boreal owl or the tawny owl. In some species a flap of skin in front of the ear can be raised to enable the bird to hear sounds from behind.

The external ears may be arranged asymmetrically, especially in owls, although this is not uniformly so across all owl species. One ear is directed partly upwards and the other downwards. The Tengmalm's owl has very marked asymmetry of the outer ear and even of the openings in the skull. This arrangement of the ear is associated with localising sound. Separation of the ears allows the bird to compute the difference in pressure of a sound received first by one ear and then by the other, enabling it to locate the direction of sound in the horizontal plane. Asymmetry in the position of the ears (one facing upwards and the other downwards) enhances the owl's ability to detect sound in the vertical plane.[4]

The middle ear

The middle ear transfers sound to the inner ear. The middle ear cavity also varies in size and researchers have found that size is related to function. Species with good to excellent hearing tend to have more spacious middle ear cavities (e.g. birds of prey and owls).[5] The first experimental demonstration of the acoustic coupling of the two ears in birds was made in 1924.[6] This occurs via a connection between the ears, and allows the bird to assess the sound impact on each ear in relation to the other. Birds also estimate differences in time of arrival of sound waves at each ear by neurological means. The middle ear cavities of both ears actively communicate with each other and this ability to compare and interpret differences in sound pressure may be a general avian principle for sound localisation.[7] However, little is understood yet of the complexity of interaction of the key functions of hearing.[8]

Functions of the ear

The avian inner ear structure has two parts with separate functions: hearing and the sense of balance.[9] The sense of balance takes place in the vestibular organ. Hearing is managed by the cochlea. In mammals, the cochlea is shaped like a coiled snail shell while in birds it is the shape of a flattened tube, varying in length according to species. Whatever the length, the avian cochlea is always considerably smaller (in proportion to body size) than the smallest cochlea of mammals. Intense sound causes hearing loss but it has been shown, at least in chicks and quails, that their ears possess the ability to repair the damage within as little as seven days.[10]

It is easier to describe the anatomy of an organ than to say how it actually functions. So far, three main functions of hearing in birds have been identified: (1) to give warning and signal the presence of a predator; (2) to provide added social functions in acoustic communication; and (3) to detect prey. Some species also use hearing for echolocation (e.g. cave swifts). The questions to look at now include how hearing is achieved, how signals are deciphered, what and how well birds can hear, and what hearing ability contributes to their survival.

A number of avian species can pinpoint the location of a sound source by listening (auditory sound cues) alone. The barn owl, barred owl and long-eared owl track prey entirely by auditory means.[11] Roger Payne's classic studies involved testing barn owls' hunting ability by providing food in different levels of light, eventually creating conditions where the food would need to be located by auditory cues alone. The owl captured the prey accurately every time.[12] Among birds tested for auditory sensitivity, owls are definitely more sensitive and far superior in hearing than diurnal birds. In fact, they can hear 300 times better than pigeons. The owl's ability to locate sound sources at a lower threshold of hearing sensitivity is about the same as that of humans and cats. The difference may be between nocturnal and diurnal species rather than specifically between owls and other birds. Other avian species hunting predominantly at night, such as frogmouths and nightjars, may also have better hearing than diurnal birds but this has not been tested yet. Graham Martin suggests that this hearing ability in owls has probably reached the absolute limit of auditory sensitivity in vertebrates.[13]

Localising sound

The owl's hearing ability is not in question, but how does it manage to localise the sound source accurately? One explanation lies in the very specialised structure of the ear, another in the way in which the owl collects sound. Owls may follow sound so that it hits frontally at the face (as if 'looking') and the flexible head assists this process. The tawny owl, for instance, locates its prey by slowly turning its head to pinpoint the sound location. Owls can turn their heads through nearly 360 degrees. By turning towards the general direction of the sound source and using the disk-like sweeping motion of parallax (just as in vision), they can locate the source of sounds very accurately. Facial disks (called ruffs) enhance the owl's ability to hear very low intensity sounds and can even determine the direction of the sound, because the disk acts as a sound collector and reflector. Disks are found not only in owls but also in other birds of prey, such as the pallid harrier, the marsh harrier and the European nightjar.

It is possible that all nocturnal birds relying on live food need extra sensitive hearing. Nocturnal living has tended to be associated with hunting but there are some nocturnal birds that are not insectivorous or carnivorous. There are, for instance, two species of parrot in Australia, the ground parrot and the night parrot, and in New Zealand the kakapo, that live exclusively on fruit and plants. We do not yet know whether 'nocturnality' itself requires especially sensitive hearing or whether hearing is largely linked to hunting live prey. Diurnal pigeons have relatively poor hearing. The topknot pigeon is one of the few nocturnal fruit-eating species but its hearing has not been investigated. Another species that feeds on fruit nocturnally is the oilbird. Instead of acute hearing over a wide acoustic range, oilbirds have developed a form of echolocation, rather like cave swiftlets. However, according to Graham Martin, their echolocation performance is poor compared with that of bats.[14] Hearing with some echolocation may be important for the oilbird largely to detect predators, but one cannot simply presume this to be so.

The kakapo is an endangered bird. It is one of the ten rarest birds on earth, disappearing because of introduced predators, including stoats and cats that seem to make an easy meal of the flightless kakapo. This suggests that kakapos are too slow to get away or cannot hear well enough to detect approaching predators. Nestlings, left on the ground, are totally defenceless. The fact alone that this species is both largely ground-feeding and ground-nesting suggests that the kakapo had no predators before the arrival of humans and their introduced species. And indeed, this is so. It may never have needed to develop acute hearing even though it is nocturnal. By contrast, we can speculate that diurnal birds that use excavating techniques for foraging might need excellent hearing to obtain some cue to the location of their invisible food. Woodpeckers, for instance, extract larvae from under the bark. How would they find them unless they heard them first? Australian magpies that strut purposefully over grassy terrain and suddenly plunge their beaks into the ground, extracting large scarab larvae, do so having heard the insect's movement first. This implies excellent hearing. In fact, recent studies have found that American robins can find worms by auditory cues alone.[15]

The perception of predators and prey may be one of the important functions of hearing in all species. In birds, hearing has another equally important function. Since birds communicate extensively by vocalisations (see Chapter 8), there is a need for auditory discrimination of sounds. What they hear and how well they can discriminate one vocalisation from another, among conspecifics and between species, has been investigated in a number of different ways.

Sound discrimination

One strong school of thought, developed in Germany in the 1920s, began to examine the hearing of birds in the context of musical sounds. These early studies often appeared in scholarly musicology journals. They questioned whether birds could distinguish between pure and noisy tones and whether their 'musicality' allowed humans to classify bird songs in human systems of music annotation. For instance, are birds capable of distinguishing intervals of a third, fourth and fifth, and can they memorise a tune and transpose it to another key?[16] This was tested in budgerigars and crossbills and it was found that these two species were capable of distinguishing between intervals that were considerably smaller than full tone steps. This ability had been established already for pigeons.[17] Memory of auditory cues was ascertained for a difference as small as 1 to 2 Hz, showing that this ability is as well developed in some birds as it is in human hearing. Moreover, these birds had no difficulty transposing a song to a different key within four octaves.[18] Another study conditioned the same birds to recognise one specific call as a food call. On completion of this training the birds were meant to be confused by embedding the specific food call in a series of known and unknown sequences of sounds and songs. The birds were able to identify the food call every time despite the scramble.[19] These findings suggest that auditory communication in birds may well be extremely subtle and complex and that the avian ear (not necessarily of all species) may well be capable of very fine discriminations. It is regrettable in many ways that this research has found few followers in the examination of these aspects of avian hearing.

Sound distortion

Most research on avian auditory perception is relatively recent. It includes attempts to explain how the avian ear can deal not only with identification of sound location but also with sound distortion.[20] This approach asks how birds are able to do this so well despite the fact that they have much smaller ears placed much closer together in their small heads than mammals. Other questions include how sounds irrelevant to the messages are filtered out and how the auditory pathways function in this process of deciphering.[21] The auditory pathways of birds were mapped out in the 1960s, including the regions of the forebrain involved in hearing. Gradually it has emerged that, despite a lack of specialisation of the avian ear itself, higher auditory centres process information that is biologically relevant to each particular species.[22]

But it is not always size that determines quality or sophistication. The derogatory meanings of 'bird-brain' and 'bird-head' may one day need to be scrapped in recognition of the fact that we have learned from the computer chip that bigger is not always better. Birds need to be organised efficiently if they are to fly but lack of size is not equal to lack of complexity. For instance, it was discovered in the 1990s that budgerigars are capable of distinguishing sounds in a large area with both ears (called 'large free-field binaural unmasking'), an ability that had been documented before only in animals with much larger heads.[23] Budgerigars, the small nomadic parakeets of inland Australia, now one of the most commonly available pet birds worldwide, also show an unusual ability to distinguish their calls against background noise (i.e. a small signal-to-noise ratio).[24] Budgerigars can also learn to classify a large number of different types of contact calls and can remember them for several months.[25] This occurs even when the calls are degraded, by filtering or truncating them.[26] The best signal-to-noise ratio attained by the budgerigar's auditory system is in a narrow spectral region of 2 to 4 kHz. This unusually sensitive hearing of budgerigars (called 'critical ratio function'), compared with that of other birds and mammals, is characteristic of the species and not a result of domestication or selective breeding.[27]

Great tits also show an unusual critical ratio function, which may have been an adaptation to coping with broadband background noise generated by wind in the canopy.[28] Budgerigars do not naturally have many trees in their arid Australian inland environment yet they have hearing comparable to that of the great tits. The reason is probably that they also have to hear against constant wind that generates broadband background noise. Having two ears is obviously an advantage for determining directionality of sound, but the sensitivity of the ear, it seems, is not entirely dependent on the size of the ear.

Smell

Compared with auditory and visual communication, relatively little is known of the importance of the sense of smell (or olfaction) in birds. It is not for want of trying—a veritable controversy raged about avian capabilities of smell in the early 19th century. The first experiments of sorts, although not well controlled, concerned largely birds of prey and vultures, the reasoning being that they are meat and carrion eaters and are therefore exposed to particularly pungent odours. Could they find their food by visual or olfactory information or by a combination of both? In 1835 some vultures (species not identified) were tested by exposing them to three different kinds of cues on food sources.[29] One was an entire skin but stuffed with grass, the second the carcass of a large hog that was extremely 'fetid' to the human nose but covered and hidden from view. The third was a dead pig hidden beneath leaves but with a trail of blood leading to the carcass. The vultures tore the skin apart and pulled out the grass but did not find the 'fetid' hog. They found the pig only by moving along the trail of blood. The author concluded that vultures have a poorly developed sense of smell. Darwin's description of an experiment with a condor in 1834 is similarly weighted against birds having an acute sense of smell, although this experiment was poorly controlled as well.[30] However, the scientific basis of knowledge about the sense of smell has been expanded dramatically over recent decades, starting with some classic studies[31] and elaborate investigations of the olfactory anatomy.[32]

All types of olfactory systems possess an olfactory epithelium (a skin with cells sensitive to chemical odours), and an olfactory bulb or lobe (part of the brain processing olfactory information; see Figure 2.2. The ratio of the size of the olfactory bulb to the overall size of the brain varies substantially from one species, and order, to the next—for example, the ratio is 3 per cent for small forest-dwelling songbirds, 8 per cent for house sparrows, 33 per cent for the kiwi and 37 per cent for some seabirds, including petrels. The larger the ratio is, the more important the sense of smell. Configurations of the nasal cavity vary greatly, by about thirteen times, and so does the size of the olfactory bulb (tested in 124 species of birds in 23 of the orders), suggesting that these quantitative differences in some way indicate differences in some aspects of function. An increase in size of the olfactory epithelium can result in an increased capacity for detailed discrimination *between* odours rather than increased sensitivity *to* odours. The short-eared owl, for instance, has an olfactory bulb that is as well developed as that of chickens, pigeons, mallards and herring gulls, suggesting that this species has some ability to discriminate between different odours. But similar size of the olfactory system may not imply that any two species perceive the same range of odours. Indeed, several species within the high-ratio group were found to respond to entirely different classes of odorants significant to that species.[33]

Bernice Wenzel noted in 1967 that the question of whether birds can smell, really contains three questions:

1. Are birds capable of perceiving olfactory stimuli?
2. Do birds naturally regulate any aspects of their behaviour in terms of olfactory cues?
3. Can birds learn to regulate certain aspects of their behaviour in terms of olfactory cues?[34]

Even today, there is only a limited amount of experimental evidence related to these questions.[35]

Birds are capable of perceiving olfactory stimuli but there are substantial variations in ability between species. For instance, thresholds of odour perception in pigeons, quails and chickens are different. The chicken is the most sensitive of the three species to pentane and hexane and the pigeon is the most sensitive to heptane. Serge Nef and colleagues isolated nine odorant receptor genes from the domestic chick. These are also found in fish, rats, mice, dogs and humans, and they are present early in embryonic development.[36] Birds can learn to regulate their behaviour following olfactory cues alone.[37]

Response to odours may be communicated to the brain by the trigeminal nerve, as well as the olfactory system, as shown in pigeons.[38] Nevertheless, overall perception of odours seems to remain poor in pigeons.[39] The same importance of the trigeminal nerve for olfaction has also been noted in studies of starlings.[40]

The role of smell

Food identification may well be one of the most important known roles of the sense of smell. Kiwis use a technique called 'extractive foraging' to obtain hidden food.[41] Not only does this method of feeding require good hearing but, in kiwis, it may rely in part or completely on smell or tactile senses. Kiwis have sensitive bristles at the base of the bill to help in foraging for food at night. In kiwis the part of the brain devoted to olfaction (the olfactory lobes) is among the largest of any bird and by far the largest of any terrestrial bird species.[42] The kiwi's acute sense of smell was confirmed in experiments as early as 1906.[43] Nevertheless, evidence for foraging by use of the sense of smell remains unusual in birds. Apart from the kiwi, there is some evidence of the importance of olfaction in the turkey vulture and possibly also in black-billed magpies.[44]

In the sea, certain plants and oils leave large odour plumes (trails) that tend to move downwind and entice pelagic (sea-dwelling) species to congregate at the source of the odour. Some ocean dwelling birds are able to locate food sources in mid-ocean by smell alone;[45] they are attracted to the odour dimethyl sulphide, which is given off by microscopic plants in sea water.[46] Many ocean birds respond to characteristic odours. Leach's storm-petrels, for instance, can discriminate between their own nest material and similar litter gathered from the forest floor, suggesting that the petrels use olfaction not only to locate their island colony but also to locate individual nest burrows in darkness.[47]

During daylight, vision and olfaction may both be used to detect possible food sources in some species of petrels and shearwaters. In one experiment, sponges were soaked either in cod liver oil or sea water and held just above the sea surface. Four species (great and sooty shearwaters, Wilson's storm-petrels, and Leach's storm-petrels) were attracted to the baits. All the species, except the sooty shearwater, showed a preference for the pungent oil-soaked sponge. Five species from two other orders of seabirds were also present (gannet, great black-backed gull, Jerring gull, Arctic tern, and puffin). When the same experiment was conducted at night, only storm-petrels were attracted and showed a strong preference for the oil-soaked sponge.[48] From this response it can be inferred that the storm-petrels were guided by olfactory cues while the other species also required visual cues. The region of the beak used for smelling in storm petrels is unique in that the nostrils open at the tip of the beak and not at the base. In addition, there are complex olfactory surfaces inside the nasal cavity, creating a large surface area for the reception of smells. Later experiments attempted to establish from how far away storm-petrels could be recruited on the basis of an olfactory lure. A team of researchers put up a test-raft with strong oily odours and waited. They were astounded by the results, finding an estimated maximum recruitment distance of about 8 kilometres at a flight speed of 30 km/h and arrival at the vessel after just 50 minutes of odour presentation.[49] This is an amazing ability which has so far not been matched by any other avian species.

Birds are able to use olfactory cues in the control of homing and navigation, as well as feeding, and olfactory landmarks may play a role in homing and migration.[50]

Habitat also shapes the evolution, development and use of the olfactory system. It has been suggested that an arboreal habitat (living in trees) tends to lead to a reduction in the sense of smell.[51] Arboreality has reduced olfactory mechanisms in primates and the same seems to be true of birds. We also know that for some species the time of year and season matter for sensory perception: the sense of smell may be better in one season than in another. For instance, in winter starlings have poorer olfactory detection and discrimination than in spring when they use their sense of smell to sniff out useful nesting material.[52]

Although it has often been ignored, birds themselves produce odours that may be important in social communication and have a function in territorial marking, partner recognition and partner choice, as in many mammals.[53] Most avian species possess a variety of secretory glands. One of these is the uropygial gland, which is used in most bird species to provide lipid secretions to render the feathers water-repellant. In some species these 'preen glands' contain a musky smell and their weight and chemical composition can vary according to season.[54] For example, the preen gland of rooks doubles in weight during the courtship and nesting period.[55] The chemical composition of the preening gland also fluctuates in female mallards and may influence breeding behaviour of the male.[56] Then there are the various and relatively unknown glands throughout the body, in the skin, at the eye and the inner ear, which secrete sebaceous (fatty) material. In addition, there are other sources of odours, such as the proventricular gland, which secretes an offensive-smelling oil in petrels, and the stomach oils of many petrels and shearwaters. The nuptial 'tangerine odour' in colonies of crested auklets is a well documented pheromonal odour (i.e. an odour used in communication). Further, there may be odour in the mucus secreted by the salivary glands under the control of hormones. It is feasible that bird species that use significant amounts of mucoid saliva for nest building (as do cave-dwelling swiftlets and oilbirds, which nest in total darkness) may be 'marking the nest' and its occupants. So far, this hypothesis of nest recognition by olfactory cues alone has been tested only for storm-petrel chicks.[57] There are also a few species, such as the various frogmouth species of Australia and Papua New Guinea, that, unlike most bird species, produce extremely pungent faeces. They spray this on intruders.[58] A good deal of work still needs to be done on how these specific odours might contribute to mate and nestling recognition, to the marking of territory, and as a defence mechanism or in courtship.

Odour discrimination and learning

In the 1990s there were a number of exciting experiments to do with learning and memory of odours. It was shown that, just as in mammals, learning about odours and tastes (chemosensory learning) takes place in chicken embryos even before hatching and that formation of an attachment to certain odours and recognising food may be aided by exposing chick embryos to particular olfactory stimuli (as discussed in Chapter 5).[59] Memory formation is part of the purpose of learning. Memory for smells is important for forming social attachments, learning to feed, avoiding predators and preventing the ingestion of harmful substances.[60]

Olfactory cues may sometimes be ignored. That is, the question is not whether a bird can detect smells but whether the detection is important in a specific context and requires a response. Chicks presented with a familiar-looking food do not attend to olfactory cues, whereas chicks presented with visually unfamiliar food will pay attention to the presence of an unknown odour.[61] There are also differences in processing olfactory information according to whether the visual stimulus is attractive or not.[62] In other words, even in species with few known abilities in odour perception, we find that odours are still very important and may have many functions. It appears too that odours can be used as a memory 'back-up' system, aiding visual information.

Other functions of olfaction are associated with danger and may warn the bird not to ingest an item. There are odours that are naturally associated with poisonous insects or plants. These are, to us, pungent or acrid odours. Even inexperienced birds can distinguish them from harmless odours such as vanilla and thiazole and quickly develop an aversion (or neophobia) to toxic stimuli.[63] The usefulness of recognising specific smells has to do with the predator–prey relationship. Many bird species are hunters of vertebrates and of a vast variety of invertebrates. Invertebrates, insects in particular, have developed an entire arsenal of defence mechanisms to ward off potential predators.

However, we need not conclude that birds must have a sense of smell to identify toxic insects. The toxins and foul smells that insects have developed might be intended for snakes or lizards with an acute sense of smell, or for the many small mammals (rodents, marsupials, lower primates) that also relish large insect food and have an excellent sense of smell. Many insects, butterflies in particular, have developed visual cues about their unpalatable taste and the toxic ones literally advertise their dangerous condition. Bright colours and patterns are conspicuous visual signals that might serve to warn birds without the additional smell component. It has been known for a long time that birds sometimes pick up a butterfly and then release it unharmed. This act is referred to as 'beak mark tasting'. When a bird has caught a butterfly it pecks a small area of the wing in order to test its palatability and, if the taste is found to be unpleasant, it is then released. This hypothesis has been in vogue for a long time, but it has also received criticism and been rejected as a reasonable explanation for this behaviour.[64] It is possible that this interaction between butterfly and bird, between prey and predator, may be based on other cues, such as tactile information received by the bird or on sudden movement by the butterfly.

Taste and tactile sense

The senses of taste and touch have been largely ignored in birds although they were described in the 19th century by a French researcher called

E. Goujon.[65] He noted that parrots had receptors around the bill that did more than just provide the bird with limited tactile information. He found that these receptors also supplied information on taste and that they were so densely packed on the inside of the upper and lower jaw (and more densely placed on the tip of the beak) that he referred to the structure as the 'bill tip organ'.

Among the first to take note of it again in the 20th century was Gottschaldt[66] who, in the 1970s, began to investigate the tactile sensitivities of the beak of the goose. He noted that the bill tip organ was widespread among bird species that used the beak for selecting and manipulating food. The bill tip organ serves a dual function of providing tactile cues and taste indications. The tactile receptors alone consist of four different types geared to react to different stimuli. The receptors have a high density of up to 1000 receptors per square millimetre and they can apparently be used to evaluate the palatibility of a food item without the need for visual cues.

Taste receptor cells are found in several locations in birds. The tastebuds on the tongue are usually packed in specific areas, such as the base of the tongue, while other parts of the tongue do not house any such receptor cells. There are also taste receptors in the lower jaw.

We might expect substantial differences in the number of tastebuds between bird species, depending on their feeding habits and specialisations. Grain feeders and whole food eaters (many insectivorous birds swallow their food whole) may not have many tastebuds while omnivorous feeders may need an extra supply of tastebuds in order to make appropriate responses, especially to a new food. We know that the kakapo has the highest density of taste receptors of any bird reported so far[67] but this is more intriguing than revealing. As ground dwellers, kakapos feed on the berries of subalpine shrubs and the stems and roots of some grasses. Kakapos also have a keen sense of smell and, like ground-dwelling mammals, scent-mark their territory.

More studies of the tongue and beak of avian species will undoubtedly reveal a greater variability and receptivity of tastes and tactile information. Toucans, such as the toco and the keel-billed toucan, have a 15-centimetre-long tongue with brush-like bristles at the end. We suspect that the different features of the brush-tipped tongue in lorikeets and crimson chats, for instance, may not just be interesting from an anatomical point of view. Their function may extend beyond the purely mechanical (manipulating food) by providing additional sensory information. Most research on taste has been confined to domestic avian species, such as ducks, geese and chickens. There is some evidence for the importance of taste in wading birds, such as four species of sandpipers (*Calidris alba*, *C. alpina*, *C. maritima* and *C. canutus*).[68]

Touch and taste sensitivity in the bill enable mallards to locate and identify food items buried beneath soft surfaces. Experiments showed that mallards were very skilled at distinguishing between real and fake peas under the sand; they picked the correct ones and left the fake ones buried in the sand.[69] Their beak has become an additional tool in food search by use of the highly sensitive 'bill tip organ' which can instantaneously assess the quality and edibility of even such tiny morsels as peas. Sound cues may be very important to most, if not all, avian species but, as the mallard responses show, there are good examples of avian species requiring no cues other than tactile responses to make accurate judgments.

Many waders and shore-birds, but also some land-foraging bird species, have developed techniques for feeding which may, to various degrees, depend on hearing and tactile cues. For instance, if feeding involves submerging the beak under water or mud, soil or leaf litter in order to find food, we would expect sensory information from the beak to be involved. In the Eurasian woodcock, the only wading bird that has taken to living in the scrub, the importance of the activities of the beak have led to the unusual evolutionary adaptation of eyes being positioned high up on its head (see Figure 6.1). In this manner, the beak can remain submerged under soil and even accommodate some banking up of leaf litter without the bird's extreme lateral vision being obscured. Like the mallard, the woodcock can view above and behind in a totally panoramic way[70] but the bird has an extremely small field of vision around the tip of the beak. This makes sense since the beak remains submerged and there is no sensory input available other than tactile and olfactory information. Touch may be the preferred sense. The bar-tailed godwit is one of many long-billed shore-bird species that can probably locate its prey exclusively by using touch-sensitive receptors in the bill tip.

Many long-billed waders are able to seize prey with the bill tip while the bill is still buried in the mud. The bill of the dunlin has a moveable upper mandible; this action of the bill is referred to as 'rhynchokinesis'. The final 5 millimetres of the upper mandible can be bent slightly upwards, separating just the tips of the mandibles. A relatively large area of the brain in the dunlin is devoted to the analysis of tactile information from this specialised bill tip. This may be likened to a tactile fovea, providing heightened sensitivity that may be common to all long-billed probing birds of the family Scolopacidae—that is, sandpipers and their allies.[71] There are also plenty of examples of storks and skimmers showing sophisticated foraging by touch sensitivity in the bill alone. American wood storks, for example, can continue to catch live fish with no apparent loss of efficiency even when completely blindfolded.[72] Some of these food-catching techniques are very stereotyped. In the Eurasian curlew we speak of 'probing' (deep insertion of beak below soil), in the bar-tailed godwit of 'stitching', describing a rapid series of shallow probes close together, and in the oystercatcher of 'sewing' as a side-to-side motion of the bill. All these bill movements may involve the tactile sense.

Apart from the bill tip organ there are also mechanical tactile receptors, called 'Herbst corpuscles' (sometimes spelled Herpst). These are found at many sites of the body surface of most species and even on the tip of the tongue, as in woodpeckers. In some species these receptors are concentrated at the bill tip rather than along its edge, suggesting that they assist in actual prey detection. Tactile cues may also be gained via the group of long rictal bristles around or at the base of the beak of the upper mandible—as seen in oilbirds, Australian ravens and tawny frogmouths.[73]

Tactile information may not just be important in avoiding danger or identifying food. In the social bonding and communication of some birds, tactile contact seems to be very important. Courtship rituals include tactile contact such as neck touching, beak fencing or, more indirectly, exchange of gifts. For some group-living species preening is a particularly important social activity. Galahs engage extensively in mutual preening. Some rub their necks against each other.

With taste, smell and touch it is not always clear whether a particular behaviour works in concert with two or three senses, or which one may be the most important sense. It is clear that complex decisions are often made by birds and that these may be based on sensory information about taste and touch alone. Birds usually need auditory feedback to maintain normal song[74] but recent experimentation has shown that this is not always true. Even if auditory and visual cues are likely to be the more important senses, it can at least be said that, by and large, no one single sense functions entirely in isolation.

part IV
THE MINDS OF BIRDS

chapter 8

HOW BIRDS COMMUNICATE

Birds are overwhelmingly sociable and engage in extensive communication. Loners are rare and many of those tend to be loners for only part of the year, retaining a strong pair bond that is renewed each breeding season (e.g. albatrosses). Communication is context-dependent. Birds communicate by using a rich variety of signals. In each field of daily life, say for breeding or territoriality, substantial variation and subtlety is employed to ensure the right nuances. For breeding, a multitude of displays and songs has evolved, designed to attract a partner or sometimes to maintain a partner or to entice a partner's interest. Visual and vocal signals are used. Some species have special copulation calls or solicitation displays.[1] Among weaverbirds the female of at least four species has specific vocalisations to solicit copulation.[2] In some species, males produce song to keep the breeding female on the nest.[3] Hearing and vision are the most important sensory modalities in communication but a few species use olfactory cues to leave messages, or scent-mark territories and nests.

The questions are: how do birds communicate about a wide range of matters; what is important for survival; is communication intentional or unintentional?

Signals and communication

The length and elaborateness of a behaviour does not tell us much about the extent and richness of its message. Consider the very elaborate displays that occur during the breeding season. Do these signals tell us much more beyond the fact that the displaying birds want to find a mate? No. In cases of courtship the communicative value may be rather limited, no matter how unique and elaborate the song or dance. A song may last for twenty minutes, a dance for five minutes and a complex display even longer. A bowerbird may take a long time to perfect his bower and place special flowers on it to give it the right appearance but these extraordinary activities may not, in fact, increase the content of the message, as compared to another species' much shorter display or song. Whether a short or long showtime, the message may still have just the same content: 'Take me. I am healthy, I am the best.' The sophistication lies in the subtleties of performance, not in any extravagance of communication. Indeed, those males of species that vie for a female via song and dance have usually evolved ritualised presentations and have thus relinquished complete individuality to make their mark.

Other ritualised visual communications that might also be quite limited in information content are greeting rituals, including greetings that are related to the protection of a brood. Species living in colonies and/or those separating from partners for long periods of time have explicit rules of greetings, partly to avoid any doubt about the identity of the approaching individual and partly to foster a reconfirmation of their bond. The wandering albatross uses extensive greeting rituals (Plate 2). Gannets 'fence' with their bills as a greeting in large colonies and do so with non-related individuals. Gentoo penguins, occupying islands around Antarctica, have extensive territorial rituals between males and also greeting rituals with their breeding partners, performing calls in an upright position, with head and beak turned skywards.

While the origin of many of these signals is clearly recognisable (territorial/pair bonding), some of the same postures and calls have evolved into a casual greeting between conspecifics. Ritual displays for the maintenance of territory may signal mainly one thing: this territory is occupied. As a greeting to non-related conspecifics, the signal might indicate that the individual is a passer-by with good intentions and not an intruder. These messages may be relayed via auditory, visual or tactile signals.

Emotional states and signals

A number of signals seem to reflect the emotional state of a bird and may or may not be intended for communication with others.[4] A bird's emotional or internal state can be influenced by hormones and this can be reflected in signalling. For instance, the amount of crowing by cockerels is influenced by the level of testosterone (a sex hormone) circulating in the bloodstream, suggesting that the hormone changes the bird's internal state. Other hormones (stress hormones) alter the internal state and affect distress calling, which is usually more frequent and louder when birds are more aroused. The more distressed a young bird feels, the more often it peeps and the louder it peeps. A similar pattern of responses accompanies increased distress in a wide range of species, including humans.

Vocal emotional aspects of signalling may also be accompanied by visual information. For example, the position of feathers on the body and head can be altered to convey an unambiguous message of displeasure, fear, anxiety, anger or general arousal (Figure 8.1). We have given elsewhere a number of examples of the meaning of feather raising.[5] Here we want to exemplify the importance of the crest. Bird species with crests may use it as a visual signal, provided the crest can be raised and lowered. It is not quite clear why some birds have crests and others do not. Every continent has some bird species with a crest and, in each case, the crest appears to make a statement. This is unrelated to size and, it seems, even to habitat.

Figure 8.1 Fear in a young tawny frogmouth. Note that the beak is half-opened, as in the threat display (see Figure 3.4).

Figure 8.2 The crest of a cockatoo (left) and of a spinifex pigeon (right). Crests are used for a wide variety of purposes in communication but it is not clear why some species have crests and others do not.

We have the small tufted titmouse and the northern cardinal in North America, the red-crested cardinal in South America, the hoopoes in Africa, the northern lapwing in Europe and the many parrot species in Australasia (Figure 8.2). The crest of the hoopoe is very high and, with its black-tipped orange-coloured feathers, very conspicuous. Although the crest may lie flat when relaxed, continuing the horizontal line of the beak, it is readily used in a range of situations, both in stationary positions and in motion. A hoopoe can hover motionlessly in front of its nest and feed the young from the air. Usually, the crest is fully erect in such difficult manoeuvres. The long beak could easily pierce the throat of the nestlings and great precision and concentration is needed in order not to fail. The crest may be raised here due to excitement or arousal but it may also be a signal to the young birds.

The pacific baza, a very small Australian and South-East Asian bird of prey, uses the crest in alarm. The wedge-tailed eagle has no crest but raises its hackles in alarm (Figure 8.3). However, the most spectacular crest, which gave the species its name, belongs to the secretary bird. Standing tall above the grasses in southern and central Africa, the black-tipped

Figure 8.3 The raised hackles of a wedge-tailed eagle indicate alarm.

plumes on the head of this unusual bird of prey are widely visible. They usually flare up at moments of high arousal, such as when catching and killing a snake, or in fear. There is no doubt that during the process of killing a snake the secretary bird is in a high state of arousal, but the bird is also entirely absorbed in its battle with the snake. Movement of the crest is therefore not necessarily linked to communication, although states of arousal may unintentionally convey a message to onlookers. Interestingly, roadrunners do not use their crest when killing a snake. They tend to raise the crest when alerted and also in courtship display.

Apart from the hoopoe, perhaps the most elaborate use of the crest is made by Australian cockatoos. We are not aware of any studies demonstrating the importance of crest movement for communication in any of these species, even though cockatoos use the crest very conspicuously in a wide variety of activities and contexts. We could speculate that the crest plays a role not only in revealing the emotional state of the individual but may also have a function in intentional communication, both to conspecifics and others. The large sulphur-crested cockatoo has a bright yellow crest that contrasts with white body feathers. Major Mitchell's cockatoos, also known as pink cockatoos, have decorative bands in red and yellow on their pink crest, while the crest of galahs and of yellow-tailed cockatoos and red-tailed black cockatoos is plainer (the same colour as the head feathers) but strongly visible nonetheless.

Unlike other crested bird species, cockatoos (among which galahs belong), are flock-living birds and semi-nomadic. The communication skills needed in flocks are paramount for maintaining important social bonds and group cohesion. Galahs have at least four positions of crest erection: barely, quarter to half, three-quarters to fully erect. A barely erect crest in a cockatoo usually indicates that the bird is cautious and alert. We have seen semi-erect crests in cockatoos in cases of fear and warning. For instance, our own galah saw a small snake on the ground while he was sitting some distance up on a perch, and was thus in no immediate danger. He tilted his head sideways while the left eye peered downwards, watching the snake intently. His crest moved up and down constantly and it was this behaviour that alerted us to the fact that something unusual was happening. The snake was removed and the crest lowered. A fully grown rat, however, making its way up the inside of an aviary, made the crest go up fully and loud screeching calls accompanied the display. There is also a fully erect crest display (of the first three rows of feathers only) that signals pure pleasure and positive interest. These responses are emotional responses to situations and objects that engender fear, anger, alarm or pleasure. The question is whether the individual bird is using the signal of the crest intentionally. We have no answer to this other than to suggest that the bird might well use the crest intentionally when interacting with conspecifics since the crest is such an actively used, mobile signal and disregard for its messages might, at times, result in substantial injury.

Generalised calls: communication across species

Some of the signals that birds have evolved appear to function well not only among conspecifics but also across other avian species. They may indeed be so generalised as to be understood by mammals and other vertebrates. Among these generalised signals are threat displays, largely visual, and auditory signals such as alarm and distress calls.[6] This is so partly because of the structure of such calls (short, repetitive, loud) and often also because of similarities in the frequency range of the calls.[7]

Alarm and distress calls that signal across species are usually given when a predator has been detected. However, a bird capable of hiding its fear will often avoid signalling. Birds shake in fear accompanied by species-specific (often barely audible) high-frequency vocalisations.

Threat signals

Signals for the purpose of instilling fear (as a threat) apply among conspecifics and may also be directed against potential predators of entirely different species (amphibians, mammals). Among conspecifics, threat displays may be employed during the breeding season and in territorial defence. Threat displays of this kind are usually linked to competition as part of the lifestyle of a species, as in sedentary (non-migratory) species that need to defend their territories. Threat displays, visual and auditory, are often not a very effective strategy for passerines and many other bird species, because they tend to be a good deal smaller than potential predators and not physically well equipped for defence. Such birds have small beaks and no teeth and, unlike birds of prey, their feet cannot be used as a weapon. A surprise display, such as extended feathers, may create a brief diversion during which the potential predator is startled and the bird may have time to get away. Most avian species, however, cannot do more than bluff their way to safety.

At best, defence and threat postures may cause the retreat of a conspecific competitor but cross-species threats often have little substance. Threat displays may work when used suddenly and spectacularly. The stone curlew, for instance, drops its wings and simultaneously fans and raises its tail feathers, facing the opponent. The overall change from the shape of a bird to something strange and unidentifiable works well enough to bestow a small but crucial advantage on the cornered curlew. Northern mockingbirds cry incessantly and, in addition, use tail flicks and fanning of the tail to warn a competitor. White-winged choughs show elaborate fanning of tail and wings (personal observation). The northern shoveler, a duck widespread throughout the Northern Hemisphere, emits a buzzing sound from its wings when taking off, which is thought to be a warning. Crested pigeons in Australia also use wing-buzzes that may well have the same function as in shovelers. A number of species use beak-clapping as a threat. Barn owls use gaping as a threat display and will also engage in repeated hissing and beak-clapping. Gaping has also been observed in the

Australian tawny frogmouth, dollarbirds, kookaburras, and most owls.[8] Quite often, though, these actions are not followed by an attack. Presumably, the intruder is meant to take the hint and disappear. Kaplan has cared for wild barn owls that initially engaged in a hissing and clapping threat display against her but never actually attacked. Clearly, the bird is sending a signal to a potential predator or an intruder. The intention is either to alert conspecifics or drive the intruder away and so protect a nest site, a food source or territory. If the display has no effect, the adult birds may fly away and watch as their brood is devoured. Or they may proceed to other displays such as feigning injury. This ritualised deception sends a false message and may deter attack by the predator.

A few bird species have effectively developed threat signals that are followed by attack. Large birds of prey, especially eagles, and flightless birds such as cassowaries, ostriches and emus will attack intruders and their display may well be no idle threat. The talons of an Egyptian vulture, a turkey vulture, a wedge-tailed eagle or condor can inflict substantial harm. In nest defence, male ostriches and emus will run to meet an intruder with outstretched wings and gaping beak (as shown in the image at the beginning of the chapter). A strike by the horny toe of an ostrich or cassowary can kill a human and certainly any smaller marauders. In Australia, cassowaries, emus and, very rarely, wedge-tailed eagles are the only avian species that can be dangerous to humans but many more dangerous birds occur in Africa and South America. Most of Europe no longer knows the power of birds as a class capable of delivering real damage except, perhaps, the experience some may have had of attack from swans and domesticated geese.

Threats are not only emitted in the context of predator–prey contacts. Competition for a food source quite often involves multi-species communication, particularly for meat and carrion-feeding species, although competition for fruit may also be intense. Birds of prey, especially species of vulture, have developed an elaborate ritual for feeding-site behaviours. Around a carcass on the African plains one can usually observe the descent of large vultures followed by the smaller ones before any hyenas, jackals or wild dogs get a feed. The scuffles in the process are never serious but vultures land with expanded wings as a gesture of warning in addition to arresting flight. Mammals and younger birds usually retreat swiftly. In vultures, the wingspan is so large that its mere size engenders fear. The largest wingspan is that of the Andean condor.

Alarm and distress calls

The phenomenon of distress and alarm calls has generated much research and publication. The question is, to what extent a distress call can help or curtail the survival of an individual bird in distress or a bird alarmed at the sight of a predator. Since the 1960s, at least four major hypotheses have been developed as to why distress calls may be useful. One is the 'request-help' hypothesis, alerting conspecifics to come to an individual's aid. A second one is the altruistic model of a 'warn-kin' hypothesis. While the individual may be doomed, at least other conspecifics can escape. This is altruism because, by calling, the bird draws attention to itself. A third hypothesis is the 'startle-predator' idea, arguing that a sudden set of loud calls will startle the predator into releasing the bird. Fourth, distress calls may attract other predators which, in turn, may distract the predator and allow the potential victim to escape. None of these hypotheses has found wide application yet. For instance, when these hypotheses were tested on predators (coyotes in this case) with playback of avian distress calls, the coyotes mounted a more intensified attack than without calling.[9]

Warning or alarm calls are clearly an example of cross-species communication. We have known for some time that many species can discriminate calls of other species as well as of their own kind.[10] Alarm calls about aerial predators have similar acoustic qualities among very different species of birds. The call is delivered with approximately similar intensity in many species and at about the same pitch of 7 kHz,[11] presumably also because it diffuses the location of the source.[12] This means that certain sets of alarm calls may become common to many species because of their physical properties. Alarm signals in some Corvidae (crows) and sparrows have similar structures and therefore induce interspecific reactions. Discovery of such rules of communication makes it more understandable why communication between very different species is possible.

The alarm call of one species may benefit a variety of other species. In some exceptional cases, the alarm call of another species is integrated into its own repertoire. This is the case, for instance, in the African coccyphas. When a predator nears an area with nestlings or defenceless juveniles, the adults emit warning signals of *other* bird species. T.B. Oatley suggested some time ago that vocal imitation of alarm calls had the function not only of warning but also of teaching the young to react to the warning calls of other species.[13]

If a signal is emitted intentionally, we would also expect that such a call would only be given under certain circumstances. Alarm calls are a case in point. If there is no other member of the bird's species around to warn, there would be no point in emitting an alarm signal. If a call merely reflects a state of arousal and is unintentional, then alarm calling should occur with or without an audience. Alarm calls are thus a special case for considering the presence or absence of an audience.

For instance, a domestic chicken emits an alarm call when it catches sight of a hawk flying overhead. Cockerels make a different warning call for a predator seen flying overhead than they do for one approaching on the ground (the aerial-predator versus the ground-predator alarm call). There is a specific screeching call for an aerial predator and a clucking call for a ground predator. By calling, the bird draws attention to itself and increases its chance of becoming prey. The call could simply be an expression of that internal state of fear (i.e. an automatic, unintentional signal of an emotional state). Even though different calls are made for aerial and ground predators, both predators induce a state of fear. It could be that an aerial predator causes more fear than a ground predator (or vice versa) and the different calls are merely a reflection of the amount of fear that the bird feels. To switch from producing one call to another completely different call as the internal state of fear increases does appear to occur in some species. For instance, two types of alarm calling have been reported for species such as the black-winged stilt, a wading bird. The type of call depends on the distance of the predator from the bird's location. Increasing fear may lead to a switch from one call type to another.[14] In other species increasing states of arousal (fear) are accompanied by making the same call more often or more loudly. Therefore, having different calls for different predators does not, in itself, prove that the bird signals about the predator to other members of its species.

Instead, the idea that the two different alarm calls of the chicken (i.e. signalling an aerial versus a ground predator) are made unintentionally has to be dismissed because of the fact that the presence or absence of an audience influences whether calling occurs or not. If the cockerel can control his vocalisations and raises the alarm only when he intends to warn other chickens, he will not call when he is alone. And, indeed, he does not. A cockerel will make an aerial alarm call only when there is another member of its own species nearby. An audience of the cockerel's own species has to be present for alarm calling to occur.[15] It could be said that the cockerel does not call when he is alone because he does not become sufficiently aroused by seeing the hawk unless another chicken is present. This does not seem to be correct because the cockerels being studied showed the same amount of looking overhead, crouching, immobility, scuttling away and sleeking down of their feathers with and without an audience. These fear behaviours show that the birds were, in fact, just as afraid when they were alone as when they had an audience. The most likely interpretation of these findings is that cockerels issue alarm calls only when there is a reason for doing so and that, when they do call, they do so with the intention of warning other members of their own species.

Communication by birds is thus not 'uncontrolled' and, although there is a range of signals that reflect the internal state of a bird, the alarm calls of some species are complex and show that they can have specific meanings that are directed towards others.[16]

Alarm and attack

Birds that live in flocks, or socially in small groups may at times be capable of driving off a predator without threat displays. They may emit a warning call and then immediately proceed with an attack. The time between warning and attack can be very short indeed and the warning call may not be made to persuade the intruder to retreat but to rouse conspecifics into action. On the approach of a climbing goanna, or monitor lizard, the chief predators of kookaburra eggs and nestlings, kookaburras band together and begin attacking, one by one. They use their beaks to ram the goanna in order to destabilise it and make it fall off the tree. Each time they do so the kookaburras risk their own lives. To deliver a powerful strike, they need to fly with maximum speed at the opponent's body and thus risk breaking their own neck on impact. Each bird will aim for the same position on the goanna's body in quick succession. As a relay team they may actually succeed in vanquishing the strong and versatile opponent.

There are also countless examples—although not all of them are documented in the scientific literature—of groups of birds from different species supporting each other in the battle against an intruder. Australian magpies and noisy miners, for instance, regularly show group mobbing. Usually, such support is done by vocalising (as in the noisy miner mobbing calls) and by flying in formation towards the intruder. Here, the communication may be very brief, but it is very effective in achieving a good outcome for a large number of birds.

Extended vocalisations and communication

Birds may well be the most versatile vocalisers, except perhaps for some sea mammals (e.g. whales and dolphins) and humans. Almost all birds can vocalise loudly enough to be audible from some distance away. Some species vocalise rarely but many are often raucous and others are extremely loud or chatty most of the time. Not all vocalisations are melodious and many last for only a few seconds.

Only a select group of birds are singers. These are the songbirds (called 'oscines'). There is overwhelming evidence that birds can discriminate between their own song (conspecific song) and that of others, called 'heterospecific song'.[17] We also know that song can be a very important component in female choice of a mate.[18] Some species have a stereotyped song, such as the eastern phoebe. Some species learn a song early in life and retain the same song all their lives, such as zebra finches.[19] Others retain the ability to learn more and vary their song (song plasticity) for at least the first year of life (e.g. Australian magpies). Starlings and the lyrebird retain plastic song all their lives. The same is true of the canary.[20] Psittacine birds, such as galahs and Grey parrots, can learn new material throughout their lives.[21] The question is, what do these vocalisations mean?

Bird vocalisations can signal about sex, territory or food. They can express anxiety or alarm, rivalry, attention, defence, flying away ('follow me') and similar short instructions. None of these may be specific to the sex of a bird, even though they are in some species. In Australian magpies, both females and males use the full song repertoire all year round.[22] Birds often have different song types that they use at different times of day or in different seasons. In Australian magpies, three song types have been distinguished: one is the dawn or dusk song identified as monotonous nocturnal song, then the territorial song and subsong.[23] In addition to time-related calls, there is a vast range of contact calls in well defined contexts, such as the begging calls of the young, alarm calls, rallying calls and others.[24] There may be calls that are not defined by season but are nevertheless distinct call types. These are the duets of bird pairs in the tropics and subtropics, and the carolling of kookaburras and Australian magpies to send a message about their territorial claims. Even the size of the repertoire of a bird can vary with season and age.[25] All these types and components have received substantial research attention over the years, chiefly to establish what their various functions might be.[26]

A bird's song also varies in complex ways along three primary dimensions: (1) the time axis (duration, tempo and phrasing); (2) frequency, perceived as pitch and varying in cadence, inflection and tone quality; and (3) intensity or amplitude, perceived as loudness and emphasis.[27] A fourth dimension could be added here as described by Dorothy Cheney and Richard Seyfarth in the vocalisation of vervet monkeys: silences in between phrases, notes and repetitions of key elements.[28] These add a dimension of possible meaning readily overlooked. Intensity of the vocalisation is sometimes ignored by researchers[29] but is also recognised as contributing to the message. Identifying the primary dimensions of song was a very important task because any variations of any of the parameters can create new meanings.

Repertoire size

The sheer number of songs a male bird in breeding season can sing might determine whether or not this male will be a successful breeder and able to maintain his territory. In a study of the European great tit, it was found that the more song types the bird sang together in a repertoire, the more effective he was.[30] One male may sing up to eight different types of song. Those with more elaborate songs are able to maintain their territory more effectively than those with less elaborate songs. This has to do with the process of decoding the messages, a complex song revealing that the singer is experienced and healthy. European robins have large and complex song repertoires. Despite this, they are able to discriminate between the songs of neighbours versus strangers and are therefore able to recognise intruders by the sound of their song alone.[31] These examples of fine discrimination strengthen the perception that song contains messages with meaning.

Distance

Sound intensity determines how far away the song can be heard. It may be very important for a bird to assess the distance of a call accurately,[32] particularly when it has lost sight of its partner, fledgling offspring or wider social group. Acoustic signals degrade progressively (meaning that they become less and less clear and audible with distance). This process can help in assessing the distance of a conspecific singer (called 'ranging'). Audible sounds have a threshold of detection and this can be expressed in decibels (dB) and metres (referred to as 'distance threshold detection' or DTD). We know that in forested environments there is a reduction of around 10 dB for each doubling of distance from the singing bird.[33] A vocalisation from another bird may well contain the message: 'I am 10 metres away from you' or 'Come here', which presupposes that the listening bird can make an adequate judgment. Whether the meaning of the message (distance) is encoded in the way the bird calls or whether it is in the decoding of the receiver is not yet fully known, and it may also vary from species to species. Carolina wrens can use overall amplitude, reverberation and relative intensities, particularly of high frequencies, as separate cues for ranging.[34] To do this depends on whether the species can make discriminations of degradation with or without prior knowledge of the song type.[35]

Communication with meaning

Although bird signals may be purely emotional, emitted without knowing awareness (cognition), it is likely that many if not most vocalisations involve both emotional and cognitive processes. The emotional contribution may be greater in some signals and the cognitive contribution greater in others. By cognitive processes we mean higher levels of brain function, those that involve decision making, memory and assessing the situation in the surrounding environment. The balance between emotion and cognition will vary with the function of the signal and the context in which it is given. Both 'emotional' and 'cognitive' signals can convey meaning.

Apart from the alarm calls we discussed above, much attention has focused on food calls. Some bird species signal to conspecifics that they have found a food source. This was discovered in the 1950s for honeyguides and herring gulls.[36] Honeyguides lead their conspecifics to the nests of wild honey bees.

Food calls vary according to how much food is found and its quality. Chickens, for example, produce food calls at higher rates when the food is what they prefer.[37] The information about quantity and quality may be generated by the emotional state of the individual producing the calls, as both more food and food of better quality may increase the bird's excitement. The presence of an audience also increases the calls that cockerels produce in the presence of food, as in the case of alarm calling. The cockerel produces a typical food call, consisting of repeated pulses of sound, when he sees food or another stimulus that he associates with food, and this attracts hens. The hens run to the male and the male drops the food, allowing the hens to eat it. Sometimes the cockerel will make the food call even when no food is present, perhaps to deceive the hen into approaching for other purposes.[38] Food calling is enhanced by the presence of a hen, compared with being alone. It was noticed that the presence of the hen had a specific effect on signalling about food but did not affect behaviour not used for signalling.[39] It would seem, therefore, that the cockerel signals with the intention of alerting the hen to the presence of food and does not simply emit calls automatically at the sight of food. The hen will even look for food on the ground when she hears the food call played through a loudspeaker. On hearing the call she puts her head close to the floor and walks around as if looking for food, even when there are no grains of food present on the floor of the cage in which she is being tested.[40] Thus, the receiver of the signal has responded in a specific manner to the meaning of the call. Although this does not prove beyond all doubt that birds communicate intentionally, it certainly indicates that they may do so. These are referential signals.

A signal is 'referential' when it has a specific meaning that is understood by other birds of the species, who also use the same signal in the same or similar context. It requires some form of cognition. So far, most research on the referential use of vocalisations in birds has focused on signalling about the presence of predators or food. We are far from understanding communication at other social levels.

Much avian communication is concerned with social relationships. Ever since the studies by Konrad Lorenz, we have been enthralled by the apparent intelligence of corvids. American crows have at least two dozen different calls and common ravens have eighteen to 64 different calls. Their repertoire includes calls for courting, assembling, scolding, threatening, dispersing and recruiting.[41] There is little doubt that many of these signals are referential.

Variations of song

To understand how important the components of song are in bird communication, a large number of playback experiments have been conducted over many decades. Of particular interest have been playback experiments using modifications of elements or of interval duration of a species' characteristic song. By altering parts of the song, it is possible to find out whether these parts or segments of a song are important to the bird (i.e. elicit a behaviour or not). Playback of modified songs altered the behaviour of the receiving bird, showing that the elements of the song are important (although not necessarily why they are important). The birds showed a reduced response. This happened, for instance, when songs were played to indigo buntings, red-winged blackbirds and the non-passerine spotted sandpiper.[42] In some species, it was found that cues to do with timing of notes (temporal cues) are not important for conspecific recognition, as in the chiffchaff,[43] because changes in cues did not lead to behavioural changes.

It appears that sound rhythm is a specific subcategory in the perception of the song of conspecifics. Jackdaws and starlings are able to distinguish two signals representing different rhythmic patterns of artificial sound sequences.[44] Many bird species can make very fine discriminatory judgments of auditory signals. For instance, in collared doves, which are not classified as songbirds, variations in the rhythm of sounds can have important communicative value: the doves listen to the rhythm of territorial cooing by conspecifics.[45]

Temporal features of rhythm may provide important cues for species recognition to those species living in the same habitat (called 'sympatrically' living species) and also contribute to delineations of territory and reproduction (referred to as 'reproductive isolation'). Hence, birds use sounds and variations of sounds within a vocal environment where species-specific characteristics are well established, widely and completely understood by conspecifics and recognised by other species.[46] Female starlings attend to variations in the songs of males when choosing a mate. Females prefer longer over shorter songs and that variation in the length of singing bouts attracts the females.[47]

The loudness of a vocalisation (amplitude) can make a substantial difference to a message. Many bird species have loud/faint pairs of song display. The loud vocalisation may be for territorial display, indicating that the caller will attack if territorial borders are infringed.[48] In fact, Carolina chickadees and Australian magpies, two songbirds in different continents, have a vocalisation display that is uttered only when the bird is ready to attack. A fainter but similar call to mates and offspring may indicate that the communicator is ready to interact but not attack.

Finally, there are dialect variations of song, so that the song of one species in a specific geographic location will be different from the song of the same species in another location. Both repertoire size and numbers of neighbours are likely to have strong influences on the distribution of song types in a population because more variation allows for more choices and errors. Geographic variation of song may be an epiphenomenon of vocal learning.[49] This means that song dialects may simply occur by chance through learning errors (imprecise copying) and different 'errors' will occur in different geographical regions. The issue in all these recent discoveries is whether there are true examples of referential meaning in bird vocalisations (i.e. for intentional communication) or whether there are other and simpler explanations for specific vocalisations.

In summary, avian species have developed a complex system of communication that enables them to live in groups, claim ownership of a patch of forest, shore or meadow, either for their nests or for a larger group, and facilitate their own survival. Beyond this, evidence is increasing that some bird species have developed capabilities well beyond simply signalling their emotions unintentionally.

chapter 9

LEARNING

Learning shapes the behaviour of each individual bird. Memories of past events are stored and kept available for future use, whether for recognising other individuals of the same species or predators, or for remembering important events. Memories may be an essential part of finding food, maintaining social bonds, finding and maintaining territories, guiding migratory flights and acquiring the vocalisations that are used for communication.

There are many different kinds of learning. Some memories are formed very rapidly after just one exposure to an event or an object or another individual. Other memories are established more slowly only after the bird has been exposed repeatedly to the same event, object or individual. Many factors determine how long learning takes and how strong a memory will be formed.[1] Age is important and so is the outcome of the event, such as obtaining a reward or being punished.

Attention is the starting point of learning and there are certain stimuli that attract some birds more than others. Some species attend to smells more than others and so are more likely to make memories of them. Species differ in the colours they find most attractive. Young domestic chicks, for example, prefer to peck at reddish grains and so learn about grains in that colour range, whereas ducklings prefer green and so learn about foods and objects that are greenish in colour.[2] These preferences channel the young bird's learning so that it learns about certain stimuli and not others, and the bird's attention to different stimuli (i.e. events, objects and other animals) changes with its stage of development and its past experience. Each memory builds on the ones before it and, in this way, each bird learns how to survive and develop its own individual 'personality'.

Imprinting

Within the first day or two after hatching, precocial birds (birds that are well developed at hatching) imprint on their siblings and parents. Imprinting is a very specific process—a rapid, powerful and stable form of learning. Imprinting can be achieved with less than an hour's exposure to an attractive stimulus, and is possible within only a few days after hatching. A young bird that is several weeks old cannot be imprinted; it can only be conditioned to certain stimuli. Imprinting thus means that a complex range of stimuli is learned and fully recognised with very little exposure at a very early stage of development.

The only species that imprint (in the true sense of the word—it is an often misused concept) are the precocial species—imprinting concerns only those species that are well developed at hatching (i.e. they are feathered and very soon can feed themselves). Young domestic chicks, ducks, quails and goslings imprint. They learn to recognise the hen and their siblings which means that the group stays together and all the chicks follow the hen when she leaves the nest. This kind of imprinting is known as 'filial imprinting' to distinguish it from sexual imprinting.

Filial imprinting takes place if the young bird is exposed to a conspicuous stimulus. No reward of food or anything else is necessary. The bird merely has to see the imprinting stimulus to imprint on what it looks like, or hear it to imprint on what it sounds like.[3] Precocial birds will also imprint on humans, if their own parent is not present; they will even imprint on a ball, balloon, watering can or other conspicuous object. Konrad Lorenz carried out some of the earliest scientific studies of imprinting in greyleg geese; his goslings would follow him to the lakeside and swim around his head when he bathed. Domestic chicks will even imprint on a flashing light.[4] Once they have done so they will always approach the object (or stimulus) on which they have imprinted and, when they cannot see it, they become very distressed and make calls to indicate this (young chicks will peep).

Although chicks will imprint on a wide range of different stimuli, they do have certain preferences that focus them on their own species. These preferences are known as 'predispositions'.[5] A domestic chick prefers to imprint on a domestic hen if given a choice. By about the third day after hatching, the chick will have learned to follow the hen. It pays attention to her visual features and learns them. It will also listen to her vocalisations and imprint on them. Hearing a sound together with seeing a conspicuous visual stimulus enhances imprinting.[6]

In addition to this visual and auditory imprinting, the young bird may imprint on the odour, or smell, of the hen. In the laboratory, this ability has been demonstrated in the domestic chick. The chick imprints on the odour of a small hanging container filled with cotton wool laced with clove oil. The imprinting can then be tested, at about three days after hatching, by presenting the chick with a choice of this odour-emanating container and one that looks the same but has no strong smell. The chick will approach and stay next to the container with the clove oil odour.[7] In the natural setting, it is possible that learning about odours takes place even before the chick hatches since exposing eggs to odours just before hatching affects the chicks' behaviour after hatching.[8] This means that a chick may hatch already familiar with the odours of its nest, siblings and hen. Also before hatching the chick embryos inside their eggs can hear the hen and they may begin to imprint on her vocalisations. Imprinting on the visual characteristics of the hen, of course, cannot take place until after the chicks have hatched.

Very young, precocial birds not only learn to recognise their mother hen but can tell one sibling from another.[9] We do not know exactly what features they use to distinguish between their siblings but it is likely to be subtle visual differences in feathers or body posture or movement, and differences in their vocalisations. These differences are not readily detected by humans. Recognition of siblings has also been shown to occur in common tern chicks. They show a preference for their siblings over chicks from neighbouring broods as early as four days after hatching.[10] This attachment between siblings ensures that they stay near each other which is a matter of survival for ground-nesting birds, like terns, living in colonies.

Imprinting on visual stimuli in ducklings, geese, quail and chicks occurs in what is referred to as a 'sensitive period' for this kind of learning.[11] Domestic chicks imprint to visual stimuli best at about 15 to 20 hours after hatching. During this period they take very little time to imprint; the imprinting memory can be established in less than an hour of exposure to the stimulus. Before the sensitive period for imprinting to a visual stimulus starts, the chicks are not able to stand up very well and they sleep much of the time, huddled next to or under the hen.[12] Once imprinting takes place, the sensitive period ends. Thus there is a window of time when imprinting can take place. A sensitive period for another kind of learning may begin after the time for imprinting.

The developing bird passes through a series of sensitive periods for different kinds of learning.[13] If a sensitive period passes without its particular type of learning taking place, it may be too late for it to happen at all; or, at least, it will be very difficult for that kind of learning to take place later.[14]

The sensitive period for sexual imprinting occurs later than that for filial imprinting.[15] Sexual imprinting refers to learning a sexual preference, and is essential for pair bonding and mating later in life. In domestic fowl, sexual imprinting takes place between 30 and 45 days after hatching. Altricial species develop more slowly and their time of sexual imprinting varies among the species; it is timed to occur when the young birds are beginning to develop the plumage colour and patterning of the adult.[16] In this way, the young bird can learn directly about the appearance of its siblings and so can recognise them as adults. In adulthood the bird will choose a sexual partner on the basis of this learning, but not one exactly like the parent. Japanese quail, for instance, prefer to mate with birds that differ slightly from their parents,[17] as do Tundra swans. This is a way of avoiding inbreeding. Families of swans have similar faces and the faces of mated pairs differ more than the faces within families.[18]

Once the young bird reaches adulthood, the specific filial attachment that it formed through imprinting in early life is no longer important to it because often it does not stay with its parent(s) and siblings. Nevertheless, the fact of its imprinting affects its social behaviour for the rest of its life.

Sexual imprinting remains important throughout the bird's life. A bird may sexually imprint on another species if it is raised by parents of another species, often preferring a member of the foster species over its own for mating. In some species the imprinted bird will still be able to mate with a member of its own species but this is not so in all species or for both sexes. Male zebra finches raised by Bengalese finches court Bengalese finches when adult, and ignore enthusiastic mating partners of their own species.[19] Male mallards that have been fostered by another species develop a learned preference for the species that fostered them, but female mallards prefer to mate with their own species irrespective of whether they have been reared by another species.[20]

Sexual imprinting on humans is a problem with hand-reared birds. Constant contact may cause the hand-reared bird to prefer to mate with humans when adult.[21] For endangered species this is a genuine problem because the purpose of rehabilitation is their survival and propagation. To overcome sexual imprinting on humans, people who raise rare birds may dress in clothes that resemble the adults of the species and hope that the young birds will find them similar enough to their own species to transfer their sexual preferences to conspecifics later in life. Konrad Lorenz described the behaviour of a hand-raised jackdaw that had sexually imprinted on him.[22] The jackdaw courted Lorenz by attempting to feed him worms, into either his mouth or his ear. Such courtship feeding is typical for the species but here it was directed to the human as a chosen partner. For Gisela Kaplan, a rehabilitation program for hand-rearing a tawny frogmouth male nearly failed because the bird sexually imprinted on her. In the evening he would make courtship calls and beak claps and then fly onto the back of the armchair in which she was sitting, preen her hair and perform copulation movements. In this case, it was possible to reverse the effects by slow re-training with a female. Sexual imprinting on humans can become irreversible, however. It is a particular problem in large birds that live in close contact with humans, such as emus. It is an alarming experience to be confronted by an emu's sexual advances but they can be deterred by walking with one hand held overhead higher than the emu's head. This stimulus has effect probably because it gives the human the appearance of being an emu, a bigger than normal emu. Sexual imprinting can occur over a wide span of time—is therefore less easy to control and can lead to birds not mating later in life.

Learning about food

From the time of hatching, precocial birds peck at stimuli that resemble quite closely the food on which they will feed. Domestic fowl chicks are not only attracted to the colour red, and ducks to green, but chicks tend to choose small spherical objects.[23] The same is true of goslings, lapwings and other precocial hatchlings. These are innate (inborn or inherited) preferences and, in the case of the chick, they focus the young bird's attention on objects that are likely to be edible grains. Learning modifies these preferences and the bird will learn to take other kinds of food, of different colours, sizes and shapes.

Social factors also determine what the young precocial bird learns about food types. Young chicks are stimulated to peck by the pecking movements of the hen and the tapping sounds made by her pecking.[24] They peck at grain similar to that pecked at by the hen.[25] In other words, they learn by observing the hen's choices in pecking. Hens also make calls to attract the chicks to food and may pick up edible objects and drop them in front of the chicks repeatedly. By doing so, the hen creates the best environment for the chicks to learn about food.

Survival depends not only on pecking food but on avoiding inedible objects and poisonous insects. For most birds only one peck at an unpleasant tasting insect is sufficient to make them avoid pecking any such object ever again. The learning has to be fast and accurate. The bird must know the difference between an inedible insect and an edible one that may look very like it. Their ability to associate specific taste and smell with a visual stimulus can be demonstrated by allowing a chick to peck at a red-coloured bead coated in a bitter-tasting substance called methyl anthranilate. Later the same chick is presented with a red bead and a blue bead, both coated only in water. The chick will peck at the blue bead and avoid the red bead even though red is its preferred colour. Both the taste and the odour of the methyl anthranilate is associated with red beads.[26] Many inedible insects assist this learning process by being brightly coloured, and red and yellow stripes seem to be the best way for an insect to advertise to a bird that it should not be eaten.

Learning about food takes place early in precocial species and, as they get older, they become increasingly less likely to sample unfamiliar food.[27]

Figure 9.1 Tawny frogmouth parents together rear one or two chicks and, even after fledging, teach them the art of hunting and finding food over many months.

By contrast, in altricial species, learning about food is often delayed until after fledging since they are fed by their parents and do not need to find their own food until some time after leaving the nest. It is different for altricial hunting birds, because whole foods are brought to the nest site and the young chicks can see and taste the prey that their parents bring to them. There is evidence from the crowned eagle, a large African raptor, that the female parent especially will offer a detailed 'commentary' on prey brought to the nest or will deliver the prey in a different manner. For instance, many vocalisations will accompany the delivery of a vervet monkey before the young eagle is allowed to feed. By contrast, she drops other prey, such as sticky meat that is easy to catch but difficult to eat without comment, forcing the young eagle to learn by trial and error how to feed on sticky meat (by cleaning the beak in between bites).

Learning about food thus involves several factors. One is trial-and-error practice by which the young bird perfects its skills in handling the food. The other is by social learning from the parents. Social learning about food by observing conspecifics feeding is important throughout life in many species. Very complex manoeuvres can be learned by one bird watching another bird performing them. In the laboratory, for example, ravens will learn to pull on a flap to slide open the lid of a box containing food by watching another raven perform this task.[28] How much detail is actually learned by the observing bird is a matter of debate but, even if only the initial aspects of approach to the box and attention to the flap are learned, this is social learning that would not occur otherwise.

Learning to feed on live prey can involve a number of steps. At first, the birds peck at a range of objects, particularly moving ones, and there is an age when this behaviour is especially noticeable. After fledging, our young tawny frogmouth would pick up any smallish object, including twigs and leaves, and bang it against hard edges in the action used by adults to kill live prey. In this way he demolished a vase of dried flowers. Vigorous pecking has also been described for loggerhead shrikes.[29] Very soon after fledging, they begin to peck at twigs and leaves, graduating about two weeks later to large objects that they manipulate with their beak and feet, and moving on to swoop down to attack insects on the ground by four weeks after fledging. Finally, the shrikes learn to sit and wait before lunging at small birds. This is a long and complex learning process. Even manipulating live prey once it has been caught is a risky business, and that too must be learned. Kookaburras and some raptors feed on venomous snakes and gripping them in the wrong place could lead to a lethal bite. Attacks need to be well oriented to the correct place on the body of the prey. As occurs in mammals, play behaviour in birds can assist learning to handle and hunt live prey. Manipulative play is common in ravens, Australian magpies and some raptors. As well as learning to hunt, play behaviour may permit the bird to learn about social rank and perfect its skills for dealing with social aggression and social bonding.

Birds that must learn to feed by diving into water have an extra difficulty to face. They have to locate the swimming prey and compensate for the bending of light rays at the surface of the water. Refraction of light makes the prey appear larger than it is and in a location slightly different from where it appears to be from above the water. This ability must be highly developed in terns since they dive from some height above the water and capture their prey expertly. There is some evidence that juvenile terns learn to fish in this way by watching their parents and practising their movements.[30] The same is true of kingfishers which usually seize their prey on the wing from below the water's surface. Watching young kookaburras trying to catch a fish can be rather comical and reveals how much skill is actually involved in a successful catch. Instead of the elegant swooping of the parent, they tend to make very inelegant belly-flops on the water, then get wet and struggle to regain flight. Young kookaburras may need to practise for weeks, watching their parents all the while, until they have perfected these skills.

Learning about predators

Many avian species will mob owls and other birds of prey and this involves flying around the potential predator while making loud vocalisations. Some birds seem to respond to owls the very first time they see them. By showing different models of owls to birds it has been possible to find out that certain features elicit mobbing behaviour—forward-looking eyes (binocular vision), the beak and the general outline of the body. Tawny frogmouths are not owls and do not prey on other birds but they have all the physical features that elicit mobbing by other avian species and sometimes they do get mobbed (e.g. by butcherbirds). The owl or frogmouth can reduce its chances of being mobbed by adopting a sleeping posture and closing its eyes.

Although mobbing of owls may be innate, mobbing of other predators has to be learned by observing other birds.[31] The alarm behaviour of young birds is enhanced by the presence of adults. The European blackbird passes on information about predators through social learning, and this has been demonstrated very effectively. If one bird sees a stuffed owl it will mob it and this will stimulate a bird in a nearby cage to mob also, even if that bird cannot see the owl. By arranging the cage so that the second bird cannot see the owl but instead can only see another harmless species or even a bottle, the second bird will learn to mob that inappropriate species or object. When, later, it sees a member of the harmless species, or the bottle, again it will raise the alarm by mobbing. This bird will now teach other blackbirds to mob the same species, or the bottle, and so the behaviour is passed on by cultural transmission. This technique has been used to great advantage by training New Zealand robins to recognise stoats, which are introduced predators.[32]

Some species mimic the calls of species that prey on them. This has been noted in many species of the African thrushes; when potential predators come close to their young, adults intersperse their own calls with mimicked calls of the predator.[33] The young may thereby learn the calls of the predator and so learn to avoid that species. Gisela Kaplan has discovered that the Australian magpie also imitates one of its predators, the barking owl, although in this case the mimicry may be used to drive off the predator rather than being a way of teaching the young to recognise the predator.

Vocal learning

In general we can say that birds learn their songs but not their calls.[34] Songbirds learn their songs by copying model songs heard early in their life, and this has been studied in detail in many species.[35] Songs are acoustically complex and often musical, whereas calls are simpler vocalisations, but the distinction between songs and calls is now questioned by many researchers.[36] Also it may not be true that all calls are inherited and not learned. There has been little direct experimentation to test whether calls are learned or not, but some field observations lead us to suggest that at least some calls are learned.

A case of natural fostering of young provides a way of testing whether calls are learned or not. Sometimes a breeding pair of pink cockatoos occupies the same nest hollow as a breeding pair of galahs and, if a conflict occurs, the galah parents are driven off. The pink cockatoos then continue to incubate both their own eggs and the galahs' eggs and they also raise the galah young. Galahs raised like this by foster parents vocalise contact and location calls that differ from those of other galahs and are very similar to those of their foster parents.[37] Cockatoos are well known mimics, which testifies to their ability to learn vocalisations, but the calls that the fostered galahs gave were not in addition to their own species-specific calls, as is often the case when parrots mimic human speech, but replaced their own calls. In other words, the galahs had not simply tacked on some new calls to their own inherited calls. The results seem to indicate that galahs raised by their own parents would also learn their calls. It is also known that young zebra finches learn their 'distance' calls, and do so from their

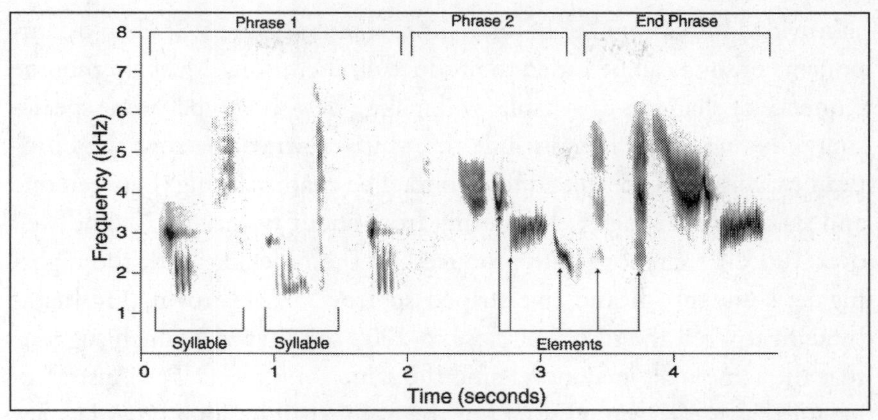

Figure 9.2 Illustration of phrase, syllable and elements in the song of a brown thornbill, a small, inconspicuous Australian bird which produces a rather powerful and melodious song that is quite complex. An element is a single sound, a syllable is a combination of several sounds, and a phrase is a distinct unit of sounds consisting of elements and syllables forming a whole. Syllables and phrase may be repeated in the same way. Songbirds often use end-phrases to indicate closure of their song, shown here in the series of descending notes.

fathers.[38] Of course, the process of acquiring or developing calls may differ from one species to the next.

The learning of calls may be characteristic of some species and not others, and also of some calls and not others. In fact, among the birds that have only calls and no song, it seems that parrots and hummingbirds are the only ones that learn their calls.[39] The calls of domestic fowl are not learned, it seems, although the contexts in which the calls are given may be refined by learning.

It appears that the ability of songbirds (oscines) to learn their species-typical vocalisations evolved just once in the common ancestor of all the oscines. Before that, birds did not sing and they did not learn their vocalisations, as is still the case for the suboscines today. Vocal learning in parrots and hummingbirds is thought to have evolved independently on their divergent lines of evolution.[40]

The learning of song by the oscines is usually confined to a limited period of life (i.e. a sensitive period) and in most species that period occurs in the first year of life.[41] A song is made up of a number of different phrases that can be subdivided into syllables, and each syllable can be subdivided into a number of different elements (Figure 9.2). These components of song can be varied to produce different songs. Just altering the sequence of elements or syllables will make a new song type. Some species sing only one song: these include the white-crowned sparrow, the European redwing and the splendid sunbird. The chaffinch sings between one and six different songs,[42] the starling from about twenty to 70, and well over 100 different songs are produced by the mocking bird, the nightingale, song thrush and five-striped sparrow.[43] The brown thrasher is thought to hold the record at close to 2000 song types,[44] which suggests that the same male may never sing the same song twice. The Australian magpie has greatly varied song but the number of its song types has not yet been determined. As both male and female Australian magpies sing,[45] unlike most European birds, it would be interesting to compare repertoire size in males and females.

We think that the singing of male oscines may signal their quality as a partner for reproduction—a male with a more elaborate song may make a better partner.[46] Perhaps the same is true for females that sing but this has not been tested. The fact that song is learned during the stages of life when nutrition is critical (nestling and fledgling stages) may mean that the physical condition of the bird influences its ability to learn about song.[47] A bird with good nutrition and good physical health during the sensitive period for song learning may, therefore, learn more songs and, in adulthood, this may signal to potential partners the fitness of that individual for mating. Some species, on the other hand, learn new songs each spring and this may also depend on their physical health and available nutrition at the time.

Nightingales have impressive memories. They learn their huge repertoires of song by 'chunking' or packaging song types, in the same way that humans learn certain sorts of information—for example, series of numbers or letters.[48] In other words, nightingales organise the elements of their songs into hierarchies and follow rules (of grammar) when they are singing. In addition, each individual bird invents its own songs and so creates aspects of singing (new phrases or 'sentences') that can be used to identify that individual bird.

Many birds learn their songs as juveniles long before they ever sing them themselves. They are silent when learning the songs by listening to other birds singing and only later do they produce the vocal repertoire that they have learned. It is known for some species that various song types are learned during a sensitive period of development.[49] The length of the sensitive period may depend on the levels of the sex hormone testosterone in the bloodstream, ending when the levels of testosterone rise.[50] The marsh wren learns a large number of songs that it heard between the age of about twenty and 70 days after hatching, the best time being from days 30 to 50.[51] Even though they hear songs after day 70, the birds do not learn them. They do, however, learn some songs in the following spring when nearby adults start to sing again.[52] In fact, marsh wrens that hatch late and so encounter the winter early learn fewer songs when young and more during the next spring. Swamp sparrows have a similar sensitive period for learning song when they are juveniles but they do not learn any more songs the next spring.[53] Nightingales have a sensitive period from two weeks after hatching to the beginning of the fourth month of life. Male nightingales first begin to rehearse their songs at about six months of age—this singing is called 'subsong'. Then European winter arrives and they become silent until about January, at which time they sing very variable song, known as 'plastic song'. After a further four months their song patterns stabilise into the adult form.[54] Unlike swamp sparrows, nightingales elaborate on their songs each year, and so do canaries.[55] With each new spring the male proves his worth as a partner by embellishing his song. These seasonal changes in the production of song are related to changes in the levels of sex hormones in the bird's bloodstream, triggered by changing day length, and they are typical of birds living in temperate regions.

It is remarkable how few times the young songbird must hear a song before it learns it. Nightingales learn a song heard only ten to fifteen times during their sensitive period for song learning.[56] Australian magpies have a similar ability to learn new song types—they can mimic sounds heard for only a very short time and integrate them into their song. In one case it was shown that a juvenile magpie was capable of an accurate rendition of kookaburra calls ('laughing') after an exposure period of only minutes.[57]

Vocal learning is influenced by social factors. Young zebra finches learn from tutors, adult males that sing. They learn better if they encounter their tutors when they are between 30 and 60 days old.[58] They learn only if they can interact with the tutor, rather than just seeing and hearing him in a nearby cage. We do not know exactly what aspects of social interaction are important for the song learning to take place but it is, surprisingly, more effective if the tutor is aggressive to his 'pupil'.[59] Indigo buntings will not learn from a tutor that they can hear but not see; they need to see the tutor, at least, and preferably interact with him socially.[60] Starlings also learn better from a tutor they can see and with whom they can interact socially and Grey parrots learn to use English labels for objects only by interacting with their human trainers and not from videotapes.[61] All these examples show that something about live interaction with a conspecific tutor, or a tutor of another species (e.g. a human), makes vocal copying possible.

Nightingales reared together in the same cage tend to share song types and, similarly, in the natural environment neighbouring birds share at least parts of their song repertoires.[62] This learning and sharing, known as 'song matching' or 'type matching', occurs in other species of songbirds too and leads to local dialects of song.[63] Song sparrows occupying neighbouring territories share two or more of their six to ten song types. Since more song matching occurs early in the song sparrow's breeding season, it appears to act as a warning related to establishing a territory for breeding.[64] Learning a neighbour's calls also occurs in some species that are not songbirds, such as the budgerigar.[65] The social interactions that occur between neighbouring birds might be important for this mutual learning of each other's song or, at least, seeing the singing neighbour rather than just hearing him may be important.

Most of the research on song in birds has involved species of the Northern Hemisphere where only the males sing. This has given the impression that only the males learn about song, but this is not so. There are many species in which the female also sings (e.g. the Australian magpie), and she too learns her song. Even in those species in which females do not sing, the females learn to recognise the songs of conspecific males. They recognise and respond to these songs, showing that they must have learned about them in detail, often in early life, just like the males. Zebra finch females distinguish their father's song from those of other males and white-crowned sparrow females choose conspecific songs of the dialect that they heard when young.[66] Female starlings have been heard to sing on occasion and they will sing complex songs if they are injected with the hormone testosterone.[67] This shows that they do learn to sing even though they do not usually do so.

There is much to be discovered about song learning in females. Some females even train their males to produce their preferred song. The female brown-headed cowbird strokes her wing when she is attracted to a male and he then sings the same song again so that, in time, the male shifts his singing to match her preference.[68] This example alone illustrates the importance of the female in song learning and performance.[69]

Flying and migrating

Many species of birds migrate seasonally over vast distances on journeys that may circumnavigate the globe or traverse the two hemispheres. How do they find their way over such long distances, sometimes returning each year to the same territory? To achieve these feats of orientation, they use compass mechanisms relying on the sun's position and the earth's magnetic field[70] or, in the case of those that migrate at night, they use the stars as a compass. For daytime migration, the sun compass is the preferred means of orientation but, when the sky is overcast, birds use their magnetic compass.[71] Use of the sun compass is complex because the sun moves across the sky and, therefore, the bird must use a timing mechanism (said to be an 'internal clock') to know which way to orient depending on the time of day. They must also take into account the azimuth (highest point in the arch of the sun's trajectory across the sky in any season) and relate this to their latitude. Birds have to learn the relationship between the sun's azimuth, latitude and the time of day. Experiments were performed on homing pigeons to see how and when they learn these relationships.[72]

The fact that pigeons learn how to use their sun compass was shown by raising a group of them under day-night conditions that were shifted to be six hours later than the normal day-night cycle.[73] A control group of pigeons was raised with their day-night cycle synchronised with the natural cycle. Then both groups were given training flights in the afternoon, when their daytime cycles overlapped. During these training flights the experimental, phase-shifted birds learned that the sun was in the south during their 'morning' and in the west at their 'noon'. They learned to home correctly using this compass information. To find this out, the pigeons were released at some distance from their home loft and the direction to which they turned in attempting to fly home was determined. They could, of course, have been relying on their magnetic compass but this was not so. The critical test was performed by then altering the day-night cycle of the experimental birds back to the natural cycle and testing their ability to orient after this. Now they flew in the wrong direction, away from their home loft. This shows they were, indeed, using the sun compass and that they had learned an abnormal compass during their initial period of training.

Other experiments have shown that pigeons learn their sun compass starting at about five weeks of age, when they first begin to make rather clumsy flights from the loft. They are able to make full use of the sun compass by the time they are three months old.[74] Giving the young pigeons more homing practice allows them to learn about their sun compass earlier. Young pigeons given several releases up to 10 kilometres from the loft, so that they had more practice in homing, had learned their sun compass at only eight or nine weeks old. This shows that they learn through the experience of orienting their flights. For the learning to be effective, they have to see the entire arch of the sun's movement across the sky and so learn where its highest point is and the time at which the sun reaches that highest point. They do this during a sensitive period in early life, but later experience can modify their sun compass.[75]

Learning in the laboratory

In the laboratory birds can be trained to perform many different kinds of tasks, including pecking at keys for a reward such as food or heat (known as 'operant conditioning'). For example, the bird may receive the reward if it pecks at a green key but not a red one, or at a key with a square on it and not one with a circle on it. Pigeons have been used extensively in such conditioning techniques. They can be trained to perform with very few mistakes and their astounding abilities to learn and remember have been demonstrated in a vast number of experimental paradigms. Pigeons can learn to distinguish 100 visual symbols that signal reward when the key on which they are displayed is pecked from over 600 other visual symbols that have no associated reward when the key is pecked.[76] They can also be trained to distinguish between symbols rotated at different orientations and to peck at keys that have photographs of water in a variety of forms—in a glass, as a droplet on a leaf, as a lake.[77] These experimental procedures have shown time and again that birds can learn complex associations in adulthood, as well as when they are young.

Many of the behaviour patterns of birds are learned. Both simple and complex behaviours can be affected by experience in early life and also later in life. Some learning is confined mainly to sensitive periods in early life, whereas other forms of learning can take place at any time in the bird's life span. Some forms of learning are powerful and almost irreversible and other forms are more flexible. In all these characteristics birds are no different from mammals. Contrary to a common belief, birds are no less reliant on learning than mammals and, in fact, some of their complexities of learning match those of higher mammals (primates).

chapter 10

ARE BIRDS INTELLIGENT?

'Intelligence' is not a unitary characteristic of an individual or a species that can be measured in one specific way.[1] Although we speak frequently of intelligence, it is not possible to rank species so that we could say one species is more intelligent than another. Of course, some species show more complex behaviour than others but each species is adapted to its particular ecological niche. Members of a species always perform well when they are tested in the context of their own niche, whereas they perform poorly, and *appear* to be less intelligent, when they are tested on tasks not relevant to that niche. Pigeons, for example, perform better than humans when they are tested on a task requiring them to recognise symbols rotated at different angles.[2] This ability is important for the pigeon's survival: as it flies over trees and buildings it must recognise them from all angles of rotation. Many other avian species might be capable of doing this too but no other species have been tested on tasks that demonstrate this ability. Such an ability is not so important for humans; in fact, we even have some difficulty in recognising faces when we see them upside down.

One way of measuring 'intelligence' across species might be to estimate how adaptable they are to different environmental contexts. In this case, the fundamental mental process that the bird would have to do is to identify the nature of the problem and develop a strategy to solve it.[3] Many species of birds are capable of learning new behaviours that allow them to adapt to a wide range of environments. Based on this definition of intelligence, the abilities of many birds are equivalent to those of chimpanzees, orang-utans and gorillas.

Making memories

Intelligence may also be described as the ability to recall the past and to have foresight of the consequences of actions but these are, generally, not considered qualities that birds might possess. Instead, birds are often thought to respond to events in ways that are instinctive, or predetermined according to inflexible programs. This is far from correct. Birds have excellent abilities to form memories and they can recall very detailed memories after long periods of time. Perhaps the best examples of these abilities come from research with species that store, or cache, their food. Many species that live in cold winter climates store their food so that they can retrieve it when needed. For example, Clark's nutcrackers store pine seeds in autumn in places from which they can be retrieved when the ground is covered in snow. They store many thousands of seeds in more than 7000 scattered locations and later they manage to retrieve the seeds with surprising accuracy.[4] To do this they must have excellent memories that take into account the spatial location of the stored seeds.[5]

Tits, chickadees and many corvids (crows) of North America also store food and retrieve it up to months later, and the same is true of related species in Europe.[6] How long they leave the stored seeds before retrieving them depends on the species. For example, in contrast to the very long-lasting memories of tits and chickadees, marsh tits have much shorter-term memories, although their memories of the locations of their stored food are just as detailed as the other species. They store several hundreds of food items in a day but retrieve them just a day later. Ravens also cache their food and retrieve it 24 hours later, this short delay being necessary because the food is meat and would perish if stored too long. Ravens have been observed to hide food during feeding binges and they try to do so when out of sight of other ravens.[7] If one raven sees another caching food, it will later pilfer the food from that site.

We might suggest that the birds search at random for their caches and only happen upon them by chance, but this is not so. Evidence for this came from experiments with marsh tits in Oxford.[8] The experimenters placed seeds at various sites around those where the tits were storing their seeds. They found that the tits visited the sites of their own stored seeds much more often than they did the control sites where seeds had been placed by the experimenter. A similar result was obtained in laboratory tests of the marsh tits. They visited their stores more often than other control sites in the aviary in which they were tested.[9] It has also been shown that Clark's nutcrackers are more successful in finding their own stores than can be accounted for by random searching.[10]

The birds use landmarks and the geometry of the environment to locate their stores.[11] We refer to this kind of memory as 'spatial memory'. It makes sense to use these more distant cues to find the caches because the local features around the site of each cache may be changed by snowfall, leaf cover or other seasonal changes. If the birds used the colour of the surrounding terrain and plants as cues to remember where they have hidden food, they would also have difficulty because of colour changes with the season; in fact, it seems that they tend to ignore colour cues.[12]

The part of the brain known as the hippocampus is particularly involved in the ability to form and retrieve spatial memories. In line with this, the hippocampus is larger in species that store their food than in closely related species that do not.[13] Even within a species that stores food, the size of the hippocampus varies with the season and from one individual to the next—it is larger in birds that have had more opportunity to store food.[14] The part of the brain used for spatial memory grows larger when it is put to use by the bird.

The remarkable ability of these species to remember the spatial location of their food stores is an adaptation to the habitat in which they live or to the type of food they eat. In many species, this is an evolutionary adaptation to surviving in environments in which highly nutritious food is abundant in only one season of the year and must be stored to be eaten in other, harsher seasons. In other species, such as ravens, short-term caching takes place when there is temporary availability of food and competition for that food. Not only do the birds remember where they stored their food items but they know how long an item can be left in storage before it will perish and become inedible. Scrub jays will cache both perishable and imperishable food and retrieve the perishable food after only a short delay. After a longer period of delay, they avoid the sites where they stored perishable foods and search only for the sites containing imperishable food items.[15] This shows that the jays remember what they have stored, and where and when they stored it.

This kind of detailed memory, taking into account 'what', 'where' and 'when', has previously been shown only in humans.[16] In humans, memory of a rather similar type is known as 'episodic memory', meaning memory of events, each of which occurs in a unique place and at a unique time, and is distinguished from semantic memory, which refers to memory of facts. The memory of the scrub jays is not exactly the same as human episodic memory but it is close to it.[17]

Of course, many species of birds do not hide food but use spatial memory for other purposes—to remember migration routes and the location of their territories or roosting sites. Homing pigeons, for example, use spatial memory to navigate back to their home loft. The hippocampus region of the brain is also involved in this spatial navigation ability, as well as in the ability of the same pigeons to remember the spatial location of food.[18]

Excellent spatial learning and memory is a notable capacity of, perhaps, most avian species. Even very young domestic chicks can learn about the spatial location of objects and they do it well.[19] Nevertheless, spatial ability is better in some species than in others, depending on habitat. Most species living in habitats that do not require this adaptation will have an equal ability to form complex memories that last for a long time but they use them for different functions. For example, songbirds remember their own complex songs as well as those of neighbouring birds for exceptionally long periods of time.[20] Male hooded warblers recognise the songs of birds holding territories next to theirs during the breeding season and they retain this memory after an eight-month period during which they migrate from North to Central America and during which time they do not sing.[21] Indeed, the complexity and detailed information that birds remember is remarkable. As we saw in Chapter 9, pigeons can learn to recognise over 600 different symbols and remember them accurately for several months. This is a remarkable feat of memory that would be difficult for many humans to perform.

Birds also demonstrate their excellent memory in many of their social behaviours. They appear to remember other individual birds for long periods of time. Memory, it seems, is a very special and highly developed aspect of the avian brain.

Solving problems

Ravens are known to be particularly 'intelligent' in solving problems and they also learn rapidly from other members of their species. This ability has been demonstrated in the laboratory by giving ravens a problem to solve and noting whether other ravens could learn by watching the raven that had solved the problem.[22] The task was to open a box by sliding its lid. Inside the box the raven would find a favourite food, three pieces of meat, and this motivated the bird to solve the problem. They had to slide the lid rather than lever it up, the latter being the way they first approached the problem. Once a raven had solved the problem, it could demonstrate its ability to other ravens. A 'pupil' raven could learn to solve the problem simply by watching a 'teacher' raven slide the lid open and then jump on the box to obtain the food reward.

Bernd Heinrich tested five ravens with pieces of meat suspended from their perches on pieces of string.[23] The birds were unable to reach the meat by bending down or by flying up to grab it. After trying for several hours to obtain the meat, the birds began to ignore it until, suddenly, one of them solved the problem: it pulled up as much string as it could, held the loop of string with a claw against the perch, and repeated this activity until the piece of meat could be hauled onto the perch and eaten. This bird had solved the problem by insight, rather than trial and error. Over the next days, all but one of the other ravens solved the problem but each in a different way; in this case they had not learned by observing the first bird's tactic.

Some birds will go to extraordinary means to find a way to obtain their favourite foods. Clark's nutcrackers, for example, have a particular fondness for pine nuts and they will even risk entering traps to get them. One researcher observed that nutcrackers dug under snow in an attempt to obtain pine nuts inside a trap placed on the snow.[24] In doing so, they approached the problem using a strategy they had not used previously.

Using tools

Many different strategies are used by birds to obtain their food in the natural environment, some of which involve tool use. Some of these skills are learned by watching other members of their species and others are acquired by problem solving. Tool use is considered to be a sign of intelligence and it was once thought that only humans used tools. We do use tools more than any other species but several species of birds are also known to use tools regularly to obtain food. They use tools to break open bones or shells and to probe into crevices and holes. The Egyptian vulture throws stones at ostrich eggs to break them open and so obtain their contents. This behaviour is learned and passed on by cultural tradition in certain groups of birds or it may be self-taught by trial and error.[25]

The lammergeier drops bones on rock surfaces to split them open so that the marrow inside can be eaten.[26] Probing for insects by using a cactus spine or a stick as a tool is a method adopted by woodpecker finches of the Galápagos Islands, and they do this particularly when other foods are scarce.[27]

Tools, it seems, are used most often to obtain food but there are examples of tools being used by birds to enhance their mating displays. The most notable is the palm cockatoo who drums with a short stick against a tree trunk as part of his mating display. The bird clasps the stick in one claw and strikes it against the tree on which he is perched as he dances and vocalises high-pitched calls. The cockatoo fashions the stick into a suitable instrument by cutting it to the right length and stripping it of leaves. Bowerbirds, it might be argued, use their bowers as tools to enhance their mating displays. But, in the case of the palm cockatoo, one object is used to strike against another object to obtain the desired result, and this fits the strictest definition of tool use.[28]

Tool using is complex behaviour but making the tool before it is used is even more complex, or more 'intelligent'. New Caledonian crows manufacture and use two different kinds of tools.[29] They make hooked tools from twigs and probing tools from pandanus leaves which they use for probing holes in trees or into the debris around trees to find insects to eat. The hooked tool is made by choosing a twig with a hooked end, which the bird then strips of leaves and works on with its beak to give it the desired shape. To use it, the bird holds the tool in its beak by the unhooked end. The other tool is made by using the beak to shear a piece off a pandanus leaf to give a tool with a particular shape, broader at the end to be held in the bird's beak. The tool is held so that the saw-toothed barbs of the pandanus leaf face towards the crow's beak and away from the tapered end.

Both tools are used to obtain prey from crevices and holes in trees. The crow carries a tool with it as it moves from tree to tree; sometimes it stores the tool in a place to which the crow returns when it needs the tool again. Storing a tool so that it can be used again may have come about because it is not easy to make these tools. The tool made from the pandanas leaf, for example, has to be sculptured from the leaf by cutting with the beak. To do this the bird must angle the beak to cut in a series of different directions. This requires skills comparable to those used by early humans to manufacture their tools.

By examining the leaves of the pandanus, it is possible to see the parts of the leaf cut out by the birds. These 'cut-outs' are the mirror image of the tools made by the crows. There are more tool 'cut-outs' on the left edges of the leaves than on the right.[30] Since more tools are cut from the left edges of the pandanas leaves and they start at the narrow end of the tool working away from the trunk, one can deduce that the birds use their right eye to guide their tool manufacture behaviour. The right eye of birds is used to classify and categorise objects.[31] This eye and the parts of the brain to which it sends visual information (i.e. the left hemisphere) are thus used to control the cutting behaviour and so ensure that the tool made matches a general 'image' of what the tool must be like. In other words, the crow must have a template for making the tool in its memory and it can best access this memory when it uses the right eye to manufacture the tool. The end result of this process is 'handedness' of the tools. This is the first demonstration of handedness in tool manufacture in a species other than humans and it demonstrates the remarkably complex behaviour of which birds are capable.

Tool use is thus not unique to humans or primates. The tool-using behaviour of crows matches and may even surpass that of apes. Most evidence of tool use in apes has come from observations of chimpanzees, although there have been observations of tool use by both free-ranging orang-utans that have had some human contact and wild orang-utans.[32] Like birds, apes use tools to obtain food by probing with twigs into termite mounds or tree holes or, in the case of chimpanzees, cracking open nuts with hammer stones. Chimpanzees may select a twig, strip it of its leaves and break it to the desired size but they end up with a straight tool without a hook.[33] One of the tools manufactured by New Caledonian crows, however, has a hook and the bird uses this hook effectively, in a way suggesting that it has a concept of the purpose of the tool. According to Hunt, humans did not begin to use hooked tools until less than 100000 years ago.[34] This comparison indicates that tool use in the crow is very sophisticated and a manifestation of their highly developed cognitive abilities.

So we see that some of the features of tool manufacture and use are not unique to humans and do not require language and the ability for symbolic thought, as many anthropologists believe. We don't know how the crows acquire the ability to make the tools but it is likely that they have a 'mental' image of the shape and function of the tool they need before they start to manufacture it. This would mean that they have symbolic 'thought', and here we use the word 'thought' while recognising that it is considered to be a unique human ability.

Concept formation

Concept formation is another facet of 'intelligence' that we have assumed to be a uniquely human quality, but we know from controlled experiments that pigeons have it too. Pigeons are able to form abstract concepts which they use to recognise objects in many different contexts.[35] They can, as said before, recognise 'water' whether it is in a glass, as a drop on a leaf or in a lake. This might sound simple because water is essential for survival but pigeons will learn to discriminate photographs of water in these various contexts from photographs showing objects and scenes without water. They can be tested by showing them the photographs on keys which they have to peck to get a food reward if water appears on the key but not if it does not appear there. Using key-pecking tasks, it has also been shown that pigeons have concepts of time and can count.[36]

Another example of concept formation involves being aware of an object that is no longer visible. To be able to do this the bird must 'think' about something that is not in its immediate presence. This is one aspect of consciousness.[37] The birds that retrieve their stored food demonstrate one example of being able to do this. Even in their first week of life, domestic chicks are able to conceptualise the presence of an object that has disappeared from sight. If the chick is imprinted on a coloured ball it will follow the ball and stay close to it. If the ball is moved out of sight behind a screen and the chick has to wait before it is released to follow the ball, the chick will retain a concept of the ball and where it is located, at least for a short time.[38] When presented with two identical screens, it approaches and goes behind the screen around which, shortly before, it had seen the ball disappear.[39] Other experiments have shown that the chick is aware not only of the existence of the ball when it is out of its sight but, using spatial memory, it also remembers the location of the ball.[40]

Categorisation and concept formation have also been shown in another species. Alex, a Grey parrot, has learned to communicate with humans using vocabulary in English.[41] If the experimenter presents Alex with objects of differing colours and shapes, he can say whether they are the same or different in terms of shape and colour. He can also say whether the objects are made of the same material or different material. This shows that he has formed concepts that apply to different objects and he understands that a single object can be classified according to more than one category (e.g. an object might be both a triangle and red in colour, and Alex refers to both of these characteristics).

Alex has been taught to use vocabulary in a meaningful way, rather than simply mimicking human speech without intent and doing so out of context like most pet parrots.[42] He learned by watching and listening to two people saying meaningful things about various objects. For example, one human would hold up a key saying 'What is this?' and the other would answer correctly or incorrectly and be praised or admonished accordingly. This training method differs from the usual way in which parrots are taught simply by repeating words and phrases over and over to them without reference to objects or contexts. When taught in the usual way, the parrot learns to mimic but not necessarily to use mimicked sounds to communicate in very complex ways or to communicate concepts.

Interestingly, parrots taught to mimic have a vocabulary related to their foot preference for holding food (see Figure 10.1).[43] Right-footed Grey

Figure 10.1 A yellow-tailed black cockatoo feeding. This individual shows clear left-foot preference for holding food. A left-foot preference is characteristic of many species of parrots and cockatoos but, among parrots kept as pets, mimicry of human speech is better if the bird has a right-foot preference.

parrots have larger vocabularies than left-footed ones. The left hemisphere is used when the bird gives a response that requires some consideration or decision making before acting. Since the left hemisphere controls the right foot, we can deduce that the birds with larger vocabularies might be using the left hemisphere. This result may, therefore, indicate that use of the left hemisphere enhances mimicry of human speech, and we are reminded of the fact that the left hemisphere of songbirds controls singing. In fact, considered together with the handedness of crows in manufacturing tools from pandanus leaves, we could say that lateralisation is an aspect of many of the higher cognitive functions of birds. Brain lateralisation may be a way of maximising 'intelligence' while keeping brain size and weight at a minimum because that is necessary for flying. The disparaging term 'bird-brained' is based on a misconception and a gross underestimation of the cognitive abilities of birds.

part V
BIRDS AND HUMANS

chapter 11

DOMESTICATION

Birds have been domesticated as pets and as a source of food for humans for a very long time and domestic fowl feature in this history as one of the most important sources of food. The domestic chicken (*Gallus gallus domesticus*) is generally believed to have descended from one or all of the four species of junglefowl (*G. gallus*, *G. varius*, *G. sonneratii*, and *G lafayettei*). Many believe that the subspecies known as the Burmese red junglefowl (*Gallus gallus spadiceus*), which occurs in South-East Asia but also in southern China, India and the islands of Sumatra, Java and Bali, was the sole ancestor of the domestic chicken.[1] Recent molecular genetic evidence shows that *Gallus gallus* alone was the ancestor of all domestic chickens and that it is likely that all the strains of domestic chickens originated from a single domestication event in Thailand and nearby areas.[2] Therefore, although the earliest records of the domestication of the junglefowl date back to 2500 BC in India and to 2200 BC in Mesopotamia[3] and to more than 5000 BC in China, it now seems that domestication of the chicken occurred earlier and in one locality, Thailand. Using the new techniques to analyse the genetic material of domestic species, it will be possible to make new discoveries about the origins of all domestic species, instead of relying solely on written records and legends.

The ancient Egyptians kept domestic fowl although not commonly until about 525 BC. From its earliest domestication the chicken might have been used for the sport of cock fighting as much as for food (Figure 11.1).[4]

Figure 11.1 Cockfighting is a widely practised sport which usually leads to serious injury or death of one or both of the fighting birds.

In some countries, Persia in particular, cocks were cherished for their crowing at dawn. In time, different breeds were selected for their differing qualities and today we have breeds that are best at laying eggs, producing meat or, in some cases, cockfighting, a sport no longer condoned by most countries. There are also breeds that are primarily collectors' items and are judged in bird shows.

Ancient legends and religions associated the cock with various powers.[5] The Greeks believed it to be a symbol of the immortality of the soul and the Chinese saw it as a symbol of both good fortune and protection of the family. Moslems have regarded the cock crow at dawn as a song in praise of Allah. The sun worshippers of Scandinavia believed that the red cock crowed in Valhalla to announce the coming of the sun. The cock crow also features in the biblical account of the Last Supper of Christ and has played a prominent role in the Christian religion, as demonstrated by the weathercock on church steeples and the sacrifice of cocks in some religious ceremonies. The cock also makes frequent appearances in literary writings, including Chaucer's *Canterbury Tales* and Shakespeare's *Hamlet*, where its powers drive away the ghost of Hamlet's father.

Other avian species domesticated for food include the turkey, guinea-fowl, pigeon, duck and goose. Like the chicken, these are all precocial birds, well developed at hatching. It is not surprising that humans domesticated precocial species as a food source since such birds could be hand-raised without difficulty when the parent bird was not available. Also, they could be handled more easily if they imprinted on humans and so would follow the farmer and come when called. All these domesticated avian species are primarily grain-eaters, which means that their food was readily available once humans had begun to cultivate grain crops.[6]

The turkey was domesticated in the West Indies, from the Mexican wild turkey.[7] This domestication was carried out by the native populations well before the Spanish arrived in that part of the world and then took the turkey back to Europe. The first pair of turkeys was offered to the Pope in the 16th century. The guineafowl was taken from Africa to Europe in the 5th century BC and became popular with the Romans.[8] The pigeon has a more ancient domestication, at about 3000 BC by the Egyptians. Domestic ducks are believed to have their origins in several parts of the Eurasian continent and, particularly, in Mesopotamia and China, the home of the Mandarin duck. The domestication of ducks may have taken place at different times in these different places but most ducks, it seems, descend from the wild mallard duck. The Muscovy duck is an exception: it has a completely separate origin in Peru.[9] Domestic geese are descended from the greylag goose, a wild species in Europe. Romans kept geese for food, especially for their livers, a culinary practice that still features in French cooking today. In fact, the inhumane practice of producing *foie gras* (fat liver) by force-feeding geese symbolises the extent to which humans have exploited domestic animals.[10]

In the past all these species were used not only for food, as they are today, but also their feathers were used to human advantage. Their down was, and still is, used to stuff quilts and their primary feathers were used as quills for writing. Geese were often plucked several times a year to provide these feathers. Apart from the pain caused by plucking the feathers, the birds would have had difficulty controlling their body temperature until the feathers grew again. The European eider duck provided the most sought-after down for quilts. Over the centuries, ostrich feathers have been used as ornaments by Europeans, worn particularly in hats, and also to make decorative fans. Later, Australian emu feathers were used for the same purpose. Birds with spectacular plumage have always been hunted because of their feathers. These feathers are used in ceremonial occasions, often only by those with high social status.

Semi-domestication of ornamental birds

Birds have also been domesticated to a certain extent for decorative purposes. Most of the swans seen on European lakes, particularly in cities, are either partly or entirely domesticated. The swan has been kept as an ornamental bird in Europe since the Middle Ages.[11] The white swans are of European origin and the black ones a more recent introduction to Europe from Australia. The Mandarin duck is also bred in similar circumstances for decorative appeal, as are other species of ducks and geese, as well as the peacock. The peacock has always been part of the religious beliefs and ceremonies of India, where it occurs in the wild. It slowly became popular in Europe during the 14th to 17th centuries.[12]

Other species were bred and released into the forests and parks of Europe as game birds for hunting. To a lesser extent, this practice continues in Europe today. The birds exploited in this way include pheasants, quails and mallards. Game birds are, of course, eaten after they have been killed but they are a specialty food item, in contrast to the fully domesticated species that are a regular source of meat and eggs. The feathers of game birds are used to decorate hats.

Birds as pets

Not all birds are eaten. Domestication has not always occurred for purely mercenary reasons. People keep pets, including birds, for company and for their pleasure. Some are kept for the beauty of their song (e.g. canaries) and others for the attractiveness of their plumage or their behavioural characteristics. Canaries and budgerigars have a long history of popularity as caged pets but, more recently, the Australian zebra finch has become as popular a pet as canaries and parrots.[13] Many bird owners spend a considerable amount of time with their birds and allow them to become part of the family, just as many dogs and cats are. Others keep birds as ornaments, sometimes in cages so small that the poor bird can barely move, let alone fly (Figure 11.2). These small cages are still on sale in pet shops,

Figure 11.2 Many large species of ornamental or companion birds, such as this macaw, are accustomed to the canopy of the vast expanses of rainforests, and so do not cope well in captivity and cannot exercise their wings adequately.

suggesting that the inhumane practice still has plenty of followers. Others are lavished with gifts and kept entertained by a devoted owner or family. It is the luck of the draw for the bird whether it is going to have a pleasant or a lonely and abused life.

Keeping birds as pets or for display in aviaries is widely practised and dates back to antiquity. A rich variety of species has been bred for this purpose. A species of parrot from India (a parakeet known as the Alexandrine parrot because it is believed to have been brought to Europe by Alexander the Great) was valued highly by the ancient Greeks and Romans.[14] It was in India and China that the first breeding of a variety of parrots took place. Apart from their brightly coloured plumage, the ability of parrots to mimic human speech and other sounds made them most attractive as pets. In Europe and later in America, the African Grey parrot was most popular for its ability to 'speak' and the macaw was, perhaps, the most popular for its plumage. African Grey parrots were used to accompany sailors on sea voyages. In the mid-19th century, parrots from Australia were sought after and the smaller budgerigar became a common household pet in Europe, and later elsewhere. Smaller parrots have traditionally been the pets of poorer people, whereas the larger and rarer species have adorned the castles and mansions of the wealthy.[15]

Over the last century, birds have also featured increasingly as live merchandise. Aviculture is an industry of sizeable proportions. In most Western countries, aviculture is now a well controlled industry that has also partly taken it upon itself to educate the public about bird keeping; and, for many species, transport is generally no longer necessary as large numbers are bred in captivity in the location for the market. For instance, budgerigars are not poached from the wild in Australia because captively bred birds are readily available in far-off Europe and North America.

Birds that are rare or not widely bred in temperate climates, however, may be shipped half-way across the world to satisfy demands from a discerning clientele, and often at extremely high cost. The supply countries are usually the tropics and the Southern Hemisphere while the consumers are largely the Northern Hemisphere countries. Prices for these embodiments of paradise (for one bird or a breeding pair) may reach the cost of a luxury car. Several countries have now prohibited export of their native species but this has not stopped the trade. Poaching of eggs and young birds and illegal exports of live birds are now commonplace and untold numbers die as a result of the methods of transport. Ironically, the definition of a rare and desirable bird is increasingly linked to the species' status of abundance. A 'rare' bird today usually means a bird that is classified vulnerable or endangered. The more endangered it is, the higher the price and the more likely it is that valuable eggs are poached. Some countries, including Australia, now have limited programs in place whereby a controlled nest-robbing exercise will raise a limited number of wild-collected eggs to young birds which are then openly offered by tender. This method has been chosen for the black cockatoo in Western Australia. It is argued that the legal sale of breeding pairs may enable some aviculturalists to breed more of these endangered birds in captivity and sell them, thereby reducing the amount of poaching.

The changed characteristics of domestic birds

It is debatable how much domestication changes the characteristics of an animal or bird. We know that domestication of the Australian zebra finch has changed some characteristics of its song compared with that of wild zebra finches.[16] And it is not surprising that over generations of selection by humans a domesticated species will change some of its characteristics, including plumage colour, certain physiological functions and behaviours other than, or in addition to, song. Some of the characteristics are actively selected by humans, such as the various colours and patterns of plumage in pet budgerigars. Other changes are due to unintentional selection by humans; that is, other characteristics may appear along with the selection of desired characteristics.[17] For example, selection of a particular plumage colour may be unexpectedly associated with a change in the temperament of the bird. Domesticated birds may also differ from their wild conspecifics because the entire domestic population has been bred from a few pairs of wild animals taken into captivity, as may well have been the case for the zebra finch.[18]

However, this does not mean that domesticated breeds are unable to show all the behaviour patterns typical of their counterparts in the wild. Sometimes domestic birds do appear to lack some of the displays that are seen in their wild relatives but this can be the effect of observing the domestic birds in the captive environment. If the domestic birds are put into a more natural setting, they show all the behaviour patterns typical of their species. For example, pekin ducks kept in a natural environment show all the behavioural displays typical of wild mallards.[19]

While it is often claimed that the domestic chicken has been selected to tolerate living in battery cages, there is no convincing evidence to support this claim.[20] Domestic chickens are capable of highly complex cognition and, given the opportunity, engage in all the patterns of behaviour typical of their species. The fact that battery hens are commonly 'debeaked' (removal of the tip of the upper beak) to prevent them from pecking at the feathers of other chickens indicates that battery cages are an unsuitable environment for the birds (Figure 11.3).

The exploitative use of birds for human profit has reached multi-billion-dollar values and it has led to human desensitisation to the cruelty often inflicted on birds. There is now increasing outrage at the cruelty involved in raising domestic birds for profit. Birds are forced to starve for an extended period to induce a moult and this practice synchronises the laying of eggs in battery chickens. After being starved, when allowed to

Figure 11.3 The inhumane living conditions of battery hens can be seen clearly here. The bird cannot move in this tight cage.

feed many chickens choke to death. There is the gruesome practice in some slaughterhouses of cutting their throats manually and putting the chickens into processing troughs while still alive.[21] Concerns over the treatment of a wide range of species have now reached such proportions that these are widely addressed by educators, policy makers, veterinarians, philosophers and many others.[22]

At the same time, there are vast and still growing numbers of bird organisations worldwide that have been established to improve the life of birds. The welfare of birds, especially of those that have been domesticated and used for food production on a massive scale, has found advocates in human society. For instance, United Poultry Concerns in Machinpongo, Virginia, is one such organisation that looks critically at the modern poultry industry and attempts to influence legislation to stop the extremes of abuse that battery practice and forced moultings involve.

The domestication of birds as farm animals and pets does not, of course, involve just poultry and slaughter, or feathers as ornaments. Pigeons are being kept for their homing abilities which makes them suitable for show, racing and homing. They are normally not killed. Pigeon keeping is a very ancient human practice. Domestic pigeons are thought to have come from the Middle East in about 3000 BC, arriving in Europe (Greece) from Syria and then dispersing to Rome, where the building of dovecots became common. They had spread to the rest of Europe by about 400 BC.[23] The ancestor of all the current breeds of domestic pigeons is thought to be the rock dove. These pigeons were used for food but pigeons were also bred for pigeon-fancying in many parts of the world. Homing, or carrier, pigeons were used to carry messages, particularly in time of war, or, in ancient Egypt, to carry messages from sailing vessels to shore. In fact, pigeons have been used to deliver messages in wars from the time of the Crusades to World War II. Today, they are big business and large associations (National Pigeon Associations) exist with their own high-volume magazines, such as *The Pigeon Debut*, advertising and reporting anything to do with pigeons, from sporting events to husbandry issues. At present, there are over 200 breeds of domestic pigeon and nearly five times that number if we include variations of these breeds.

Pigeons are very beautiful birds and, worldwide, there are over 500 species of them living in the wild. The greatest number of pigeon and dove species is found in Australia and on tropical islands. Many of them are tropical and subtropical birds, often with the most breath-taking, iridescent or colourful plumage. We only have to think of the superb fruit dove, the wompoo fruit-dove, the rose-crowned fruit-dove or the emerald-dove to realise that they are every bit as beautiful as other tropical birds and parrots.

Somehow, though, pigeons and doves have been devalued by their human use. Domestic pigeons have also spread into the wild and they belong to the few species of bird that have not only endured human encroachment on their territory but have actually succeeded in settling in human-made environments. Anywhere in the Northern Hemisphere they can be found occupying roof tops in cities and congregating in parks and other public places. Some, like the passenger pigeon of North America, were also much hunted.

Pigeons are, sometimes, even thought of as 'rats of the air',[24] precisely because they are hardy and have multiplied in human spaces, to the deep resentment of many. Yet it was their domestication in the first place that brought these birds into close proximity with humans. Pigeons and doves, largely rainforest dwellers, are naturally shy. We have some on our subtropical property and the closest we have ever managed to get to them was at the distance of binoculars. In a few pockets they can still survive unmolested and they retain a necessary fear of humans, their greatest predator.

chapter 12

BIRDS, HUMANS AND CONSERVATION

Human expansion across the globe has led to substantial clashes with wild bird populations. One of the first clashes between birds and humans occurred with the development and expansion of agriculture, and the problem remains today. Avian species that are known, or believed, to eat or damage crops have been culled and persecuted.[1] The most remarkable mass killing of birds in their millions happened under Mao Tse Tung's rule and instruction. Harvests were poor so the birds were blamed for this failure and, apparently with Mao's approval, farmers began to kill as many birds as they could and thus help the harvest along. There was a holocaust on a scale that has rarely been seen in recorded human history. Then harvest time came: and the harvest, instead of being improved, was much poorer than it had ever been before. Neither Mao nor his advisers had suspected that birds might actually help the harvest. The extremely poor harvest, with its threat of famine, was because they had killed the birds eating the pests that destroyed the crops. The next year, no one shot or trapped a bird and over a long period of time the birds returned and the crops improved.

Flocks of crop-eating birds are still being shot or poisoned today, and there are others that are poisoned accidentally or maliciously.[2] Shooting of birds continues for two other reasons: one is for sport (game birds) and another is specifically directed against birds of prey. Most countries have now set in place laws against shooting raptors but policing of this can be difficult. The main focus on changing attitudes to raptors world-wide has been to educate the public that usually they are no threat to livestock.

The sport of shooting ducks, geese and other game birds is still based on an attitude that, we believe, we can ill-afford in the 21st century. This is the assumption that we can treat 'nature' as a supermarket and take from the wild *what* we want, even if hunting seasons are now restricted and no longer allow the taking of everything *when* we want it. Treating nature as a supermarket has already served as the single largest reason for the ever increasing list of extinctions of plants, fish and mammals. In timber production and fish harvesting there are the first sustained signs that attitudes are changing, with the establishment of new branches of industry such as plantations and fish farms. Unfortunately, this has not stopped the destruction of old growth forests, nor has it stopped the persecution of birds or, at least, the total disregard of birds' needs.

Most of the clashes between humans and birds have resulted in losses for birds, just as there have been losses of many other animals, from insects to mammals. The highest concentration of birds is still found in wetlands and in the rainforests of the world, which occur around the tropical belts and in the Southern Hemisphere. Unfortunately, for the world's populations of birds, this is little comfort. The most powerful nations inhabit the Northern Hemisphere while the species most in need of protection are located in the Southern Hemisphere. This mismatch between power and needs creates two problems at once: the Northern Hemisphere continues to use the Southern Hemisphere and tropical countries as supply centres for its own overwhelming needs (i.e. needs that are disproportionately higher than for the remaining 80 per cent of the world's population). For instance, Indonesian exports of tropical rainforest timber provide 80 per cent of the plywood needs of the United States alone.[3] Japan and Korea are the main customers for Borneo's primary timber, to be used as disposable crates in the building industry.[4] Old growth forests are being dismantled and multinational companies move in to harvest while profits go elsewhere. Forests lie devastated and dysfunctional when the loggers depart. Even though loggers no longer take every bit of timber, they do take the very best to satisfy customer demands. The debris left behind is a jumble of fallen trees, exposed soil, destruction of undergrowth and erosion. The second problem is that the source of destruction is too far away from Northern Hemisphere countries and so rarely gets reported. People in Europe, North America and Japan are not well informed about the sheer magnitude of destruction wrought elsewhere for their short-term benefit, even though international organisations are now actively engaged in projects to relieve the carnage. It may well be a little too late.[5]

Water management

The 20th century has bequeathed extraordinary habitat changes involving the destruction, modification (pollution) or extraction of components (such as water) of whole ecosystems. Worldwide, many wetlands and river systems have problems because their waters are used for crop irrigation. Other, more benign reasons, such as control of insects, particularly mosquitoes, may have ramifications far beyond our present knowledge. Current mosquito control in wetlands includes insecticides such as target-specific Bti or methoprene.[6] The result is a massive 50 to 80 per cent reduction of insect density and biomass, and not just of the target species. Insects are a major component of wetland food webs and changes in food chains and predator–prey relationships are expected.[7] A reduction in insects at the beginning of the food chain inevitably means a reduction of food for birds. Some birds feed directly on insects but suffering is also caused to birds that feed on species relying on insects, such as frogs, lizards and fish.

Even in areas where wildernesses are now being maintained for the sake of sustaining populations of wildlife, there is evidence of detrimental human intervention. Unfortunately, in today's world, environments are being modified to suit human needs and the disappearance of wetlands and forests is distrastrous for the future of birds. Some of these changes are based on sudden interventions in the environment, such as clearing of forests, pollution of bird habitat, removal of food sources and depletion of waterways. The influencing factors can be quite subtle at times. For instance, the wood storks of the wetlands of Florida's Everglades have declined by 95 per cent because a change in waterflow made the birds postpone their breeding to a different season when the fish disperse and hence provide no food for their chicks.[8]

Clearing forests

Many forests have been cleared to make way for agriculture, cities or roads. All avian species that require existing nest-holes in trees have experienced breeding difficulties, to some degree, in countries with high levels of agricultural and urban development. Tree holes tend to develop only in mature old trees. The more old trees that are felled to make clearings for agriculture or space for new housing projects, the lower will be the reproductive success of some species. Most owls and parrots of the world are under threat from this kind of encroachment on their habitat. Many parrots are rainforest species and, as a result of rainforest logging around the globe, one-third of all parrot species (out of about 330 species) are now threatened in the wild. Often natural forests are replaced by monocultures of non-native trees for which the local wildlife finds very little use, neither for feeding nor nesting. Among the largest of these monoculture forests, for instance, are the vast pine plantations in South Africa.

In many birds, shelter is a prerequisite to everything else. Ground-foraging species, for instance, may need a particular kind of shelter to give them sufficient cover or background for camouflage. If they are easily detectable, even the best food supply will not ensure survival. Harry Recher predicts that ground-foraging birds are at risk and will feature next on the list for extinction.[9] Shelter, nest sites and appropriate food supplies are basic and important criteria in determining where birds live and where they thrive. Tragically, the most contested areas on the surface of the globe, environmental and political 'hot-spots' such as the Amazon basin and the wilderness of Borneo, are also those with the highest concentration of birds. The Birdlife International Biodiversity Project identified 221 endemic bird areas covering 5 per cent of the earth's land surface where 75 per cent of the world's 300 and more threatened species occur.[10] In 1999 a Birdlife International Partnership meeting was held in Malaysia by several umbrella organisations of the world. It found that, in the 21st century, one in every eight of the world's bird species would be in danger of extinction.

Human technology

Only in a few places around the world are there any funded programs that specifically address the effect that modern technology has on wildlife, particularly birds (Plate 12). Power lines, cars, airplanes, boats, tracking stations, wire (especially barbed wire) and electric fences kill large numbers of birds or, at the very least, have negative effects on birds and other animals.[11] Road casualties of birds have become commonplace. In many regions of the world, birds are not even listed as protected. By law, drivers who kill birds on the road are usually not required to stop. A pet clinic at the veterinary faculty in Zurich found that in ten years, between 1985 and 1994, 47 per cent of all bird admissions were trauma cases and half of them suffered from fractures, usually caused by car accidents.[12] Yet there is little evidence so far, anywhere in the world, that minor legislative amendments in favour of bird and wildlife survival are being made. Refractors on car lights and wind-friction devices on the bumper-bar would suffice to warn birds (and mammals) of an approaching car. These, or similar proven devices, could be part of the compulsory equipment of a car, at a small cost to the individual driver, at no cost to governments but at a premium for animals, saving probably millions of animal lives.

Fire management

Occasional natural disasters, like fire, do not usually inflict harm on animal populations in the long term (even with high death rates) because they occur irregularly and allow the species to recover. By contrast, in recent practice, fires have become a tool for regular forest 'management', as a way of fuel-load reduction. The argument in favour of controlled burn-offs is that reducing fuel load can prevent a major fire. Most people are appeased by this explanation. It makes sense and may save property and even human lives.

Most people involved in the management of fires are convinced that controlled fire is the best method of managing major bushfires. And while they may be experts in their field, engineers and practitioners in fire management are not usually trained in the flora and fauna of the area they manage. Leaving aside problematic aspects of repeated burn-offs such as creating clearings and fostering the growth of non-native weeds, these controlled burn-offs in Australia are often undertaken too late in the season and thus seriously interfere with bird breeding. Consideration of the breeding cycles of birds is rarely if ever apparent. The problem is that experts in one area rarely speak to those in others, so environments do not often get the benefit of being managed 'holistically'.

Major fires, even those that occur naturally through lightning strikes, do not happen in the same area in consecutive years. They are spaced far apart and, like most natural catastrophes, they have built-in evolutionary safeguards, at least where Australian flora and fauna are concerned. Some plants need fire for seeds to germinate. Many animals have adapted to fire by building elaborate underground shelters (e.g. wombats). Most birds have finished nesting and their offspring have fledged before the natural fire season starts. Still, major fires affect breeding for at least two seasons after the fire before full recovery is made.[13] Controlled burning shifts the natural paradigm in two ways. First, it reduces the fire cycle from approximately five years to one year and, second, it shifts the fire season from post-breeding to the breeding season. In one rainforest property in the hinterland of Coffs Harbour, the owner burnt off every year during the mild winter months. There were hardly any birds. That same property has now been without burning for four years and this year was the first year that an abundance of birds became apparent. Burning off every year has serious long-term effects on bird populations in the burnt-off regions.

Industry and the environment

No one doubts any more that human productivity has caused the degradation of the global environment, and is responsible for many pollutants in water, soil and air. Although regulations are now in place in most Western countries to curb air pollution and the emptying of toxic wastes into waterways, these measures alone are not sufficient to reverse the damage. It is easy to see how human industrial activity has affected many hundreds of thousands of individual birds and countless species. We hear of vast oil slicks caused by shipping disasters, resulting in many pelagic species with soiled feathers. They are destined for a cruel death.[14] We rarely hear of the common shipping practice of emptying old oil supplies into the middle of the ocean but jettisoned waste also kills birds.

Increasingly, accidents from large mining companies cause ecological disasters. In 1998 there was the Doñana disaster in south-west Spain.

Metals are extracted by using sulphuric acid and this highly acidic metal-contaminated waste is stored in massive tailing ponds. The pond dike collapsed and released about 5 million cubic metres into the tributaries leading directly into the World Heritage site of the Doñana National Park, contaminating sensitive ecological areas.[15] There have been mine disasters in Papua New Guinea and, in 1999, a similar dike-break of highly toxic waste from a tailing pond occurred in Hungary, emptying its contents into the Danube and other waterways. In Australia, mining companies have sought permission to mine in the heritage area of the Kakadu National Park in the Northern Territory, gaining a sympathetic ear from politicians, while local people understand that disastrous accidents are far from rare or implausible. Each time such a disaster happens, the bird populations, as well as all other animals, are severely affected. When they happen in heritage areas, endangered species are usually also affected.

Because birds have such a variety of requirements and specificity of feeding habits, they are very effective indicators of environmental diversity and general habitat health.[16] Unfortunately, relatively few international organisations have taken diversity into account when considering the economy and land use with regard to environmental deterioration and other problems.[17] Popular opinion is very much in favour of birds and, more than ever, people are demanding safe areas for birds and other native species of flora and fauna. We have to take the challenge and arrive at a new balance between short-term human needs and long-term ecological necessities.

Feral animals and birds

Damage to wildlife has been caused partly by the introduction of non-native animals such as rats and cats, arriving with the early settlers. Other species were purposely introduced for agriculture or pleasure. When they escaped into the wild they multiplied and caused the decimation of many native species. European expansion and voyages of discovery have not only plundered and destroyed native human populations but also the native flora and fauna across the globe. Europeans introduced non-native species to parts of the world where the environment was not suited to them. These included goats, rats, stoats, cats, foxes, rabbits, a host of plants, insects, fish, amphibians and reptiles. Today, there is hardly an island on the world's surface that does not have to grapple with the effects of introduced species. Ironically, some of the 'cures' to deal with introduced feral species cause further harm to birds by becoming part of the food chain. Poisons are laid for foxes and other rodents but birds at the upper end of the food chain, particularly birds of prey, may die as a consequence of poisoned bait. In Australia, almost all owls are endangered and we seem to be losing the battle to save them. Herbicides and insecticides, sometimes sprayed excessively, affect birds feeding on insect or grain diets.

Moreover, an unhealthy ecosystem may also be indicated by an increase in native predators. They move in because feral animals are often feeders that leave plenty of scraps. Predators (birds, reptiles and mammals) move in to feast on the abundance. Under these conditions, rate of multiplication tends to increase beyond sustainable limits. They stay and multiply in proportions that the particular habitat would not normally support. So the scraps that lured them in the first place will soon not be enough and the predators turn to their natural food sources, including preying on birds and their nests. Only now there are many more of them. This is what is called 'predator overload'. Once predator overload sets in this leads to the diminishment of passerines and other landbirds.

Parasites also move in as defences of breeding birds are low or as they lose competitors. For instance, in North America the population of cowbirds was documented by annual counts and over a century it increased exponentially.[18] Cowbirds are parasites which themselves have lost predators and they now, through eco-imbalance, inadvertently become party to the destruction of native bird populations. In healthy ecosystems, they have no overall detrimental effects on bird populations that are parasitised or preyed upon.

Ironically, many human organisations then point the finger at nest-raiding native birds and birds of prey, 'blaming' them for the decline of the songbird! A typical 'solution' suggested is the culling (killing) of these last native bird populations of predators.

This mentality is widespread in Australia—for example, the long and heated debate about currawongs and 'their' damage to songbirds. Killing one native species in order to save other native species is a short-sighted 'blame the victim' strategy. Such a strategy may have political benefits and, unbelievably, has even been argued as a 'save the wildlife' measure. However, it will not lead to eradication of the source of the problem. Human behaviour is the problem, not the native birds. Also, some environmental measures are undertaken without any understanding of bird behaviour. If wildlife managers knew that currawongs assemble and remain in areas purely because of exotic fruiting shrubs they might consider removing the exotic shrubs (or prevent them from fruiting) instead of proposing to cull the native birds. Even local governments are responsible for planting exotic trees and shrubs to line the streets of their towns and cities, attracting semi-nomadic currawongs to feed, to disperse exotic seeds and to stay in the areas, often in large numbers. In our struggle to find answers to the problems in our environment, it may at times be easier to blame the animals than to alter the perceptions and lifestyles of humans.

Ecotourism and bird behaviour

We now live with a new set of contradictions. At no time in modern human history has there been so great an interest in wildlife and wildernesses. Ironically, this interest may well be inversely related to the speed with which such wildernesses and wildlife in general are disappearing from the globe and from our own backyards. In response to the dramatic decline of wilderness areas, two main industries have sprung up which are lucrative, innovative and provide new genres of entertainment and education: wildlife documentaries and ecotourism.

There is now a wide range of popular wildlife documentaries and wildlife magazines. We have access to superbly coloured and photographed information about the private lives of animals and plants. We can see in our living rooms aspects of the behaviour of birds that we would rarely, if ever, see with our own eyes. We are invited to take a close-up look at birds, in a way we would never be privileged to experience in the wild, and we are told about their behaviours, habits and lifestyle.

Such luxury and such valuable information may come at a price. One of the costs is that wildlife photography is at a premium. Wildlife photographers compete fiercely for a title page or a report because that is how they earn their income. In the process, expectations of quality have increased enormously and sometimes short cuts are taken that may seriously contribute to further damage and risk for living animals. One short cut is to use flash even when it is seriously irresponsible. On a field trip to Borneo a wildlife photographer who joined us took out a flash the size of a suitcase and photographed directly into the dappled light of the jungle, into the eyes of orang-utans. Orang-utan eyes are like ours and very large flashes can blind them. Photography of nocturnal bird species is also usually done with flash.

Another method is to photograph animals in zoos rather than in the wild. While the photographs may be of the highest standard, the subject matter often shows animals that are depressed or not in good health. This has happened a good deal in photography of great apes, less so in birds. The public gets used to seeing animals that are not the norm in the wild and subliminally accepts the appearance of captive animals as the norm.

We know of no ethical standards for wildlife photography and have seen no magazines that carry a label stating that editorial policy conforms to the minimum ethical standards of its own profession. As long as the 'shot' is good, it will get published, no matter how it was obtained. There are banks of wildlife photography that can be accessed by publishers of magazines and books. To our knowledge, none of them carries ethical assurances. The same criticisms apply to wildlife documentaries although there are usually more people involved and they may require some form of permission. However, it is not always clear what ethical norms are being applied. Ethical standards for wildlife photography and documentaries are seriously overdue. Thankfully, there are also magazines and documentary makers that make it their business to argue for the conservation and preservation of fauna and they have a very important role to play.

Wildlife documentaries may have another and, we believe, mostly unintended negative side effect. Increasingly, we are troubled by what is implied by portraying a bird or other animal in a pristine natural environment, enjoying the perfect lifestyle. When films are made of areas that we have visited personally, there is often a mismatch of our experience of the locality and what is shown in the film. For example, a film was made about Madagascar, portraying it as the jewel of the Indian Ocean as it was once rightly called. When we visited the eastern coast and the centre of Madagascar, we found that the sparkle had gone, the forests had disappeared and bare and eroded soil greeted the traveller everywhere. The highly unusual lemurs scarcely lived anywhere in the wild but found refuge in small overcrowded sanctuaries, small regions of forest remnants that gave us a glimpse of how Madagascar might once have been. Many lemur species and particularly birds of prey face extinction there, and tireless and dedicated groups of people are trying to prevent this from happening. The documentary was made in several of these very small sanctuaries but not once did it reveal that these were the last refuges for wildlife. Viewers are therefore given the false impression of an intact world (the 'heile Welt' syndrome). Presenting a film like this is a great disservice to the public and to the animals. As viewers and consumers, we get no news of the desperate state in which some species find themselves and, because the photography is so attractive, we also want our share of it in the real world. Wildlife documentaries now supplement the vast industry of ecotourism, sometimes by sniffing out a few real gems of wilderness, sometimes by arousing our interest even when the reality might look very different indeed.

Ecotourism is also a double-edged sword. Discovering 'paradise' at the very time it is so nearly lost belongs to the contradictions of development and symbolises the emerging environmental tragedies of the 20th and 21st centuries. Adventure tourism, as it was once called, entertained a small group of intrepid people. Now all known areas of high forest and animal density have become tourist spots in one way or another. Large aircraft and well organised ground transport allow for safe and fast access to wildernesses.[19] On the positive side, it is true that some spots of wilderness have avoided the fate of being cut for timber because of tourism. There is plenty of evidence that the existence of some national parks and wildlife reserves is now secured by the income they generate from ecotourism.[20] National parks feature widely as tourist attractions. The secret places of pristine nature are fast disappearing. In many cases, information is readily available on the Internet.[21]

A distinction has to be made between specific interest groups and tourism. Birdwatching, for instance, has always been an active outdoor hobby pursued enthusiastically by large numbers of clubs and individuals worldwide. Many birdwatching clubs have accepted the voluntary task of counting birds, and so contribute to our information on species abundance and distribution. Birdwatchers have developed a certain decorum in the presence of birds. Since they want to observe them, they usually walk quietly in the bush, are naturally supportive of birds and behave in a manner that disturbs them least. Tourists have no such restraints. They come as consumers to do what they have been promised in the brochures; they often have no specialised knowledge or interest in the species they are seeing but are on the trip because they were enticed by the range of activities and attractive countryside.

To balance tourist dollars against avian needs is one of the many challenges facing us this century. It is generally agreed by organisations working with and writing about birds that we need to take better care of birds in the wild. If we want to know how well we handle our stewardship of the world, we need only observe the birds.

NOTES

CHAPTER 1: SPECIAL FEATURES OF BIRDS

1 Bibby, C.J. (1999) Making the most of birds as environmental indicators. In *Proc. 22 Int. Ornithol. Congress*, eds N.J. Adams and R.H. Slotow, vol. 70, Ostrich, Durban, pp. 81–88.
2 Rüppell, G. (1977) *Bird Flight*, Van Nostrand Reinhold Company, London.
3 Hinde, R.A. (1956) The biological significance of territories in birds. *Ibis*, 98, 340–369.
4 Boag, P.T. and Grant, P.R. (1981) Intense natural selection in a population of Darwin's finches (Geospizinae) in the Galápagos. *Science,* 214, 82–85; Grant, P.R. (1986) *Ecology and Evolution of Darwin's Finches*, Princeton University Press, Princeton, New Jersey.
5 Clayton, D.H. and Cotgreave, P. (1994) Relationship of bill morphology to grooming behaviour in birds. *Animal Behaviour*, 47, 195–201.
6 Clayton, D.H. (1991) Coevolution of avian grooming and ectoparasite avoidance. In *Bird–Parasite Interactions: Ecology, Evolution and Behavior*, eds J.E. Loye and M. Zuk, Oxford University Press, Oxford, pp. 258–289.
7 Clayton and Cotgreave (1994), op. cit.
8 Ibid.
9 Clayton, D.H. and Wolfe, N.D. (1993) The adaptive significance of self-medication. *Trends in Ecology Evolution,* 8, 60–63; Murray, M.D. (1990) Influence of host behaviour on some ectoparasites of birds and mammals. In *Parasitism and Host Behaviour*, eds C.J. Barnard and J.M. Behnke, Taylor and Francis, London, pp. 286–311.
10 Lucas, A.M. and Stettenheim, P.R. (1972) *Avian Anatomy: Integument*, US Government Printing Office, Washington, DC.
11 Brush, A.H. (1993) The evolution of feathers: a novel approach. *Avian Biology*, 9, 121–162.
12 Rüppell (1977), op. cit.
13 Ibid.
14 Bell, H.L. (1984) A bird community of lowland rainforest in New Guinea: foraging ecology and community structure of the avifauna. *Emu*, 84, 142–158.
15 Noske, R.A. (1996) Abundance, zonation and foraging ecology of birds in mangroves of Darwin Harbour, Northern Territory. *Wildlife Research*, 23, 443–474.
16 Noske, R.A. (1983) *Comparative Behaviour and Ecology of Some Australian Bark-foraging Birds*, PhD thesis, Dept of Zoology, University of New England, Armidale, NSW.

17 Saunders, T. and Ydenberg, R. (1995) Consumption and caching of food in the Northwestern Crow (Corvus caurinus). *Auk*, 112, 778–780.
18 Martin, G. (1990) *Birds by Night*, T. & A.D. Poyser, London.
19 Birdlife International. (1996) *Global Directory of Endemic Bird Areas*, Birdlife International, Cambridge.
20 Hinde (1956), op. cit.
21 Dunham, M.L., Warner, R.R. and Lawson, J.W. (1995) The dynamics of territory acquisition: a model of two coexisting strategies. *Theoretical Population Biology*, 47, 347–364; Stamps, J.A. and Krishnan, V.V. (1999) A learning-based model of territory establishment. *Quarterly Review of Biology*, 74, 291–307.
22 Giraldeau, L.A. and Ydenberg, R. (1987) The center-edge effect: the result of a war of attrition between territorial constraints. *Auk*, 104, 535–538.
23 Johnson, L.S. and Kermott, L.H. (1990) Possible causes of territory takeovers in a north-temperate population of house wrens. *Auk*, 107, 781–784.

CHAPTER 2: THE EVOLUTION OF BIRDS

1 Wellenhofer, P. (1990) Archaeopteryx. *Scientific American*, May, 42–49.
2 Ibid.
3 Feduccia, A. (1996) *The Origin and Evolution of Birds*, Yale University Press, New Haven.
4 Ibid.
5 Ibid.
6 Ibid.
7 Sereno, P.C. (1999) The evolution of dinosaurs. *Science*, 284, 2137-2147.
8 Ji, Q., Curries, P.J., Norell, M.A. and Ji, S-A. (1998) Two feathered dinosaurs from northeastern China. *Nature*, 393, 753–761.
9 Barsbold, R., Currie, P.J., Myhrvold, N.P., Osmólska, H., Tsogtbaatar, K. and Watabe, M. (2000) A pygostyle from a non-avian theropod. *Nature*, 403, 155–156.
10 Hou, L., Martin, L.D., Zhou, Z. and Feduccia, A. (1996) Early adaptive radiation of birds: evidence from fossils from northeastern China. *Science*, 274, 1164–1167. Wang, J. (1998) Scientists flock to explore China's 'site of the century'. *Science*, 279, 1626.
11 Hou, L., Martin, L.D., Zhou, Z, Feduccia, A. and Zhang, F (1999) A diapsid skull in a new species of the primitive bird *Confuciusornis*. *Nature*, 399, 679–682.
12 Barsbold et al. (2000), op. cit.
13 Normile, D. (2000) New feathered dino firms up bird links. *Science*, 288, 1721.
14 Chatterjee, S. (1991) Cranial anatomy and relationships of a new Triassic bird from Texas. *Philosophical Transactions of the Royal Society of London*, 332B, 277–342.
15 Padian, K. and Chiappe, L.M. (1998) The origin and early evolution of birds. *Biological Reviews of the Cambridge Philosophical Society*, 73, 1–42.
16 Garner, J.P., Taylor, G.K. and Thomas, A.L.R. (1999) On the origins of birds: the sequence of character acquisition in the evolution of avian flight. *Philosophical Transactions of the Royal Society of London, B*, 266, 1259–1266.
17 Ostrom, J.H. (1979) Bird flight: how did it begin? *Scientific American*, 67, 46–56.
18 Sereno (1999), op. cit.
19 Rogers, L.J. and Kaplan, G. (1998) *Not Only Roars and Rituals: Communication in Animals*, Allen & Unwin, Sydney.
20 Sereno (1999), op. cit.
21 Feduccia (1996), op. cit.
22 Novas, F.E. and Puerta, P.F. (1997) New evidence concerning avian origins from the late Cretaceous of Patagonia. *Nature*, 387, 390–392.
23 Hou et al. (1999), op. cit.
24 Walker, C.A. (1981) New subclass of birds from the Cretaceous of South America. *Nature*, 292, 51–53.

25 Gibbons, A. (1996) Early birds rise from China fossil beds. *Science*, 274, 1083.
26 Sanz, J.L., Chiappe, L.M., Pérez-Moreno, B.P., Buscalioni, A.D., Moratalla, J.J., Ortega, F. and Poyato-Ariza, F.J. (1996) An early Cretaceous bird from Spain and its implications for the evolution of avian flight. *Nature*, 382, 442–445; Sanz, J.L., Chiappe, L.M., Pérez-Moreno, B.P., Moratalla, J.J., Hernández-Carrasquilla, F., Buscalioni, A.D., Ortega, F., Poyato-Ariza, F.J., Rasskin-Gutman, D. and Martínez-Delclos, X. (1997) A nestling bird from the lower Cretaceous of Spain: implications for avian skull and neck evolution. *Science*, 276, 1543–1546.
27 Sanz et al. (1996), op. cit.
28 Feduccia (1996), op. cit.
29 Sibley, C.G. and Ahlquist, J.E. (1990) *Phylogeny and Classification of Birds: A Study of Molecular Evolution*, Yale University Press, New Haven.
30 Cooper, A. and Penny, D. (1997) Mass survival of birds across the Cretaceous–Tertiary Boundary: molecular evidence. *Science*, 275, 1109–1113; Gibbons, A. (1997) Did birds sail through the K-T extinction with flying colors? *Science*, 275, 1068.
31 Cooper and Penny (1997), ibid.
32 Sibley and Ahlquist (1990), op. cit.; Shetty, S., Griffin, D.K. and Marshall-Graves, J.A. (1999) Comparative painting reveals strong chromosome homology over 80 million years of bird evolution. *Chromosome Research*, 7, 289–295.
33 Sereno (1999), op. cit.
34 Cooper and Penny (1997), op. cit.
35 Feduccia, A. (1995) Explosive evolution in tertiary birds and mammals. *Science*, 267, 637–638.
36 Ibid.
37 Boles, W.E., Godthelp, H., Hand, S. and Archer, M. (1994) Palaeontological note. *Alcheringa*, 18, 70; Boles, W.E. (1995) The world's oldest songbird. *Nature*, 374, 21–22.
38 Vickers-Rich, P., Baird, R.F., Monaghan, J. and Rich, T.H. (eds) (1991) *Vertebrate Palaeontology of Australasia*, Thomas Nelson, Melbourne.
39 Ibid.
40 Boles, W.E. (1997) Fossil songbirds (Passeriformes) from the Early Eocene of Australia. *Emu*, 97, 43–50.
41 Gill, F.B. (1995) *Ornithology*, 2nd edn, W.H. Freeman, New York.
42 Feduccia (1996), op. cit.
43 Glickstein, M.E. (1990) Brain pathways in the visual guidance of movement and the behavioral functions of the cerebellum. In *Brain Circuits and Functions of the Mind*, ed. C. Trevarthen, Cambridge University Press, Cambridge.
44 Feduccia (1996), op. cit.
45 Rogers, L.J. (1997a) *Minds of Their Own: Thinking and Awareness in Animals*, Allen & Unwin, Sydney.
46 Clayton, N.S. and Krebs, J.R. (1994) Hippocampal growth and attrition in birds affected by experience. *Proceedings of the National Academy of Sciences*, 91, 7410–7414.
47 Basil, J.A., Kamil, A.C., Balda, R.P. and Fite, K.V. (1996) Differences in hippocampal volume among food-storing corvids. *Brain, Behavior and Evolution*, 47, 156–164.
48 Vander Wall, S.B. and Balda, R.P. (1977) Coadaptations of Clark's nutcracker and the pinyon pine for efficient seed harvest and dispersal. *Ecological Monographs*, 47, 89–111.
49 Deng, C., Kaplan, G. and Rogers, L.J. (2001) Similarity of the song nuclei of male and female Australian magpies (*Gymnorhina tibicen*). *Behavioural Brain Research*, in press.
50 DeVoogd, T.J., Krebs, J.R., Healy, S.D. and Purvis, A. (1993) Relations between song repertoire size and the volume of the brain nuclei related to song: comparative evolutionary analyses amongst oscine birds. *Proceedings of the Royal Society of London, B*, 254, 75–82.

51 Nishikawa, K.C. (1997) Emergence of novel functions during brain evolution: using a cladistic approach to investigate how new brain functions evolve. *Bioscience*, 47, 341–345.
52 Nottebohm, F. (1989) From bird songs to neurogenisis. *Scientific American*, February, 56–61.
53 Barnea, A. and Nottebohm, F. (1994) Seasonal recruitment of hippocampal neurons in adult, free-ranging black-capped chickadees. *Proceedings of the National Academy of Sciences*, 91, 11217–11221.
54 Krebs, J.R., Clayton, N.S., Healy, S.D., Cristol, C.A., Patel, S.N. and Jolloffe, A.R. (1996) The ecology of the avian brain: food-storing memory and the hippocampus. *Ibis*, 138, 34–46.
55 Rogers, L.J. (1996) Behavioral, structural and neurochemical asymmetries in the avian brain: a model system for studying visual development and processing. *Neuroscience and Biobehavioral Reviews*, 20, 487–503.
56 Evans, C.S., Evans, L. and Marler, P. (1993) On the meaning of alarm calls: functional references in an avian vocal system. *Animal Behaviour*, 46, 23–28.
57 Andrew, R.J., Mench, J. and Rainey, C. (1982) Right–left asymmetry of response to visual stimuli in the domestic chicks. In *Analysis of Visual Behavior*, eds D.J. Ingle, M.A. Goodale and R.J.W. Mansfield, MIT Press, Cambridge, MA, pp. 197–209.
58 Rogers, L.J. (1997b) Early experiential effects on laterality: research on chicks has relevance to other species. *Laterality*, 2, 199–219.
59 Güntürkün, O. and Kesch, S. (1987) Visual lateralization during feeding in pigeons. *Behavioural Neuroscience*, 101, 433–435.
60 Nottebohm, F. (1977) Asymmetries in neural control of vocalization in the canary. In *Lateralization in the Nervous System*, eds S. Harnard, R.W. Doty, L. Goldstein, J. Jaynes and G. Krauthamer, Academic Press, New York, pp. 23–44.
61 Floody, O.R. and Arnold, A.P. (1997) Song lateralization in the zebra finch. *Hormones and Behavior*, 31, 25–34.
62 Nottebohm, F., Allvarez-Buylla, A., Cynx, J., Kirn, J., Ling, C.Y. and Nottebohm, M. (1990) Song learning in birds: the relation between perception and production. *Philosophical Transactions of the Royal Society of London, B*, 329, 115–124.
63 Cynx, J., Williams, H. and Nottebohm, F. (1992) Hemispheric differences in avian song discrimination. *Proceedings of the National Academy of Science*, 89, 1372–1375.
64 Rogers, L.J. (2000) Evolution of hemispheric specialisation: advantages and disadvantages. *Brain and Language*, 73, 236–253.
65 Bisazza, A., Rogers, L.J. and Vallortigara, G. (1998) The origins of cerebral asymmetry: a review of evidence of behavioral and brain lateralization in fishes, reptiles and amphibians. *Neuroscience and Biobehavioral Reviews*, 22, 411–426; Vallortigara, G., Rogers, L.J., Bisazza, A., Lippolis, G. and Robins, A. (1998) Complementary right and left hemifield use for predatory and agonistic behavior. *Neuroreport*, 9, 3341–3344.
66 Rogers (2000), op. cit.
67 Robins, A., Lipollis, G., Bisazza, A., Vallortigara, G. and Rogers, L.J. (1997) Lateralization of agonistic responses and hind-limb use in toads. *Animal Behaviour*, 56, 875–881.
68 Feduccia (1996), op. cit.; Wroe, S. (1999) The bird from hell? *Australia Nature*, Summer, 56–63.
69 Feduccia (1996), op. cit.
70 Ibid.
71 Murray, P.F. and Megirian, D. (1998) The skull of dromornithid birds: anatomical evidence for their relationship to Anseriformes. *Records of the South Australian Museum*, 31, 51–97.
72 Wroe (1999), op. cit.
73 Feduccia (1996), op. cit.
74 Ibid.

75 Cracraft, J. (1973) Continental drift, paleoclimatology, and the evolution and biogeography of birds. *Journal of Zoology*, 169, 455–545.
76 Steadman, D.W. (1995) Prehistoric extinctions of Pacific island birds: biodiversity meets zooarchaeology. *Science*, 267, 1123–1131.

CHAPTER 3: CHOOSING A MATE

1 Dunn, P.O. and Cockburn, A. (1999) Extrapair mate choice and honest signalling in cooperatively breeding superb fairy-wrens. *Evolution*, 53, 938–946.
2 Black, J.M. (ed.) (1996) *Partnership in Birds*, Oxford University Press, Oxford.
3 Kendeigh, S.C. (1952) *Parental Care and Its Evolution in Birds*, The University of Illinois Press, Urbana, USA.
4 Milius, S. (1998c) When birds divorce: who splits, who benefits, and who gets the nest. *Science News*, 153, 153–156.
5 Coulson, in McNamara, J.M. and Forslund, P. (1996) Divorce rates in birds: predictions from an optimization model. *The American Naturalist*, 147, 609–640.
6 Catry, P. and Furness, R.W. (1997) Territorial intrusions and copulation behaviour in the great skua. *Animal Behaviour*, 54, 1265–1272.
7 McNamara, J.M. and Forslund, P. (1996) Divorce rates in birds: predictions from an optimization model. *The American Naturalist*, 147, 609–640.
8 Kaplan, G. (2000) Enchanting Frogmouths. *GEO*, 22, 45–50.
9 Newton, I. (ed.) (1989) *Lifetime Reproduction in Birds*, Academic Press, London.
10 McKinney, F., Derrickson, S.R. and Mineau, P. (1983) Forced copulation in waterfowl. *Behaviour*, 86, 250–294.
11 Austin, J.J., Carter, R.E. and Parkin, D.T. (1993) Genetic evidence for extra-pair fertilisation in socially monogamous short-tailed shearwaters, *Puffinus tenuirostris* (Procellariiformes: Procellariidae), using DNA fingerprinting. *Australian Journal of Zoology*, 41, 1–11; Austin, J.J. and Parkin, D.T. (1996) Low frequency of extra-pair paternity in two colonies of the socially monogamous short-tailed shearwater *Puffinus tenuirostris*. *Molecular Ecology*, 5, 145–150.
12 Alatalo, R.V., Gustafsson, L. and Lundberg, A. (1984) High rate of cuckoldry in pied and collared flycatchers. *Iokos*, 42, 41–47; Hoffenberg, A.S., Power, H.W., Lombardo, L.G., Lombardo, M.P. and McGuire, T.R. (1988) The frequency of cuckoldry in the European Starling. *Wilson Bulletin*, 100, 60–69.
13 Birkhead, T.R., Pellat, J. and Hunter, F.M. (1988) Extra-pair copulation and sperm competition in the Zebra Finch. *Nature*, 327; Fujioka, M. and Yamagishi, S. (1981) Extramarital and pair copulations in the Cattle Egret. *Auk*, 98, 134–144; Gavin, T.A. and Bolinger, E.K. (1985) Multiple paternity in a territorial passerine: the Bobolink. *Auk*, 102, 550–555. Moller, A.P. (1987) Behavioural aspects of sperm competition in swallows. *Behaviour*, 100, 92–104.
14 Dhondt, A.A. (1989) Blue Tit. In *Lifetime Reproduction in Birds*, ed. I. Newton, Academic Press, London, pp. 15–33.
15 Milius, S. (1998a) Chickadees sneak up the social ladder. *Science News*, 154, 27.
16 Dunn and Cockburn (1999), op. cit.
17 Petrie, M., Halliday, T. and Sanders, C. (1991) Peahens prefer peacocks with elaborate trains. *Animal Behaviour*, 41, 323–331.
18 Van de Pitte, M.M. (1998) The female is somewhat duller—the construction of the sexes in ornithological literature. *Environmental Ethics*, 20, 23–39.
19 Kaplan (2001), personal observation.
20 Frith, C.B. and Frith, D.W. (1993) Courtship display of the tooth-billed bowerbird (*Scenopoeetes dentirostris*). *Emu*, 93, 129–136.
21 Zahavi, A. and Zahavi, A. (1997) *The Handicap Principle*, Oxford University Press, Oxford.

22 Vallet, E., Beme, I. and Kreutzer, M. (1998) Two-note syllables in canary songs elicit high levels of sexual display. *Animal Behaviour*, 55, 291–297.
23 Yamaguchi, A. (1999) Auditory experience does not shape sexual preferences for songs in female northern cardinals. *Behaviour*, 136, 309–329.
24 Lack, D. (1968) *Ecological Adaptations for breeding in birds*, Methuen & Co., London.
25 Saetre, G.-P. and Slagsvold, T. (1992) Evidence of sex recognition from plumage colour by the pied flycatcher *Ficedula hypoleuca. Animal Behaviour*, 44, 293–299.
26 Lehrman, D.S. (1965) Interaction between hormonal and external environments in the regulation of the reproductive cycle of the ring dove. In *Sex and Behaviour*, ed. F.A. Beach, Wiley, New York.
27 Saetre and Slagsvold (1992), op. cit.
28 Briskie, J.V. and Montgomerie, R. (1997) Sexual selection and the intromittent organ in birds. *Journal of Avian Biology*, 28, 73–86.
29 McKinney et al. (1983), op. cit.
30 Briskie and Montgomerie (1997), op. cit.
31 Briskie, J. (1998) Why kissing is for the birds. *Nature Australia*, 26, 24–29.
32 Bennett, A.T.D. and Cuthill, I.C. (1994) Ultraviolet vision in birds—what is its function? *Vision Research*, 34, 1471–1478.
33 Andersson, S., Ornborg, J. and Andersson, S. (1998) Ultraviolet sexual dimorphism and assortative mating in blue tits. *Proceedings of the Royal Society, London B*, 265, 445–450.
34 Bennett, A.T.D., Cuthill, I.C., Partridge, J.C. and Meier, E.J. (1996) Ultraviolet vision and mate choice in zebra finches. *Nature*, 380, 433–435.
35 Hunt, S., Cuthill, I.C., Swaddle, J.P. and Bennett, A.T.D. (1997) Ultraviolet vision and band-colour preferences in female zebra finches, *Taeniopygia guttata. Animal Behaviour*, 54, 1383–1392.
36 Tinbergen, N. (1935) Field observations of East Greenland birds. 1. The behavior of the red-necked phalarope (*Phalaropus lobatus* L.) in spring. *Ardea*, 24, 1–42.
37 Jansen, A. (1999) Home ranges and group territoriality in chowchillas (*Orthonyx spaldingii*). *Emu*, 99, 280–290; Lack (1968), op. cit.; Armstrong, E.A. (1965) *Bird Display and Behavior*, Dover Publications, New York.
38 Sheldon, W.G. (1967) *The Book of the American Woodcock*, University of Massachusetts Press, Amherst.
39 Frith and Frith (1993), op. cit.
40 Robinson, F.N. and Curtis, H.S. (1996) The vocal displays of the lyrebird (*Menuridae*). *Emu*, 96, 258–275.
41 Armstrong, D.A. (1996) Territorial behaviour of breeding white-cheeked and New Holland honeyeaters: conspicuous behaviour does not reflect aggressiveness. *Emu*, 96, 1–11.
42 Huxley, J.S. (1914) The courtship habits of the great crested grebe (*Podiceps cristatus*). *Proceedings of the Zoological Society, London*, 491–562.
43 Nuechterlein, G.L. (1982) Western Grebes: the birds that walk on water. *National Geographic*, 161, 624–637.
44 Armstsrong, E.A. (1965) *Birds Display and Behavior*, Dover Publications, New York.
45 Darling, F.F. (1938) *Bird Flocks and the Breeding Cycle: A Contribution to the Study of Avian Sociality*, Cambridge University Press, Cambridge.
46 Armstrong, E.A. (1965) *Bird Display and Behavior*, Dover Publications, New York.
47 Millais, J.G. (1913) *British Diving Ducks*, Longmans & Co., London.
48 Darwin, C. (1872) *The Expression of the Emotions in Man and Animals*, John Murray, London.
49 Heinrich, B. (1999) *Mind of the Raven. Investigations and Adventures with Wolf-birds*, Cliff Street Books, New York.
50 Kaplan (2000), op. cit.; Chisholm, A.H. (1934) *Bird Wonders of Australia*, Angus and Robertson, Sydney.

CHAPTER 4: REPRODUCTION

1 McCleery, R.H. and Perrins, C.M. (1989) Great Tit. In *Lifetime Reproduction in Birds*, ed. I. Newton, Academic Press, London, pp. 33–53.
2 Sternberg, H. (1989) Pied Flycatcher. In *Lifetime Reproduction in Birds*, ed. I. Newton, Academic Press, London, pp. 55–74.
3 Ibid.
4 Birkhead, T.R. and Goodburn, S.F. (1989) The Magpies. In *Lifetime Reproduction in Birds*, ed. I. Newton, Academic Press, London, pp. 173–182.
5 Lack, D. (1940) Habitat selection and speciation in birds. *British Birds*, 34, 80–84.
6 Walsberg, G.E. (1985) Physiological consequences of microhabitat selection. In *Habitat Selection in Birds*, ed. M.L. Cody, Academic Press, London, pp. 389–434.
7 Drent, R.H. (1975) Incubation. *Avian Biology*, 5, 333–419; Walsberg (1985), op. cit.
8 Rothstein, S.I. and Robinson, S.K. (1998) *Parasitic Birds and Their Hosts*, Oxford University Press, Oxford.
9 Payne, R.B. (1998) Brood parasitism in birds: strangers in the nest. *Bioscience*, 48, 377–390.
10 Brooker, M. and Brooker, L. (1996) Acceptance by the splendid fairy-wren of parasitism by Horsefield's bronze-cuckoo: further evidence for evolutionary equilibrium in brood parasitism. *Behavioral Ecology*, 7, 395–407.
11 Lowther, P.E. (1993) Brown-headed cowbird (*Molothrus ater*). In *The Birds of North America*, eds A. Poole. and F. Gill, The Academy of Natural Sciences, Philadelphia.
12 Mermoz, M.E. and Reboreda, J.C. (1999) Egg-laying behaviour by shiny cowbirds parasitizing brown-and-yellow marshbirds. *Animal Behaviour*, 58, 873–882.
13 Sealy, S., Neudord, D.L. and Hill, D.P. (1995) Rapid laying by brown-headed cowbird *Molothrus ater* and other parasitic birds. *Ibis*, 137, 76–84.
14 Rothstein and Robinson (1998), op. cit.
15 Robert, M., Sorci, G., Møller, AP., Hochberg, M.E. and Pomiankowski, A. (1999) Retaliatory cuckoos and the evolution of host resistance to brood parasites. *Animal Behaviour*, 58, 817–824.
16 Soler, M., Soler, J.J., Martinez, J.G. and Møller, A.P. (1995) Magpie host manipulation by great spotted cuckoos: evidence for an avian mafia? *Evolution*, 49, 770–775.
17 Robert et al. (1999), op. cit.
18 Mermoz and Reboreda (1999), op. cit.
19 Scott, D.M., Weatherhead, P.J. and Ankney, C.D. (1992) Egg-eating by female brown-headed cowbirds. *Condor*, 94, 579–584.
20 Joseph, L. and Drummond, R. (1982) Food item of the black butcherbird. *Sunbird*, 12, 49–50.
21 Prawiradilaga, D.M. (1996) Foraging ecology of pied currawongs (*Strepera graculina*) in recently colonised areas of their range. In *Ecology*, Australian National University, Canberra.
22 Buchanan, R. (1978) Pied Currawongs: their diet and weed dispersal in some urban bushland. *Bulletin of the Ecological Society of Australia*, 8, 6; Kaplan, G. (1999) Behavioural snapshot: pied currawong (*Strepera graculina*). *Interpretive Birding Bulletin*, vol. 2.
23 Brigham, R.M. and Geiser, F. (1997) Breeding biology of Australian owlet-nightjars *Aegotheles cristatus* in eucalypt woodland. *Emu*, 97, 316–321.
24 Goodfellow, P. (1977) *Birds as builders*, David & Charles, London.
25 Coddington, C.L. and Cockburn, A. (1995) The mating system of free-living emus. *Australian Journal of Zoology*, 43, 365–372.
26 Goodfellow (1977), op. cit.
27 Körtner, G. and Geiser, F. (1999) Nesting behaviour and juvenile development of the tawny frogmouth *Podargus strigoides*. *Emu*, 99, 212–217.

28 White, F.N., Bartholomew, G.A. and Kinney, J.L. (1978) Physiological and ecological correlates of tunnel nesting in the European bee-eater, *Merops apiaster. Physiological Zoology*, 51, 140–154.
29 White, F.N., Bartholomew, G.A. and Howell, T.R. (1975) The thermal significance of the nest of the sociable weaver *Philetairus socius*: Winter observations. *Ibis*, 117, 171–179.
30 Goodfellow (1977), op. cit.
31 Collias, N.E. and Collias, E.C. (1984) *Nest Building and Bird Behavior*, Princeton University Press, Princeton, NJ.
32 Skutch, A.F. (1976) *Parent Birds and Their Young*, University of Texas Press, Austin.
33 Bertram, B. (1992) *The Ostrich Communal Nesting System*, Princeton University Press, Princeton.
34 Dugatkin, L.A. (1997) *Cooperation Among Animals. An Evolutionary Perspective*, Oxford University Press, New York; Stacey, P.B. and Koenig, W.D. (1990) *Cooperative Breeding in Birds: Long-Term Studies of Ecology and Behaviour*, Cambridge University Press, Cambridge.
35 Darling, F.F. (1938) *Bird Flocks and the Breeding Cycle: A Contribution to the Study of Avian Sociality*, Cambridge University Press, Cambridge.
36 Wittenberger, J.F. and Hunt, G.L.J. (1985) The adaptive significance of coloniality in birds. *Avian Biology*, 8, 1–78.
37 Verwey, J. (1930) Die Paarungsbiologie des Fischreihers. *Zoologisches Jahrbuch, Abt. allgemeine Zoologisch Physiologie*, 48, 1–120.
38 Williamson, K. (1941). First brood of swallows assisting to feed second brood. *British Birds*, 34, 221.
39 Farabaugh, S.M., Brown, E.D. and Hughes, J.M. (1992) Cooperative territorial defence in the Australian magpie, *Gymnorhina tibicen* (Passiformes, Cracticidae), a group-living songbird. Ethology, 92, 283–292. Veltman, C.J. (1989) Flock, pair and group-living lifestyles without cooperative breeding by Australian magpies *Gymnorhina tibicen. Ibis*, 131, 601–608.
40 Stacey and Koenig (1990), op. cit.
41 Brown, J.L. (1987) *Helping and Communal Breeding in Birds*, Princeton University Press, Princeton.
42 Ford, H.A. (1989) *Ecology of Birds. An Australian Perspective*, Surrey Beatty & Sons, Sydney.
43 Stacey and Koenig (1990), op. cit.
44 Poiani, A. and Pagel, M. (1997) Evolution of avian cooperative breeding: comparative tests of the nest predation hypothesis. *Evolution*, 51, 226–240.
45 Cresswell, W. (1997) Nest predation: the relative effects of nest characteristics, clutch size and parental behaviour. *Animal Behaviour*, 53, 93–103.
46 Martin, T.E. (1992) Interaction of nest predation and food limitation in reproductive strategies. *Current Ornithology*, 9, 163–197.
47 Ibid.
48 Lundberg, S. (1985) The importance of egg hatchability and nest predation in clutch size evolution in altricial birds. *Oikos*, 45, 110–117; Møller, A.P. (1990) Nest predation selects for small nest size in the blackbird. *Oikos*, 57, 237–240.
49 Poiani, A. (1993) Small clutch sizes as a possible adaptation against ectoparasitism: a comparative analysis. *Oikos*, 68, 455–462.
50 Ford, H.A. (1998) Faithfulness of breeding site and birthplace in noisy friarbirds *Philemon corniculatus. Emu*, 98, 269–275; Tomkovich, P.S. and Soloviev, M.Y. (1994) Site fidelity in high arctic breeding waders. *Ostrich*, 65, 174–180.
51 Tinbergen, N. (1935) Field observations of East Greenland birds. 1. The behavior of the red-necked phalarope (*Phalaropus lobatus* L.) in spring. *Ardea*, 24, 1–42.
52 Armstrong, E.A. (1965) *Bird Display and Behavior*, Dover Publications, New York.

53 Allen, A.A. (1934) Sex rhythm in the ruffed grouse (*Bonasa umbellus* Linn.) and other birds. *Auk*, 51, 180–199.
54 Armstrong (1965), op. cit.
55 Makkink, G.F. (1936) An attempt at an ethogram of the European avocet (*Recurvirostra avosetta* L.), with ethological and psychological remarks. *Ardea*, 31, 23–74.
56 Tinbergen, N. (1960) *The Herring Gull's World*. Basic Books, N.Y.
57 Armstrong (1965), op. cit.
58 Beebe (1925) The variegated tinamou (*Crypturus v. variegatus*, Emelin). *Zoologica*, 6, 195–227.
59 Thorpe, W.H. (1972) Duetting and Antiphonal Song in Birds. Its Extent and Significance. I. *Behaviour. An International Journal of Comparative Ethology, Leiden*, Supplement XVIII.
60 Levin, R.N. (1996b) Song behaviour and reproductive strategies in a duetting wren, *Thryothorus nigricapillus*. I. Removal experiments. *Animal Behaviour*, 52, 1093–1106; Levin, R.N. (1996a) Song behaviour and reproductive strategies in a duetting wren, *Thryothorus nigricapillus*. I. Playback experiments. *Animal Behaviour*, 52, 1107–1117.
61 Laskey, A.R. (1944) A study of the cardinal in Tennessee. *Wilson Bulletin*, 56, 27–44.
62 Armstrong (1965), op. cit.
63 Lorenz, K. (1931) Beiträge zur Ethologie sozialer Corviden. *Journal of Ornithology*, 79, 67–127.
64 Dugatkin (1997), op. cit.
65 Armstrong (1965), op. cit.
66 Eastman, W.R. (1970) *The Life of the Kookaburra and Other Kingfishers*, Angus & Robertson, Sydney.
67 Mock, D.W. and Parker, G.A. (1997) *The Evolution of Sibling Rivalry*, Oxford University Press, Oxford.
68 Whitmore, M.J. (1986) Infanticide of nestling noisy miners, communally breeding honeyeaters. *Animal Behaviour*, 34, 933–935.
69 Armstrong, D.A. (1991) Aggressiveness of breeding territorial honeyeaters corresponds to seasonal changes in nectar availability. *Behavioural Ecology and Sociobiology*, 29, 103–111.

CHAPTER 5: DEVELOPMENT

1 Dekker, R.W.R.J. and Brom, T.G. (1992) Megapode phylogeny and the interpretation of incubation strategies. *Zoologische Verhandelingen*, 278, 19–31.
2 Birks, S.M. (1997) Paternity in the Australian brush-turkey, *Alectura lathami*, a megapode bird with uniparental male care. *Behavioral Ecology*, 8, 560–568.
3 Dekker and Brom (1992), op. cit.
4 Rahn, H., Paganelli, C.V. and Ar, A. (1975) Relation of avian egg to body weight. *Auk*, 92, 750–765; Ricklefs, R.E. and Starck, J.M. (1998) Embryonic growth and development. In *Avian Growth and Development*, eds J.M. Starck and R.E. Ricklefs, Oxford University Press, New York, pp. 31–58.
5 O'Connor, R.J. (1984) *The Growth and Development of Birds*. John Wiley & Sons, Chichester.
6 O'Connor (1984), op. cit.
7 Dekker and Brom (1992), op. cit.
8 Williams, T.D. (1994) Intraspecific variation in egg size and egg composition in birds: effects on offspring fitness. *Biological Reviews*, 68, 35–59.
9 Potti, J. (1999) Maternal effects and the pervasive impact of nestling history on egg size in a passerine bird. *Evolution*, 53, 279–285.
10 Potti, J. and Merino, S. (1996) Causes of hatching failure in pied flycatchers. *Condor*, 98, 328–336.

11 Smith, H.G. and Wettermark, K-J. (1995) Heritability of nestling growth in cross-fostered European starlings *Sturnus vulgaris*. *Genetics*, 141, 657–665.
12 Cunningham, E.J.A. and Russell, A.F. (2000) Egg investment is influenced by male attractiveness in the mallard. *Nature*, 404, 74–77.
13 Ricklefs and Starck (1998), op. cit.
14 Ibid.
15 Starck, J.M. (1999) Functional capacities of extraembryonic organs in bird embryos. In *Proceedings of the 22nd International Ornithological Congress 16–22 August 1998, Durban*, eds N.J. Adams and R.H. Slotow, Birdlife South Africa, S46.5.
16 Schwabl, H. (1993) Yolk is a source of maternal testosterone for developing birds. *Proceedings of the National Academy of the Sciences USA*, 90, 11444–11450.
17 Schwabl, H. (1996) Maternal testosterone in the avian egg enhances postnatal growth. *Comparative Biochemistry and Physiology*, 114A, 271–276.
18 Gil, D., Graves, J., Hazon, N. and Wells, A. (1999) Male attractiveness and differential testosterone investment in zebra finch eggs. *Science*, 286, 126–128.
19 Schwabl, H., Mock, D.W. & Gieg, J.A. (1997) A hormonal mechanism of parental favouritism. *Nature*, 386, 231.
20 Schwabl, H. (1997) Maternal steroid hormones in the egg. In *Perspectives in Avian Endocrinology*, eds R. Etches and S. Harvey, Journal of Endocrinology Ltd, Bristol, pp. 3–13.
21 Oppenheim, R.W. (1974) The ontogeny of behavior in the chick embryo. In *Advances in the Study of Behavior*, vol. 5, eds D.S. Lehram, J.S. Rosenblatt, R.A. Hinde and E. Shaw, Academic Press, N.Y., pp. 133–171; Rogers, L.J. (1995) *The Development of Brain and Behaviour in the Chicken*, CAB International, Wallingford, UK.
22 Gottlieb, G. (1968) Prenatal behavior of birds. *Quarterly Reviews in Biology*, 43, 148–174; Rogers (1995), op. cit.
23 Tolhurst, B.E. and Vince, M.A. (1976) Sensitivity to odours in the embryo of the domestic fowl. *Animal Behaviour*, 24, 772–779; Burne, T.H.J. and Rogers, L.J. (1999) Changes in olfactory responsiveness by the domestic chick after early exposure to odorants. *Animal Behaviour*, 58, 329–336.
24 Seymour, R.S. and Ackerman, R.A. (1980) Adaptations to underground nesting in birds and reptiles. *American Zoology*, 20, 437–447.
25 Lickliter, R. (1990) Premature visual stimulation accelerates intersensory functioning in bobwhite quail neonates. *Developmental Psychobiology*, 23, 15–27.
26 Tuculescu, R.A. and Griswold, J.G. (1983) Prehatching interactions in domestic chicks. *Animal Behaviour*, 31, 1–10.
27 Vince, M.A. (1966) Potential stimulation produced by avian embryos. *Animal Behaviour*, 14, 34–40; Vince, M.A. (1973) Some environmental effects on the activity and the development of the avian embryo. In *Behavioural Embryology*, ed. G. Gottlieb, Academic Press, NY, pp. 285–323.
28 MacCluskie, M.C., Flint, P.L. and Sedlinger, J.S. (1997) Variation in incubation periods and egg metabolism in mallards: intrinsic mechanisms to promote hatch synchrony. *Condor*, 99, 224–228; Viñuela, J. (1997) Laying order affects incubation duration in the black kite (*Milvus migrans*): counteracting hatching asynchrony? *Auk*, 114, 192–199.
29 Bekoff, A. (1992) Neuroethological approaches to the study of motor development in chicks: achievements and challenges. *Journal of Neurobiology*, 23, 1486–1505.
30 Oppenheim, R.W. (1972) Prehatching and hatching behaviour in birds: a comparative study of altricial and precocial species. *Animal Behaviour*, 20, 644–655.
31 Ibid.
32 Bryant, D.M. and Tatner, P. (1990) Hatching asynchrony, sibling competition and siblicide in nestling birds: studies of swiftlets and bee-eaters. *Animal Behaviour*, 39, 657–671.
33 Stoleson, S.H. (1999) The importance of early onset of incubation for the maintenance

of egg viability. In *Proceedings of the 22nd International Ornithological Congress 16–22 August 1998, Durban*, eds N.J. Adams and R.H. Slotow, Birdlife South Africa, S11.2.
34 Viñuela, J. and Carrascal, L.M. (1999) Hatching patterns in precocial birds: a preliminary comparative analysis. In *Proceedings of the 22nd International Ornithological Congress 16–22 August 1998, Durban*, eds N.J. Adams and R.H. Slotow, Birdlife South Africa, S11.1.
35 Krebs, E.A., Cunningham, R.B. and Donnelly, C.F. (1999) Complex patterns of food allocation in asynchronously hatching broods of crimson rosellas. *Animal Behaviour*, 57, 753–763.
36 Mock, D.W. and Parker, G.A. (1997) *The Evolution of Sibling Rivalry*, Oxford University Press, Oxford.
37 Bryant and Tatner (1990), op. cit.
38 Teather, K.L. (1992) An experimental study of competition for food between male and female nestlings of the red-winged blackbird. *Behavioral Ecology and Sociobiology*, 31, 81–87.
39 Krebs et al. (1999), op. cit.
40 Ibid.
41 Ibid.
42 Hohtola, E. and Visser, G.H. (1998) Development of locomotion and endothermy in altricial and precocial birds. In *Avian Growth and Development*, eds J.M. Starck and R.E. Ricklefs, Oxford University Press, New York, pp. 157–173.
43 Visser, G.H. (1998) Development of temperature regulation. In *Avian Growth and Development*, eds J.M. Starck and R.E. Ricklefs, Oxford University Press, NY, pp. 117–156.
44 Ricklefs, R.E. and Hainsworth, F.R. (1969) Temperature regulation in nesting cactus wren: the nest environment. *Condor*, 70, 32–37.
45 Rogers (1995), op. cit.
46 Tinbergen, N. (1960) *The Herring Gull's World*. Basic Books, NY.
47 Apanius, V. (1998) Ontoneny of immune function. In *Avian Growth and Development*, eds J.M. Starck and R.E. Ricklefs, Oxford University Press, New York, pp. 203–222.
48 Düttmann, H., Bergmann, H-H. and Engländer, W. (1998) Development of behavior. In *Avian Growth and Development*, eds M. Starck and R.E. Ricklefs, Oxford University Press, New York, pp. 223–246.
49 McBride, G., Parer, I.P. and Foenander, F. (1969) The social organisation and behaviour of the feral domestic fowl. *Animal Behaviour Monographs*, 2, 127–181.
50 Rowley, I. (1990) The galah: behavioural ecology of the galah, *Eolophus roseicapillus*. Surrey Beatty & Sons, Sydney.
51 Rüppell, G. (1977) *Bird Flight*. Van Nostrand Reinhold, NY.
52 Schwabl, H. (1998) Developmental changes and among-sibling variation of corticosterone levels in an altricial avian species. *General and Comparative Endocrinology*, 116, 403–408.
53 Ellsworth, E.A. and Belthoff, J.R. (1999) Effects of social status on the dispersal behaviour of juvenile western screech-owls. *Animal Behaviour*, 57, 883–892.
54 Belthoff, J.R. and Dufty, A.M. (1998) Corticosterone, body condition and locomotor activity: a model for dispersal in screech owls. *Animal Behaviour*, 55, 405–415.
55 Rogers (1995), op. cit.

CHAPTER 6: VISION

1 Martin, G.R. and Katzir, G. (1999) Visual fields in short-toed eagles, *Ciraetus gallicus* (Accipitridae), and the function of binocularity in birds. *Brain, Behavior and Evolution*, 53, 55–66.
2 McFadden, S.A. (1993) Constructing the three-dimensional image. In *Vision, Brain,*

and Behavior in Birds, eds H.P. Zeigler and H-J. Bischof, MIT Press, Cambridge, MA, pp. 47–61.

3 Miles, F.A. (1998) The neural processing of 3-D visual information: evidence from eye movements. *European Journal of Neuroscience*, 10, 811–822.

4 Martin, G.R. (1986) Total panoramic vision in the mallard duck, *Anas platyrhynchus*. *Vision Research*, 26, 1303–1305; Martin, G.R. (1994) Visual fields in woodcocks *Scolopax rusticola* (Scoloacidae charariiformes). *Journal of Comparative Physiology A—Sensory, Neural and Behavioral Physiology*, 174, 787–793.

5 Martin, G.R. and Katzir, G. (1994) Visual fields and eye movements in herons (Ardeidae). *Brain, Behavior and Evolution*, 44, 74–85.

6 Martin (1994), op. cit.

7 Martin and Katzir (1994), op. cit.

8 Martin, G.R. and Katzir, G. (1995) Visual fields in ostriches. *Nature*, 374, 19–20.

9 Pettigrew, J.D. and Konishi, M. (1976) Neurones selective for orientation and binocular disparity in the visual Wulst of the barn owl (*Tyto alba*). *Science*, 193, 675–678; Vander-willigen, R.F., Frost, B.J. and Wagner, H. (1998) Stereoscopic depth perception in the owl. *Neuroreport*, 9, 1233–1237.

10 Martin and Katzir (1999), op. cit.

11 Ibid.

12 Martin, G.R. (1985) Eye. In *Form and Function in Birds*, vol. 3, eds A.S. King and J. McLelland, Academic Press, London, pp. 311–373.

13 Wallman, J. and Pettigrew, J.D. (1985) Conjugate and disjunctive saccades in two avian species with contrasting occulomotor strategies. *Journal of Neuroscience*, 5, 1418–1428.

14 Pettigrew, J.D., Wallman, J. and Wildsoet, C.F. (1990) Saccadic oscillations facilitate ocular perfusion from the avian pecten. *Nature*, 343, 362–363.

15 Martin (1985), op. cit.

16 Nalbach, H-O, Wolf-Oberhollenzer, F. and Remy, M. (1993) Exploring the image. In *Vision, Brain, and Behavior in Birds*, eds H.P. Zeigler and H-J Bischof, MIT Press, Cambridge.

17 Rogers, L.J. (1995) *The Development of Brain and behaviour in the Chicken*. CAB International, Wallingford, Oxon.

18 Schaeffel, F., Howland, H.C. and Farkas, L. (1986) Natural accommodation: the growing chicken. *Vision Research*, 26, 1977–1993.

19 Hodos, W. and Erichsen, J.T. (1990) Lower-field myopia in birds: an adaptation that keeps the ground in focus. *Vision Research*, 30, 653–657.

20 Martin, G.R. (1999) Eye structure of foraging King penguins (*Aptenodytes patagonicus*). *Ibis*, 141, 444–450.

21 Rogers, L.J. and Kaplan, G. (1998) *Not Only Roars and Rituals: Communication in Animals*, Allen & Unwin, Sydney.

22 Martin (1985), op. cit.

23 Davies, M.N.O. and Green, P.R. (1988) Head-bobbing during walking, running and flying: relative motion perception in the pigeon. *Journal of Experimental Biology*, 138, 71–91.

24 Frost, B.J., Wylie, D.R. and Wang, Y.C. (1994) The analysis of motion in the visual system of birds. In *Perception and Motor Control in Birds: an Ecological Approach*, eds M.N.O. Davies and P.R. Green, Springer-Verlag, Berlin, pp. 248–269.

25 Friedman, M.B. (1975) How birds use their eyes. In *Neural and Endocrine Aspects of Behaviour in Birds*, eds P. Wright, P.G. Caryl and D.M. Vowles, Elsevier, Amsterdam, pp. 181–204.

26 Land, M.F. (1999) Motion and vision: why animals move their eyes. *Journal of Comparative Physiology A*, 185, 341–352.

27 Casperson, L. (2000) Head movement and vision in underwater-feeding birds of stream, lake, and seashore. *Bird Behavior*, 13, 31–46.
28 Varela, F.J., Palacios, A.G. and Goldsmith, T. (1993) Color vision in birds. In *Vision, Brain, and Behavior in Birds*, eds H.P. Zeigler and H-J. Bischof, MIT Press, Cambridge, MA, pp. 77–98; Bowmaker, J.K., Wilkie, S.E. and Hunt, D.M. (1999) Photoreceptors and molecular genetics of visual pigments. In *Proceedings of the 22nd International Ornithological Congress 16–22 August 1998, Durban*, eds N.J. Adams and R.H. Slotow, Birdlife South Africa, S45.3.
29 Rojas, L.M., McNeil, R., Cabana, T. and Lachaoelle, P. (1997) Diurnal and nocturnal visual function in two tactile foraging waterbirds: the American White Ibis and the Black Skimmer. *Condor*, 99, 191–200.
30 Bowmaker, J.K. (1998) Evolution of colour vision in vertebrates. *Eye*, 12, 541–547.
31 Neumeyer, C. (1990) Evolution of colour vision. In *Evolution of the Eye and Visual System*, eds J.R. Cronly-Dillon and R.L. Gregory, Macmillan, London.
32 Marchetti, K. (1993) Dark habitats and bright birds illustrate the role of the environment in species divergence. *Nature*, 362, 149–152.
33 Endler, J.A. and Thery, M. (1996) Interacting effects of lek placement, display behavior, ambient light, and color patterns in three neotropical forest-dwelling birds. *American Naturalist*, 148, 421–452.
34 Bowmaker, J.K., Heath, L.A., Wilkie, S.E. and Hunt, D.M. (1997) Visual pigments and oil droplets from six classes of photoreceptor in the retinas of birds. *Vision Research*, 37, 2183–2194.
35 Bowmaker, Wilkie and Hunt (1999), op. cit.
36 Bennett, A.T.D. and Cuthill, I.C. (1994) Ultraviolet vision in birds—what is its function? *Vision Research*, 34, 1471–1478.
37 Burkdardt, D. (1996) Ultraviolet perception by bird eyes and some implications. *Naturwissenschaften*, 83, 492–497.
38 Viitala, J., Korpimaki, E., Palokangas, E. and Koivula, M. (1995) Attraction of kestrels to vole scent marks visible in ultraviolet light. *Nature*, 373, 425–427.
39 Andersson, S., Ornborg, J. and Andersson, M. (1998) Ultraviolet sexual dimorphism and assortative mating in blue tits. *Proceedings of the Royal Society of London, B*, 265, 445–450.
40 Cuthill, I.C., Bennett, A.T.D., Partridge, J.C. and Maier, E.J. (1999a) Plumage reflectance and the objective assessment of avian sexual dichromatism. *American Naturalist*, 153, 183–200.
41 Bennett, A.T.D., Cuthill, I.C., Partridge, J.C. and Maier, E.J. (1996) Ultraviolet vision and mate choice in zebra finches. *Nature*, 380, 433–435.
42 Hunt, S., Cuthill, I.C., Swaddle, J.P. and Bennett, A.T.D. (1997) Ultraviolet vision and band-colour preferences in female zebra finches, *Taeniopygia guttata*. *Animal Behaviour*, 54, 1383–1392.
43 Andersson, S. (1999) Morphology of UV reflectance in a whistling-thrush: implications for the study of structural colour signalling in birds. *Journal of Avian Biology*, 30, 193–204.
44 Cuthill, I.C., Partridge, J.C. and Bennett, A.T.D. (1999b) UV vision and its functions in birds. In *Proceedings of the 22nd International Ornithological Congress 16–22 August 1998, Durban*, eds N.J. Adams and R.H. Slotow, Birdlife South Africa, S45.4.
45 Wilschko, W., Munro, U., Ford, H. and Wilschko, R. (1993) Red light disrupts magnetic orientation of migratory birds. *Nature*, 364, 525–527.
46 Wehner, R. (1989) Neurobiology of polarization vision. *Trends in Neurosciences*, 9, 353–359.
47 Phillips, J.B. and Moore, F.R. (1992) Calibration of the sun compass by sunset polarized light patterns in a migratory bird. *Behavioral Ecology and Sociobiology*, 31, 189–193.

48 Åkesson, S. and Bäckman, J. (1999) Orientation in pied flycatchers: the relative importance of magnetic and visual information at dusk. *Animal Behaviour*, 57, 819–828.

CHAPTER 7: HEARING, SMELL, TASTE AND TOUCH

1 Kühne, R. and Lewis, B. (1985) External and middle ears. In *Form and Function in Birds*, eds A.S. King and J. McLelland, Academic Press, London, pp. 227–272.
2 Emlen, J.T. and DeJong, M.J. (1992) Counting birds: the problem of variable hearing disabilities. *Journal of Field Ornithology*, 63, 26–31.
3 Konishi, M. (1993) Listening with two ears. *Scientific American*, 268, 66; Kühne and Lewis (1985), op. cit.
4 Bradshaw, J.L. and Rogers, L.J. (1993) *The Evolution of Lateral Asymmetries, Language, Tool Use, and Intellect*, Academic Press, New York.
5 Kühne and Lewis (1985), op. cit.
6 Ibid.
7 Knudsen, E.I. and Konishi, M. (1979) Mechanisms of sound localisation in the barn owl (*Tyto alba*). *Journal of Comparative Physiology*, 133, 13–21.
8 Kühne and Lewis (1985), op. cit.
9 Smith, C.A. (1985) Inner ear. In *Form and Function in Birds*, eds A.S. King and J. McLelland, Academic Press, London, pp. 273–310.
10 Adler, H.J., Niemiec, A. J., Moody, D.B. and Raphael, Y. (1995) Tectorial membrane regeneration in acoustically damaged birds: an immunocytochemical technique. *Hearing Research*, 86, 43–46.
11 Kuhne and Lewis (1985), op. cit.
12 Payne, R.S. (1962) How the barn owl locates prey by hearing. *Living Bird*, 1, 151–159; Payne, R.S. (1971) Acoustic location of prey by barn owls (*Tyto alba*). *Journal of Experimental Biology*, 54, 535–573.
13 Martin, G. (1990) *Birds by Night*, T. and A.D. Poyser, London.
14 Ibid.
15 Montgomerie, R. and Weatherhead, P.J. (1997) How robins find worms. *Animal Behaviour*, 54, 143–151.
16 Knecht, S. (1939) Über den Gehörsinn und die Musikalität der Vögel. *Zeitschrift für vergleichende Physiologie*, 27, 169–232.
17 Wassiljew, M.P. (1933) Über das Unterscheidungsvermögen der Vögel für die hohen Töne. *Zeitschrift für vergleichende Physiologie*, 19, 424–438.
18 Knecht (1939), op. cit.
19 Ibid.
20 Taschenberger, G., Gallo, L. and Manley, G.A. (1995) Filtering of distortion-product otoacoustic emissions in the inner ear of birds and lizards. *Hearing Research*, 91, 87–92.
21 Klinke, R., Müller, M., Richter, C.-P. and Smolders, J. (1994) Preferred intervals in birds and mammals: a filter response to noise? *Hearing Research*, 74, 238–246.
22 Konishi, M. (1974) Hearing and vocalization in songbirds. In *Birds: Brain and Behavior*, eds I.J. Goodman and M.W. Schein, Academic Press, New York.
23 Dent, M.L., Larsen, O.N. and Dooling, R.J. (1997) Free-field binaural unmasking in budgerigars (*Melopsittacus undulatus*). *Behavioral Neuroscience*, 111, 590–598.
24 Farabaugh, S.M., Dent, M.L. and Dooling, R.J. (1998) Hearing and vocalizations of wild-caught Australian budgerigars (*Melopsittacus undulatus*). *Journal of Comparative Psychology*, 112, 74; Okanoya, K. and Dooling, R.J. (1987) Hearing in passerine and psittacine birds: a comparative study of absolute and masked auditory thresholds. *Journal of Comparative Psychology*, 101.
25 Park, T.J. and Dooling, R.J. (1985) Perception of species-specific contact calls by budgerigars (*Melopsittacus undulatus*). *Journal of Comparative Psychology*, 99, 391–402.

26 Park, T.J. and Dooling, R.J. (1986) Perception of degraded vocalizations by budgerigars (*Melopsittacus undulatus*). *Animal Learning and Behaviour*, 14, 359–364.
27 Farabaugh et al. (1998), op. cit.
28 Langemann, U., Gauger, B. and Klump, G.M. (1998) Auditory sensitivity in the great tit—perception of signals in the presence and absence of noise. *Animal Behaviour*, 56, 763–769.
29 Audubon, J.J. (1826) Account of the habits of the turkey buzzard (*Vultur aura*), particularly with the view of exploding the opinion generally entertained of its extraordinary power of smelling. *Edinb. New Phil. J.*, 2, 172–184.
30 Darwin, C. (1896) *Naturalist's voyage round the world*, D. Appleton & Co., New York.
31 Wenzel, B.M. (1967) Olfactory perception in birds. In *Olfaction and Taste*, ed. T. Hayashi, Pergamon Press, New York, pp. 203–217; Wenzel, B.M. (1968) The olfactory prowess of the kiwi. *Nature*, 220, 1133–1134; Wenzel, B.M. and Sieck, M.H. (1972) Olfactory perception and bulbar electrical activity in several avian species. *Physiology and Behavior*, 9, 287–293; Wenzel, B.M. (1987) The olfactory and related systems in birds. *Annals of the New York Academy of Science*, 519, 137–149.
32 Bang, B.G. and Cobb, S. (1968) The size of the olfactory bulb in 108 species of bird. *Auk*, 85, 55–61; Bang, B.G. (1971) Functional Anatomy of the olfactory system in 23 orders of birds. *Acta Anatomica*, 79, 1–76; Bang, B.G. and Wenzel, B.M. (1985) Nasal cavity and olfactory system. In *Form and Function in Birds*, eds A.S. King and J. McLelland, Academic Press, London and New York, pp. 195–225.
33 Bang (1971), op. cit.
34 Wenzel (1967), op. cit.
35 Malakoff, D. (1999) Following the scent of avian olfaction. *Science*, 286, 704–705.
36 Nef, S., Allaman, I., Fiumelli, H., De Castro, E. and Nef, P. (1996). Olfaction in birds—differential embryonic expression of nine putative odorant receptor genes in the avian olfactory system. *Mechanisms of Development*, 55, 65–77.
37 Stattelman, A.J., Talbot, R.B. and Coulter, D.B. (1975) Olfactory thresholds of pigeons (*Columba livia*), quail (*Colinus virgianus*) and chickens (*Gallus gallus*). *Comparative Biochemical Physiology*, 50A, 807–809.
38 Walker, J.C., Tucker, D. and Smith, J.C. (1979) Odor sensitivity mediated by the trigeminal nerve in the pigeon. *Chemical Senses and Flavour*, 4, 107–116.
39 Walker, J.C., Walker, D.B., Tambiah, C.R. and Gilmore, K.S. (1986) Olfactory and nonolfactory odor detection in pigeons: elucidation by a cardiac acceleration paradigm. *Physiology and Behavior*, 38, 575–580.
40 Mason, J. and Clark, L. (1995) Capsaicin detection in trained European starlings: the importance of olfaction and trigeminal chemoreception. *Wilson Bulletin*, 107, 165.
41 Wenzel (1968), op. cit.
42 Bang (1971), op. cit.
43 Benham, W. B. (1906) The olfactory sense in Apteryx. *Nature*, 74, 222–223.
44 Stager, K.E. (1964) The role of olfaction in food location by the Turkey vulture (*Carthates aura*). *Los Angeles County Museum Contributions in Science*, 81, 1–63; Buitron, D. and Nuechterlein, G.L. (1985) Experiments on olfactory detection of food caches by black-billed magpies. *Condor*, 87, 92–95.
45 Lequette, B., Verheyden, C. and Jouventin, P. (1989) Olfaction in subantarctic seabirds: its phylogenetic and ecological significance. *Condor*, 91, 732–735; Grubb, T.C. (1972) Smell and foraging in shearwaters and petrels. *Nature*, 237, 404–405; Hutchison, L.V. and Wenzel, B.M. (1980) Olfactory guidance in foraging by procellariiforms. *Condor*, 82, 314–319.
46 Malakoff (1999), op. cit.

47 Martin (1990), op. cit.
48 Grubb (1972), op. cit.
49 Verheyden, C. and Jouventin, P. (1994) Olfactory behavior of foraging Procellariiforms. *Auk*, 111, 285–291.
50 Gagliardo, A. and Teyssedre, A. (1988) Interhemispheric transfer of olfactory information in homing pigeon. *Behavioural Brain Research*, 27, 173–178; Papi, F. (1990). Olfactory navigation in birds. *Experimentia*, 46, 352–363; Waldvogel, J.A. (1989) Olfactory orientation by birds. In *Current Ornithology*, vol. 6, M. Power, D. ed., Plenum Press, New York, pp. 269–321.
51 Bang (1971), op. cit.
52 Clark, L. and Smeraski, C.A. (1990) Seasonal shifts in odor acuity of starlings. *Journal of Experimental Zoology*, 255, 22–29.
53 Bang (1971), op. cit.
54 Kennedy, R.J. (1971) Preen gland weights. *Ibis*, 113, 369–372.
55 Ibid.
56 Jacob, J., Balthazart, J. and Sachoffeniels, E. (1979) Sex differences in the chemical composition of uropygial gland waxes in domestic ducks. *Biochemical Systematics and Ecology*, 7, 149–153.
57 Mínguez, E. (1997) Olfactory nest recognition by British storm-petrel chicks. *Animal Behaviour*, 53, 701–707.
58 Rogers, L.J. and Kaplan, G. (1998) *Not only Roars and Rituals: Communication in Animals*, Allen & Unwin, Sydney.
59 Sneddon, H., Hadden, R. and Hepper, P.G. (1998) Chemosensory learning in the chicken embryo. *Physiology and Behavior*, 64, 133–139; Burne, T.H.J. and Rogers, L.J. (1999) Changes in olfactory responsiveness by the domestic chick after early exposure to odorants. *Animal Behaviour*, 58, 329–336.
60 Vallortigara, G. and Andrew, R.J. (1994) Olfactory lateralization in the chick. *Neuropsychologia*, 32, 417–423; Jones, R.B. and Roper, T.J. (1997) Olfaction in the domestic fowl: a critical review. *Physiology and Behavior*, 62, 1009–1018.
61 Marples, N.M. and Roper, T.J. (1996) Effects of novel colour and smell on the response of naive chicks towards food and water. *Animal Behaviour*, 51, 1417–1424.
62 Rogers, L.J., Andrew, R.J. and Burne, T.H.J. (1998) Light exposure of the embryo and development of behavioural lateralisation in chicks, I: olfactory responses. *Behavioural Brain Research*, 97, 195–200.
63 Marples, N.M. and Roper, T.J. (1997) Response of domestic chicks to methyl anthranilate odour. *Animal Behaviour*, 53, 1263–1270.
64 Kassarov, L. (1999) Are birds able to taste and reject butterflies based on 'beak mark tasting'? A different point of view. *Behaviour*, 136, 8.
65 Goujon (1958) 1869.
66 Gottschaldt, K.-M. (1985) Structure and function of avian somatosensory receptors. In *Form and Function in Birds*, vol. 3, eds A.S.King and J. McLelland, Academic Press, London and New York, pp. 375–461.
67 Berkhoudt, H. (1985) Structure and function of avian taste receptors. In *Form and Function in Birds*, vol. 3, eds A.S. King and J. McLelland, Academic Press, London and New York, pp. 463–496.
68 Van Heezik, Y.M., Gerritsen, A.E.C. and Swennen, C. (1983) The influence of chemoreception on the foraging behaviour of two species of sandpiper, *Calidris alba* and *Calidris alpina*. *Netherland Journal of Sea Research*, 17, 47–56; Gerritsen, A.F.C., Van Heezik, Y.M. and Swennen, C. (1983) Chemoreception in two further *Calidris* species (*C.maritima* and *C. canutus*) with a comparison of the relative importance of chemoreception during foraging in *Calidris* species. *Netherland Journal of Zoology*, 33, 485–496.

69 Zweers, G.A. and Wouterlood, F.G. (1973) Functional anatomy of the feeding apparatus of the mallard (*Anas platyrhynchos*). *Proceedings of the 3rd Eur. Anat. Congr., Manchester*, 88–89; Martin (1990), op. cit.
70 Martin, G. (1986) Total panoramic view vision in the mallard duck (*Anas platyrhynchos*). *Vision Research*, 26, 1303–1305.
71 Pettigrew, J.D. and Frost, B.J. (1985) A tactile fovea in the *Scolopacida*? *Brain Behavior and Evolution*, 26, 185–195.
72 Kahl, M.P. and Peacock, L.J. (1963) The bill-snap reflex: a feeding mechanism in the American Wood Stork. *Nature*, 199, 505–506.
73 Martin (1990), op. cit.
74 Watanabe, A. and Aoki, K. (1998) The role of auditory feedback in the maintenance of song in adult male Bengalese finches Lonchura striata var. domestica. *Zoological Science*, 15, 837–841.

CHAPTER 8: HOW BIRDS COMMUNICATE

1 Leboucher, G., Kreutzer, M.L. and Dittami, J. (1994) Copulation solicitation displays in female canaries (*Serinus canaria*): are estradiol implants necessary? *Ethology*, 97, 190–197.
2 Crook, J.H. (1969) Function and ecological aspects of vocalisation in weaver birds. In *Bird Vocalisations*, ed. R.E. Hinde, Cambridge University Press, Cambridge, pp. 265–289.
3 Dunn, P.O., Cockburn, A. and Mulder, R.A. (1995) Fairy-wren helpers often care for young to which they are unrelated. *Proceedings of the Royal Society of London, B*, 259, 339–343.
4 Rogers, L.J. (1997) *Minds of Their Own: Thinking and Awareness in Animals*, Allen & Unwin, Sydney; also Westview, Boulder, Colorado.
5 Rogers, L.J. and Kaplan, G. (1998) *Songs, Roars and Rituals: Communication in birds, mammals and other animals*, Harvard University Press, Boston.
6 Stefanski, R.A. and Falls, J.B. (1972) A study of distress calls of song, swamp and white-throated sparrows (Aves: Fringillidae). I. Intraspecific responses and functions. *Canadian Journal of Zoology*, 50, 1501–1512.
7 Marler, P. (1955) Characteristics of some animal calls. *Nature*, 176, 6–8.
8 Kaplan, G. (2000) Enchanting Frogmouths. *GEO*, 22, 45–50; Chisholm, A.H. (1934) *Bird Wonders of Australia*, Angus and Robertson, Sydney.
9 Wise, K.K., Conover, M.R. and Knowlton, F.F. (1999) Response of coyotes to avian distress calls: testing the startle-predator and predator-attraction hypotheses. *Behaviour*, 136, 935–949.
10 Dooling, R.J., Brown, S.D., Klump, G.M. and Okanoya, K. (1992) Auditory perception of conspecific and heterospecific vocalizations in birds. *Journal of Comparative Psychology*, 106, 20–28.
11 Marler (1955), op. cit.
12 Rogers and Kaplan (1998), op. cit.
13 Oatley, T.B. (1971) The functions of vocal imitation by African coccyphas. *Ostrich*, Sup. 8, 85–89.
14 Emlen, S. (1972) An experimental analysis of the parameters of bird song eliciting species recognition. *Behaviour*, 41, 130–171.
15 Marler, P. and Evans, C. (1996) Bird calls: just emotional displays or something more? *Ibis*, 138, 26–33; Rogers and Kaplan, op. cit.
16 Evans, C.S. (1997) Referential signals. *Perspectives in Ethology*, 12, 99–143.
17 Dooling et al. (1992), op. cit.; Wisniewski, A.B. and Hulse, S.H. (1997) Auditory scene analysis in European starlings (*Sturnus vulgaris*): discrimination of song segments, their segregation from multiple and reversed conspecific song, and evidence for conspecific song categorization. *Journal of Comparative Psychology*, 111, 337–350.

18 Riebel, K. and Slater, P.J.B. (1998) Testing female chaffinch song preferences by operant conditioning. *Animal Behaviour*, 56, 1443–1453.

19 Catchpole, C.K. and Slater, P.J.B. (1995) *Bird Song. Biological Themes and Variations*, Cambridge University Press, Cambridge.

20 Nottebohm, F., Stokes, T.M. and Leonard, C.M. (1976) Central control of song in the canary, *Serinus canaria. Journal of Comparative Neurology*, 165, 457–485; Nottebohm, F. (1981) A brain for all seasons: cyclical anatomical changes in song-control nuclei of the canary brain. *Science*, 214, 1368–1370.

21 Pepperberg, I. (1990) Some cognitive capacities of an African grey parrot. *Advances in the Study of Behavior*, 19, 357–409.

22 Brown, E.D. and Farabaugh, S.M. (1991) Macrogeographic variation in alarm calls of the Australian magpie *Gymnorhina tibicen. Bird Behaviour*, 9, 64–68; Brown, E.D., Farabaugh, S.M. and Veltman, C.J. (1988) Song sharing in a group-living songbird, the Australian magpie, *Gymnorhina tibicen*, I. Vocal sharing within and amongst social groups. *Behaviour*, 104, 1–28.

23 Sanderson, K. and Crouche, H. (1993) Vocal Repertoire of the Australian Magpie *Gymnorhina tibicen* in South Australia. *Australian Bird Watcher*, 15, 162–164.

24 Robinson, A. (1956) The annual reproductive cycle of the magpie, *Gymnorhina dorsalis* Campbell, in south-western Australia. *Emu*, 56, 233–336.

25 Hartshorn, C. (1973) *Born to Sing*, Indiana University Press, Bloomington; Ince, S.A. and Slater, P.J.B. (1985) Versatility and continuity in the songs of thrushes *Turdus. Ibis*, 127, 355–364.

26 Thorpe, W.H. (1972) Duetting and antiphonal song in birds. Its extent and significance. I. *Behaviour. An International Journal of Comparative Ethology, Leiden*, Sup. XVIII; Levin, R.N. (1996b) Song behaviour and reproductive strategies in a duetting wren, *Thryothorus nigricapillus*. I. Removal experiments. *Animal Behaviour*, 52, 1093–1106; Levin, R.N. (1996a) Song behaviour and reproductive strategies in a duetting wren, *Thryothorus nigricapillus*. I. Playback experiments. *Animal Behaviour*, 52, 1107–1117.

27 Emlen, J.T. and DeJong, M.J. (1992) Counting birds: the problem of variable hearing disabilities. *Journal of Field Ornithology*, 63, 26–31.

28 Cheney, D.L. and Seyfarth, R.M. (1985) Vervet monkey alarm calls: manipulation through shared information? *Behaviour*, 94, 150–166.

29 Emlem (1972), op. cit.

30 Krebs, J.R., Ashcroft, R. and Webber, M. (1978) Song repertoires and territory defence in the great tit. *Nature*, 271, 539–542.

31 Brindley, E. (1991) Response of European robins to playback of song: neighbour recognition and overlapping. *Animal Behaviour*, 41, 503–512.

32 Naguib, M. (1996) Auditory distance estimation in song birds: implications, methodologies and perspectives. *Behavioural Processes*, 38, 163–168.

33 Marten, K. and Marler, P. (1977) Sound transmission and its significance for animal vocalization. I. Temperate habitats. *Behavioral Ecology and Sociobiology*, 2, 271–290.

34 Naguib (1996), op. cit.; Naguib, M., Klump, G.M., Hillmann, E., Griessmann, B. and Teige, T. (2000) Assessment of auditory distance in a territorial songbird: accurate feat or rule of thumb? *Animal Behaviour*, 59, 715–721.

35 McGregor, P.K. and Falls, J.B. (1984) The response of western meadowlarks (*Sturnella neglecta)* to the playback of degraded and undegraded songs. *Canadian Journal of Zoology*, 62, 212–225.

36 Friedman, H. (1955) The honey guides. *US National Museum Bulletin*, 208, 1–279; Frings, H. and Frings, M. (1956) Auditory and visual mechanisms in food-finding behaviour of the herring gull. *Wilson Bulletin*, 67, 155–170.

37 Evans (1997), op. cit.

38 Gyger, M. and Marler, P. (1988) Food calling in the domestic fowl, *Gallus gallus*: the role of external referents and deception. *Animal Behaviour*, 36, 358–365.
39 Evans, C. and Marler, P. (1994) Food calling and audience effects in male chicken, *Gallus gallus*: their relationship to food availability, courtship and social facilitation. *Animal Behaviour*, 47, 1159–1170.
40 Evans (1997), op. cit.
41 Moss, M.B. (1996). Cunning corvids: ravens and crows are some of the smartest birds in the sky, and they can teach backwoods travelers quite a bit. *Backpacker*, 24, 16 (14).
42 Emlen (1972), op. cit.; Brenowitz, E.A. (1983) The contribution of temporal song cues to species recognition in the red-winged blackbird. *Animal Behaviour*, 31, 1116–1127; Heidemann, M.K. and Oring, L.W. (1976) Functional analysis of spotted sandpiper (*Actitis macularia*) song. *Behaviour*, 56, 18–193.
43 Becker, P.H., Thielcke, G. and Wüstenberg, K. (1980) Der Tonhöhenverlauf ist eintscheidend für das Gesangserkennen des miteeleuropäischen Zilpzalps (*Phylloscopus collybita*). *Journal of Ornithology*, 121, 229–244.
44 Reinert, J. (1965) Takt-und Rhytmusunterscheidungen bei Dohlen. *Zeitschrift für Tierpsychologie*, 22, 623–671; Hulse, S.H., MacDougall Shackleton, S.A. and Wisniewski, A.B. (1997) Auditory scene analysis by songbirds: stream segregation of birdsong by European starlings (*Sturnus vulgaris*). *Journal of Comparative Psychology*, 111, 3–13; Wisniewski and Hulse (1997), op. cit.
45 Slabbekoorn, H. and Cate, C.T. (1999) Collared dove responses to playback: slaves to the rhythm. *Ethology*, 105, 377–391.
46 Kroodsma, D.E. and Byers, B.E. (1991) The function of birdsong. *American Zoology*, 31, 318–328.
47 Gentner, T.Q. and Hulse, S.H. (2000) Female European starling preference and choice for variation in conspecific male song. *Animal Behaviour*, 59, 443–458.
48 Andrew, R.J. (1961) The displays given by passerines in courtship and reproductive fighting. A review. *Ibis*, 103, 549–579.
49 Williams, J.M. and Slater, P.J.B. (1990) Modelling bird song dialects: the influence of repertoire size and numbers of neighbours. *Journal of Theoretical Biology*, 145, 487–496.

CHAPTER 9: LEARNING

1 Clayton, N.S. and Soha, J.A. (1999) Memory in avian food caching and song learning: a general mechanism or different processes? *Advances in the Study of Behavior*, 28, 115–173.
2 Goodwin E.H. and Hess, E.H. (1969) Innate visual form preferences in the pecking behaviour of young chickens. *Behaviour*, 34, 223–237; Kear, J. (1964) Colour preference in young Anatidae. *Ibis*, 106, 361–369.
3 Bolhuis, J.J. (1991) Mechanisms of avian imprinting: a review. *Biological Reviews*, 66, 303–345.
4 Bateson, P.P.G. and Wainwright, A.A.P. (1972) The effects of prior exposure to light on the imprinting process in domestic chicks. *Behaviour*, 42, 279–290.
5 Bolhuis (1991), op. cit.
6 van Kampen, H.S. and Bolhuis, J.J. (1993) Interaction between auditory and visual learning during filial imprinting. *Animal Behaviour*, 45, 623–625.
7 Burne, T.H.J. and Rogers, L.J. (1995) Odours, volatiles and approach avoidance behaviour of the domestic chick (*Gallus gallus domesticus*). *International Journal of Comparative Psychology*, 8, 99–114; Vallortigara G. and Andrew, R.J. (1994) Olfactory lateralization in the chick. *Neuropsychologia*, 32, 417–423.
8 Burne, T.H.J. and Rogers, L.J. (1999) Changes in olfactory responsiveness by the domestic chick after early exposure to odorants. *Animal Behaviour*, 58, 329–336.

9 Vallortigara, G. and Andrew, R.J. (1991) Lateralization of response by chicks to change in a model partner. *Animal Behaviour*, 41, 187–194.
10 Palestis, B.G. and Burger, J. (1999) Individual sibling recognition in experimental broods of common tern chicks. *Animal Behaviour*, 58, 375–381.
11 Bateson, P.P.G. (1979) How do sensitive periods arise and what are they for? *Animal Behaviour*, 27, 470–486; Rogers, L.J. (1995) *The Development of Brain and Behaviour in the Chicken*, CAB International, Wallingford, Oxon.
12 Bateson, P.P.G. (1987) Imprinting as a process of competitive exclusion. In *Imprinting and Cortical Plasticity: Comparative Aspects of Sensitive Periods*, eds J.P. Rauscheker and P. Marler, John Wiley, New York, pp. 151–168.
13 Rogers (1995), op. cit.
14 Parsons, C.H. and Rogers, L.J. (1997) Pharmacological extension of the sensitive period for imprinting in *gallus domesticus*. *Physiology and Behavior*, 62, 1303–1310.
15 Schutz, F. (1965) Sexuelle Prägung bei Anatiden. *Zeitschrift für Tierpsycologie*, 22, 50–103; Vidal, J.M. (1980) The relations between filial and sexual imprinting in the domestic fowl: effects of age and social experience. *Animal Behaviour*, 28, 880–891.
16 Bateson, P.P.G. (1979) How do sensitive periods arise and what are they for? *Animal Behaviour*, 27, 470–486; Rogers, L.J. (1995) *The Development of Brain and Behaviour in the Chicken*. CAB International, Wallingford, Oxon.
17 Bateson, P.P.G. (1980) Optimal outbreeding and the development of sexual preferences in Japanese quail. *Zieschrift für Tierpsycologie*, 53, 231–244.
18 Bateson, P.P.G., Lotwick, W. and Scott, D.K. (1980) Similarities between the faces of parents and offspring in Bewick's swans and the differences between mates. *Journal of Zoology, London*, 191, 61–74.
19 Immelmann, K. (1972) Sexual and other long-term aspects of imprinting in birds and other species. In *Advances in the Study of Behavior*, vol. 4, eds D.S. Lehrman, R.A. Hinde and E. Shaw, Academic Press, New York, pp. 147–174.
20 Schutz, F. (1971) Prägung des Sexualverhaltens von Enten und Gänsen durch Sozialeindrücke während der Jugendphase. *Journal of Neuro-visc. Rel. Supplement*, 10, 339–357.
21 Immelmann (1972), op. cit.
22 Lorenz, K.Z. (1952) *King Solomon's Ring*, Crowell, New York.
23 Dawkins, R. (1968) The ontogeny of a pecking preference in domestic chicks. *Zeitschrift für Tierpsychologie*, 25, 170–186.
24 Tolman, C.W. (1967) The effect of tapping sounds on feeding behaviour of domestic chicks. *Animal Behaviour*, 15, 145–148.
25 McBride, G., Parer, I.P. and Foenander, F. (1969) The social organisation and behaviour of the feral domestic fowl. *Animal Behaviour Monographs*, 2, 127–181; Suboski, M.D. and Bartashunas, C. (1984) Mechanisms for social transmission of pecking preferences to neonatal chicks. *Journal of Experimental Psychology*, 10, 189–192.
26 Burne, T.H.J. and Rogers, L.J. (1997) Relative importance of odour and taste in the one-trial passive avoidance learning bead task. *Physiology and Behavior*, 62, 1299–1302.
27 Desforges, M.F. and Wood-Gush, D.G.M. (1975) A behavioural comparison of domestic and mallard ducks. Habituation and flight reactions. *Animal Behaviour*, 23, 692–697.
28 Fritz, J. and Kotschal, K. (1999) Social learning in common ravens, *Corvus corax*. *Animal Behaviour*, 57, 785–793.
29 Smith, S.M. (1973) A study of prey attack behaviour in the Loggerhead shrike, *Lanius ludovicianus* L. *Behaviour*, 44, 113–141.
30 LeCroy, M. (1972) Young Common and Roseate Terns learning to fish. *Wilson Bulletin*, 84, 201–202.
31 Curio, E. (1988) Cultural transmission of enemy recognition by birds. In *Social Learning:*

Psychological and Biological Perspectives, eds T.R. Zentall and B.G. Galef Jr, Lawrence Erlbaum, Hillsdale, pp. 75–97.
32 Maloney, R.F. and McLean, I.G. (1995) Historical and experimental learned predator recognition in free-living New Zealand robins. *Animal Behaviour*, 50, 1193–1201.
33 Oatley, T.B. (1971) The functions of vocal imitation by African coccyhas. *Ostrich* Sup., 8, 85–89.
34 Kroodsma D.E. and Miller, E.H. (eds) (1996) *Ecology and Evolution of Acoustic Communication in Birds*, Cornell University Press, Ithaca.
35 Kroodsma D.E. and Miller, E.H. (eds) (1982) *Acoustic Communication in Birds*, vol. 2, Academic Press, New York; Marler, P. (1990) Song learning: the interface between behaviour and neuroethology. *Philosophical Transactions of the Royal Society of London, B*, 329, 109–114.
36 Brown, E.D. and Farabaugh, S.M. (1997) What birds with complex social relationships can tell us about vocal learning: vocal sharing in avian groups. In *Social influences on Vocal Development*, eds C.T. Snowdon and M. Hausberger, Cambridge University Press, Cambridge, pp. 98–127.
37 Rowley, I. and Chapman, G. (1986) Cross-fostering, imprinting and learning in two sumpatric species of cockatoo. *Behaviour*, 96, 1–16.
38 Zann, R. (1997) Vocal learning in wild and domesticated zebra finches: Signature cues for kin recognition or epiphenomena? In *Social influences on Vocal Development*, eds C.T. Snowdon and M. Hausberger, Cambridge University Press, Cambridge, pp. 85–97.
39 Baptista, L.F., Nelson, D.A. and Gaunt, S.L.L. (1998) Cognitive processes in avian vocal acquisition. In *Animal Cognition in Nature: The Convergence of Psychology and Biology in the Laboratory and Field*, eds R.P. Balda, I.M. Pepperberg and A.C. Kamil, Academic Press, San Diego, pp. 245–273.
40 Nowicki, S., Peters, S. and Podos, J. (1998) Song learning, early nutrition and sexual selection in songbirds. *American Zoologist*, 38, 179–191.
41 Marler (1990), op. cit.
42 Slater, P.J.B. (1981) Chaffinch song repertoires: observations, experiments and a discussion of their significance. *Zietschrift für Tiërpsychologie*, 56, 1–24.
43 Catchpole, C.K. and Slater, P.J.B. (1995) *Bird Song: Biological Themes and Variations.* Cambridge University Press, Cambridge.
44 Kroodsma, D.E. and Parker, L.D. (1977) Vocal virtuosity in the brown thrasher. *Auk*, 94, 783–785.
45 Brown and Farabaugh (1997), op. cit.
46 Catchpole, C.K. (1996) Song and female choice: good genes and big brains? *Trends in Ecology and Evolution*, 11, 358–360.
47 Nowicki et al. (1998), op. cit.
48 Todt, D. and Hultsch, H. (1996) Acquisition and performance of repertoires: ways of coping with diversity and versatility. In *Ecology and Evolution of Communication*, eds D.E. Kroodsma and E.H. Miller, Cornell University Press, New York, pp. 79–96.
49 Nelson, D.A. (1997) Social interaction and sensitive phases for song learning: a critical review. In *Social influences on Vocal Development*, eds C.T. Snowdon and M. Hausberger, Cambridge University Press, Cambridge, pp. 7–22.
50 Whaling, C.S., Soha, J.A., Nelson, D.A., Lasley, B. and Marler, P. (1998) Photoperiod and tutor access affect the process of vocal learning. *Animal Behaviour*, 56, 1075–1082.
51 Kroodsma, D.E. (1978) Aspects of learning in the ontogeny of birdsong. In *The Development of Behavior: Comparative and Evolutionary Aspects*, eds G.M. Burghardt and M. Bekoff, Garland, New York, pp. 215–230.
52 Kroodsma, D.E. and Pickert, R. (1980) Environmentally dependent sensitive periods for avian vocal learning. *Nature*, 288, 477–479.

53 Marler, P. and Peters, S. (1987) A sensitive period for song acquisition in the song sparrow, *Melospiza melodia*: a case of age-limited learning, *Ethology*, 76, 89–100.
54 Hultsch, H. and Todt, D. (1982) Temporal performance roles during vocal interactions in nightingales. *Behavioral Ecology and Sociobiology*, 11, 253–260.
55 Nottebohm, F., Nottebohm, M.E. and Crane, L.A. (1986) Developmental and seasonal changes in canary song and their relation to changes in the anatomy of song control nuclei. *Behavioral and Neural Biology*, 46, 445–471.
56 Hultsch, H. and Todt, D. (1989) Memorization and reproduction of songs in nightingales: evidence for package formation. *Journal of Comparative Physiology A*, 165, 197–203.
57 Kaplan, G. (1996) Selective learning and retention: song development and mimicry in the Australian magpie. *International Journal of Psychology*, 31, 233; Kaplan, G. (1999) Song structure and function of mimicry in the Australian magpie (*Gymnorhina tibicen*): compared to the lyrebird (*Menura ssp.*). *International Journal of Comparative Psychology*, 12, 219–241.
58 Eals, L.A. (1985) Song learning in zebra finches: some effects of song model availability on what is learnt and when. *Animal Behaviour*, 33, 1293–1300.
59 Weary, D. and Krebs, J. (1987) Birds learn song from aggressive tutors. *Nature*, 329, 485.
60 Payne, R.B. (1981) Song learning and social interaction in indigo buntings. *Animal Behaviour*, 29, 688–697.
61 Hausberger, M. (1997) Social influences on song acquisition and sharing in the European starling (*Sturnus vulgaris*). In *Social Influences on Vocal Development*, eds C.T. Snowdon and M. Hausberger, Cambridge University Press, Cambridge, pp. 128–156. Pepperberg, I.M., Gardiner, L.I. and Luttrell, L.J. (1999) Limited contextural vocal learning in the grey parrot (*Psittacus erithacus*): effect of interactive co-viewers on videotaped instruction. *Journal of Comparative Psychology*, 113, 158–159.
62 Hultsch, H. and Todt, D. (1981) Repertoire sharing and song post distance in nightingales. *Behavioral Ecology and Sociobiology*, 8, 182–188.
63 Catchpole and Slater (1995), op. cit.
64 Beecher, M.D., Campbell, S.E., Burt, J.M., Hill, C.E. and Nordby, J.C. (2000) Song-type matching between neighbouring song sparrows. *Animal Behaviour*, 59, 21–27.
65 Farabaugh, S.M., Linzenbold, A. and Dooling, R.J. (1994) Analysis of warble song of the budgerigar (*Melopsittacus undulatus*): evidence for social factors in the learning of contact calls. *Journal of Comparative Psychology*, 108, 81–92.
66 Miller, D.B. (1979) Long-term recognition of father's song by female zebra finches. *Nature*, 280, 389–391; Baker, M.C. (1983) The behavioral response of Nuttall's white-crowned sparrows to male song of natal and alien dialects. *Behavioral Ecology and Sociobiology*, 12, 309–315.
67 Hausberger, M. (1997) Social influences on song acquisition and sharing in the European starling (*Sturnus vulgaris*). In *Social influences on Vocal Development*, eds C.T. Snowdon and M. Hausberger, Cambridge University Press, Cambridge, pp. 128–156.
68 King, A.P. and West, M.J. (1988) Searching for the functional origins of cowbird song in eastern Brown-headed Cowbirds (*Molothrus ater ater*). *Animal Behaviour*, 36, 1575–1588.
69 West, M.J., King, A.P. and Freeberg, T.M. (1997) Building a social agenda for the study of bird song. In *Social influences on Vocal Development*, eds C.T. Snowdon and M. Hausberger, Cambridge University Press, Cambridge, pp. 41–56.
70 Wiltschko, W. and Wiltschko, R. (1998) The navigation system of birds and its development. In *Animal Cognition in Nature: The Convergence of Psychology and Biology in the*

Laboratory and Field, eds R.P. Balda, I.M. Pepperberg and A.C. Kamil, Academic Press, San Diego, pp. 155–199.
71 Keeton, W.T. (1969) Orientation by pigeons: is the sun necessary? *Science*, 165, 922–928.
72 Wiltschko, R. and Wiltschko, W. (1981) The development of sun compass orientation in young homing pigeons. *Behavioral Ecology and Sociobiology*, 9, 135–141.
73 Wiltschko and Wiltschko (1998), op. cit.
74 Wiltschko and Wiltschko (1981), op. cit.
75 Wiltschko and Wiltschko (1998), op. cit.
76 von Fersen, L. and Güntürkun, O. (1990) Visual memory lateralization in pigeons. *Neuropsychologia*, 28, 1–7.
77 Delius, J.D. (1987) Sapient sauopsids and hollering hominids. In *Geneses of Language*, ed. W. Koch, Brockmeyer, Bochum; Rogers, L.J. (1997) *Minds of Their Own: Thinking and Awareness in Animals*, Allen & Unwin, Sydney.

CHAPTER 10: ARE BIRDS INTELLIGENT?

1 Rogers, L.J. (1997) *Minds of Their Own: Thinking and Awareness in Mammals*, Allen & Unwin, Sydney.
2 Delius, J.D. (1987) Sapient sauropsids and hollering hominids. In *Geneses of Language*, ed. W. Koch, Brockmeyer, Bochum.
3 Snyder, P.J. (2000) Uncovering the intellectual and emotional lives of birds. *Science Spectra*, 19, 8–14.
4 Balda, R.P. and Kamil, A.C. (1998) The ecology and evolution of spatial memory in corvids of the southwestern USA: the perplexing Pinyon Jay. In *Animal Cognition in Nature: The Convergence of Psychology and Biology in the Laboratory and Field*, eds R.P. Balda, I.M. Pepperberg and A.C. Kamil, Academic Press, San Diego, pp. 29–64.
5 Shettleworth, S.J. (1983) Memory in food-hoarding birds. *Scientific American*, March, 85–94.
6 Shettleworth, S.J. (1990) Spatial memory in food-storing birds. *Philosophical Transactions of the Royal Society, London, B*, 143–151.
7 Heinrich, B. and Pepper, J.W. (1998) Influence of competitors on caching behaviour in the common raven, *Corvus corax. Animal Behaviour*, 56, 1083–1090.
8 Cowie, R.J., Krebs, J.R. and Sherry, D.F. (1981) Food storing by marsh tits. *Animal Behaviour*, 29, 1252–1259.
9 Sherry, D.F., Krebs, J.R. and Cowie, R.J. (1981) Memory for the location of stored food in marsh tits. *Animal Behaviour*, 29, 1260–1266.
10 Tomback, D.F. (1980) How nutcrackers find their seed stores. *Condor*, 82, 10–19.
11 Cheng, K. and Sherry, D.F. (1992) Landmark-based spatial memory in birds (*Parus atricapillus* and *Columba livia*): the use of edges and distances to represent spatial positions. *Journal of Comparative Psychology*, 106, 331–341; Sherry, D.F. and Duff, S.J. (1996) Behavioural and neural bases of orientation in food-storing birds. *Journal of Experimental Biology*, 199, 165–172.
12 Shettleworth, S.J. and Hampton, R.R. (1998) Adaptive specialisations of spatial cognition in food-storing birds? Approaches to testing a comparative hypothesis. In *Animal Cognition in Nature: The Convergence of Psychology and Biology in the Laboratory and Field*, eds R.P. Balda, I.M. Pepperberg and A.C. Kamil, Academic Press, San Diego, pp. 65–98.
13 Krebs, J.R. (1990) Food-storing birds: adaptive specialization in brain and behaviour? *Philosophical Transactions of the Royal Society, London, B*, 329, 153–160; Hampton, R.R. and Shettleworth, S.J. (1996) Hippocampus and memory in a food-storing and in a nonstoring bird species. *Behavioral Neuroscience*, 110, 946–964.
14 Smulders, T.V., Sasson, A.D. and DeVoogd, T.J. (1995) Seasonal variation in hippocampal volume in a food-storing bird, the black-capped chickadee. *Journal of Neurobiology*, 27, 15–25; Krebs, J.R., Clayton, N.S., Healy, S.D., Cristol, C.A., Patel, S.N. and Jolliffe,

A.R. (1996) The ecology of the avian brain: food-storing memory and the hippocampus. *Ibis*, 138, 34–36; Clayton, N.S. and Lee, D.W. (1998) Memory and the hippocampus in food-storing birds. In *Animal Cognition in Nature: The Convergence of Psychology and Biology in the Laboratory and Field*, eds R.P. Balda, I.M. Pepperberg and A.C. Kamil, Academic Press, San Diego, pp. 99–118.

15 Clayton, N.S. and Dickinson, A. (1998) Episodic-like memory during cache recovery by scrub jays. *Nature*, 395, 272–274.

16 Jeffery, K. and O'Keefe, J. (1998) Worm-holes and avian space-time. *Nature*, 395, 215–216.

17 Griffiths, D., Dickinson, A. and Clayton, N.S. (1999) Episodic memory: what can animals remember about their past? *Trends in Cognitive Sciences*, 3, 74–80.

18 Bingman, V.P. and Jones, T-J (1994) Sun compass-based spatial learning impaired in homing pigeons with hippocampal lesions. *Journal of Neuroscience*, 14, 6687–6694; Strasser, R. and Bingman, V.P. (1999) The effects of hippocampal lesions in homing pigeons on a one-trial food association task. *Journal of Comparative Physiology A*, 185, 583–590.

19 Rashid, N. and Andrew, R.J. (1989) Right hemisphere advantage for topographical orientation in the domestic chick. *Neuropsychologia*, 27, 937–948; Vallortigara, G., Zanforlin, M. and Pasti, G. (1990) Geometric modules in animals' spatial representations: a test with chicks (*Gallus gallus domesticus*). *Journal of Comparative Psychology*, 104, 248–254.

20 Clayton, N.S. and Soha, J.A. (1999) Memory in avian food caching and song learning: a general mechanism or different processes? *Advances in the Study of Behaviour*, 28, 115–173.

21 Godard, R. (1991) Long-term memory of individual neighbours in a migratory songbird. *Nature*, 350, 228–229.

22 Fritz, J. and Kotrschal, K. (1999) Social learning in common ravens, *Corvus corax*. *Animal Behaviour*, 57, 785–793.

23 Heinrich, B. (1995) An experimental investigation of insight in common ravens (*Corvus corax*). *Auk*, 112, 994–1003.

24 Balda and Kamil (1998), op. cit.

25 Lawick-Goodall, J. Van. (1968) Tool-using bird: the Egyptian vulture. *National Geographic*, 1968, 631–641; Thouless, C.R., Fanshawe, J.H. and Bertram, B.C.R. (1989) Egyptian vultures *Neophron percopterus* and ostrich *Struthio camelus* eggs: the origins of stone-throwing behavior. *Ibis*, 131, 9–15.

26 Feduccia, A. (1996) *The Origin and Evolution of Birds*, Yale University Press, New Haven.

27 Millikan, C.G. and Bowman, R.I. (1967) Observations on Galápagos tool-using finches in captivity. *The Living Bird*, 6, 23–41; Rogers (1997), op. cit.

28 Beck, B.B. (1980) *Animal Tool Behavior: The Use and Manufacture of Tools by Animals*, Garland Press, New York.

29 Hunt, G.R. (1996) Manufacture and use of hook-tools by New Caledonian crows. *Nature*, 379, 249-251.

30 Hunt, G.R. (2000) Human-like, population-level specialization in the manufacture of pandanus tools by New Caledonian crows, *Corvus moneduloides*. *Proceedings of the Royal Society*, 267, issue 1441.

31 Rogers, L.J. (1996) Behavioural, structural and neurochemical asymmetries in the avian brain: a model system for studying visual development and processing. *Neuroscience and Biobehavioral Reviews*, 20, 487–503.

32 McGrew, W.C. (1992) Tool-use by free-ranging chimpanzees: the extent of diversity. *Journal of Zoology, London*, 228, 689–694; Kaplan, G. and Rogers, L.J. (1999) *The Orang-utans*, Allen & Unwin, Sydney; also published by Perseus Press, Boston, 2000; Van Schaik, C.P. and Fox, E.A. (1996) Manufacture and use of tools in wild Sumatran orang-utans. *Naturwissenschaften*, 83, 186–188.

33 Hunt (2000), op. cit.
34 Ibid.
35 Delius (1987), op. cit.; Rogers (1997), op. cit.
36 Roberts, W.A. (1997) Does a common mechanism account for timing and counting phenomena in the pigeon? In *Time and Behaviour: Psychological and Neurobehavioural Analyses,* eds C.M. Bradshaw and E. Szabadi, Elsevier Science, Amsterdam.
37 Rogers (1997), op. cit.
38 Vallortigara, G., Regolin, L., Rigoni, M. and Zanforlin, M. (1998) Delayed search for a concealed imprinted object in the domestic chick. *Animal Cognition*, 1, 17–24.
39 Regolin, L., Vallortigara, G. and Zanforlin, M. (1995a) Detour behaviour in the domestic chick: searching for a disappearing prey or a disappearing social partner. *Animal Behaviour*, 50, 203–211.
40 Regolin, L., Vallortigara, G. and Zanforlin, M. (1995b) Object and spatial representations in detour problems by chicks. *Animal Behaviour*, 49, 195–199.
41 Pepperberg, I.M. (1990) Conceptual of some nonprimate species, with an emphasis on an African Grey parrot. In *Language and Intelligence in Monkeys and Apes*, eds S.T. Parker and K.R. Gibson, Cambridge University Press, Cambridge.
42 Pepperberg, I.M. (1998) The African Grey parrot: how cognitive processing might affect allospecific vocal learning. In *Animal Cognition in Nature: The Convergence of Psychology and Biology in the Laboratory and Field*, eds R.P. Balda, I.M. Pepperberg and A.C. Kamil, Academic Press, San Diego, pp. 381–409.
43 Snyder, P.J. and Harris, L.J. (1997) Lexicon size and its relation to foot preference in the African Grey parrot (*Psittacus erithacus*). *Neuropsychologia*, 35, 919–926.

CHAPTER 11: DOMESTICATION

1 Collias, N.E. and Collias, E.C. (1967) A field study of the Red Jungle Fowl in North-central India. *Condor*, 69, 360–386; Wood-Gush, D.G.M. (1971) *The Behaviour of the Domestic Fowl*, Heinemann, London.
2 Fumihito, A., Mitake, T., Takada, M., Shingu, R., Endo, T, Gojbori, T., Kondo, N. and Ohno, S. (1996) Monphyletic origin and unique dispersal patterns of domestic fowls. *Proceedings of the National Academy of Sciences USA*, 93, 6792–6796.
3 Wood-Gush, D.G.M. (1959) A history of the domestic chicken from antiquity to the 19th century. *Poultry Science*, 38, 321–326.
4 Barloy, J.J. (1978) *Man and Animal*, Gordon and Cremonesi, London.
5 Ibid.
6 Hale, E.B. (1969) Domestication and the evolution of behaviour. In *The Behaviour of Domestic Animals*, ed. E.S.E. Hafez. Balliere, Tindall and Cassell, London, pp. 22–42.
7 Ibid.
8 Barloy (1978), op. cit.
9 Hale (1969), op. cit.
10 Orlans, F.B., Beauchamp, T.L., Dresser, R., Morton, D.B. and Gluck, J.P. (1998) *The Human Use of Animals: Case Studies in Ethical Choice*. Oxford University Press, Oxford.
11 Barloy (1978), op. cit.
12 Ibid.
13 Immelmann, K. (1982) *Australian Finches*, Angus & Robertson, London.
14 Freud, A. (1981) *All About the Parrots*, Howell Book House, NY.
15 Serpell, J. (1996) *In the Company of Animals: A Study of Human–Animal Relationships*, Cambridge University Press, Cambridge.
16 Zann, R. (1993) Structure sequence and evolution of song elements in wild Australian zebra finches. *Auk*, 110, 702–715.
17 Jackson, S. and Diamond, J. (1996) Metabolic and digestive responses to artificial selection in chickens. *Evolution*, 50, 1638–1651.

18 Zann (1993), op. cit.
19 Miller, D.B. (1977) Social displays of mallard ducks: effects of domestication. *Journal of Comparative and Physiological Psychology*, 91, 221–232; Lickliter, R. and Ness, J.W. (1990) Domestication and comparative psychology: Status and strategy. *Journal of Comparative Psychology*, 104, 211–218.
20 Rogers, L.J. (1995) *The Development of Brain and Behaviour in the Chicken*, CAB International, Wallingford, Oxon.
21 Davis, K. (1997) *Poisoned chickens, poisoned eggs. An inside look at the modern poultry industry* , The Book Publishing Company, Machipongo, VA, USA.
22 Orlans et al. (1998), op. cit.
23 Uschuk, P. (1999) Hot times, pigeons in the city. *Parabola*, Spring, 91–95.
24 Ibid.

CHAPTER 12: BIRDS, HUMANS AND CONSERVATION

1 Linz, G.M., Bergman, D.L. and Bleier, W.J. (1997) Estimating survival of song bird carcasses in crops and woodlots. *The Prairie Naturalist*, 29, 7–13.
2 McKenzie, R.A., Lanham, A.E.L., Taylor, J.D., Gibson, J.A. and Pierce, R.J. (1996) Fenthion poisoning of native birds in southern Queensland. *Australian Veterinary Journal*, 74, 321–323; Allender, W.J. (1994) Fenamiphos poisoning of native geese. *Vet hum toxicol*, 36, 305–306.
3 *Environment* (1999) Borneo rain forest on verge of total destruction, *http://www.enn.com*.
4 Kaplan, G. and Rogers, L.J. (2000) *The Orang-Utans*, Allen & Unwin, Sydney and Perseus, New York.
5 Bibby, C.J. (1999) Making the most of birds as environmental indicators. In *Proceedings of the 22nd International Ornithological Congress*, vol. 70, eds N.J. Adams and R.H. Slotow, Ostrich, Durban, pp. 81–88.
6 Niemi, G.J., Hershey, A.E., Shannon, L., Hanowski, J.M., Lima, A., Axler, R.P. and Regal, R.R. (1999) Ecological effects of mosquito control on zooplankton, insects, and birds. *Environmental Toxicology and Chemistry*, 18, 549–559.
7 Ibid.
8 Duplaix, N. (1990) South Florida water: paying the price. *National Geographic*, 178, 89–114.
9 Recher, H.F. (website, n.d.) Ground-dwelling and ground-foraging birds: the next round of extinctions? University of New England, Armidale, NSW. http://www.environment.gov.au/life/general-info/biolinks/biolink4.html
10 Heywood, V.H. (1995) *Global Biodiversity Assessment*, Cambridge University Press, Cambridge.
11 Goldingay, R. L. and Whelan, R. J. (1997) Powerlines easements: do they promote edge effects in eucalypt forest for small mammals? *Wildlife Research. CSIRO Australia*, 24, 737–744.
12 Duplaix (1990), op. cit.
13 Russell, E.M. and Rowley, I. (1993) Demography of the cooperatively breeding splendid fairy-wren, *Malurus splendens* (Maluridae). *Australian Journal of Zoology*, 41, 475–505.
14 McOrist, S. and Lenghaus, C. (1992) Mortalities of little penguins (*Eudyptula minor*) following exposure to crude oil. *Veterinary Records, Journal of the British Veterinary Association*, 130, 161–162.
15 Pain, D.J., Sanchez, A. and Meharg, A.A. (1998) The Donana ecological disaster: contamination of a world heritage estuarine marsh ecosystem with acidified pyrite mine waste. *Science of the Total Environment*, 222, 45–54.
16 Furness, R.W. and Greenwood, J.J.D. (eds) (1993) *Birds as Monitors of Environmental Change*, Chapman & Hall, London.
17 Bibby (1999), op. cit.

18 Terborgh, J. (1992) Perspectives on the conservation of neotropical migrant landbirds. In *Ecology and Conservation of Neotropical Migrant Landbirds*, eds J.M. Hagan and D.W. Johnston, Smithsonian Institution Press, Washington.
19 Kaplan, G. (1998) Economic development and ecotourism in Malaysia. In *The Shaping of Malaysia*, eds A. Kaur and I. Metcalfe, Macmillan, London and St. Martin's Press, New York.
20 McNeely, J.A. and Thorsell, J.W. (1989) Jungles, mountains and islands. How tourism can help conserve the natural environment. In *Tourism: A Vital Force for Peace*, eds L.J. D'Amore and J. Jafari, D'Amore and Associates, Montreal.
21 Briggs, J. (1991) *Parks of Malaysia*, Longman, Malaysia, Petaling Jaya, Selangor.

SELECT BIBLIOGRAPHY

Balda, R.P., Pepperberg, I.M. and Kamil, A.C. (1998) *Animal Cognition in Nature: The Convergence of Psychology and Biology in Laboratory and Field*, Academic Press, San Diego.

Black, J.M. (ed.) (1996) *Partnership in Birds*, Oxford University Press, Oxford.

Catchpole, C.K. and Slater, P.J.B. (1995) *Bird Song: Biological Themes and Variations*, Cambridge University Press, Cambridge.

Cody, M.L. (ed.) (1985) *Habitat Selection in Birds*, Academic Press, London.

Dugatkin, L.A. (1997) *Cooperation Among Animals: An Evolutionary Perspective*, Oxford University Press, New York.

Feduccia, A. (1996) *The Origin and Evolution of Birds*, Yale University Press, New Haven.

Ford, H. (1989) *Ecology of Birds: An Australian Perspective*, Surrey Beatty and Sons, Sydney.

Furness, R.W. and Greenwood, J.J.D. (eds) *Birds as Monitors of Environmental Change*, Chapman and Hall, London.

Grant, P.R. (1986) *Ecology and Evolution of Darwin's Finches*, Princeton University Press, Princeton.

Hagan, J.M. and Johnston, D.W. (eds) (1992) *Ecology and Conservation of Neotropical Migrant Landbirds*, Smithsonian Institution Press, Washington.

Heinrich, B. (1999) *Mind of the Raven: Investigations and Adventures with Wolf-birds*, Cliff Street Books/HarperCollins, New York.

King, A.S. and McLelland, J. (eds) (1985) *Form and Function in Birds*, Academic Press, London.

Kroodsma, D.E. and Miller, E.H. (eds) (1996) *Ecology and Evolution of Communication*, Cornell University Press, New York.

Martin, G.R. (1990) *Birds by Night*, T. and A.D. Poyser, London.

Newton, I. (ed.) (1989) *Lifetime Reproduction in Birds*, Academic Press, London.

Rogers, L.J. (1995) *The Development of Brain and Behaviour in the Chicken*, CAB International, Wallingford, Oxon.

Rogers, L.J. (1997) *Minds of Their Own: Thinking and Awareness in Animals*, Allen & Unwin, Sydney.

Rogers, L.J. and Kaplan, G. (1998) *Not Only Roars and Rituals: Communication in Animals*, Allen & Unwin, Sydney.

Rothstein, S.I. and Robinson, S.K. (1998) *Parasitic Birds and Their Hosts*, Oxford University Press, Oxford.

Rowley, I. (1982) *Bird Life*, 2nd edition, Australian Naturalist Library, Collins, Sydney.

Rowley, I. (1990) *The Galah: Behavioural Ecology of the Galah*, Eolophus roseicapillus, Surrey Beatty and Sons, Sydney.

Rüppell, G. (1977) *Bird Flight*, Van Nostrand Reinhold, London.

Serpell, J. (1996) *In the Company of Animals*, Cambridge University Press, Cambridge.

Skutch, A.F. (1996) *The Minds of Birds*, Texas A and M University Press, College Station.

Snowdon, C.T. and Hausberger, M. (1997) *Social Influences on Vocal Development*, Cambridge University Press, Cambridge.

Stacey, P.B. and Koenig, W.D. (1990) *Cooperative Breeding in Birds: Long-term Studies of Ecology and Behaviour*, Cambridge University Press, Cambridge.

Stark, J.M. and Ricklefs, R.E. (1998) *Avian Growth and Development: Evolution within the Altricial Precocial Spectrum*, Oxford University Press, Oxford.

Tinbergen, N. (1960) *The Herring Gull's World: A Study of the Social Behaviour of Birds*, Basic, New York.

ILLUSTRATION SOURCES

Chapter opening photos and photo in the Preface by Gisela Kaplan

Figure

1.1	Adapted from a 1996 poster issued by Birdlife International, 'Putting Biodiversity on the Map'. Drawing Craig Lawlor
1.2	Photos Gisela Kaplan
1.3	Drawing Craig Lawlor
1.4	Prepared by Chao Deng
2.1	Drawing Craig Lawlor
2.2	Drawing Craig Lawlor
2.3	Drawing Craig Lawlor
3.1	Jay Sarson/Lochman Transparencies
3.2	Photo Gisela Kaplan
3.3	Frank Park/A.N.T. Photo Library
3.4	Photo Gisela Kaplan
4.1	Photo Gisela Kaplan
4.2	Photo Gisela Kaplan
5.1	Photos Gisela Kaplan and Hans & Judy Beste/Lochman Transparencies
5.2	Photo John Roberts
5.3	Photos Gisela Kaplan
6.1	Modified from Martin, G.R. (1994) *Journal of Comparative Physiology* A, 174, 787–793, and Martin, G.R. and Katzir, G.

	(1999) *Brain, Behavior and Evolution,* 53, 55–66. Drawing by Craig Lawlor
6.2	Photo Gisela Kaplan
6.3	Modified from Martin, G.R. (1985) *Form and Function in Birds*. Vol. 3, edited by A.S. King and J. McLelland, Academic Press. Drawing Craig Lawlor
6.4	Photo Gisela Kaplan
6.5	Photo Gisela Kaplan
6.6	Prepared by Craig Lawlor
8.1	Photo Gisela Kaplan
8.2	Photos Lesley Rogers and Jiri Lochman/Lochman Transparencies
8.3	Photo B.G. Thomson/A.N.T. Photo Library
9.1	Photo Gisela Kaplan
9.2	Sonogram Gisela Kaplan
10.1	Photo Jiri Lochman/Lochman Transparencies
11.1	Photo Gisela Kaplan
11.2	Photo Lesley Rogers
11.3	Photo Lesley Rogers

Plate

1	Photo Jiri Lochman/Lochman Transparencies
2	Photo Gisela Kaplan
3	Photo Gisela Kaplan
4	Photos Gisela Kaplan
5	Photo Gisela Kaplan
6	Photo Gisela Kaplan
7	Photo Gisela Kaplan
8	Photo Jack Cameron/A.N.T. Photo Library
9	Photo Gisela Kaplan
10	Photo Gisela Kaplan
11	Photo Gisela Kaplan
12	Photo Lesley Rogers
13	Photo Gisela Kaplan

SCIENTIFIC NAMES OF BIRDS

Acanthiza pusilla, brown thornbill
Accipiter fasciatus, brown goshawk
Acrocephalus palustris, marsh warbler
Acryllium vulturinium, vulturine guineafowl
Actitis macularia, spotted sandpiper
Aechmophorus occidentalis, western grebe
Aegolius funereus, Tengmalm's owl
Aegotheles cristatus, Australian owlet-nightjar
Aegotheles novaezealandiae, New Zealand owlet-nightjar (extinct)
Aepyornis maximus, elephant bird (extinct)
Aerodramus spp., cave swiftlets
Aethia cristadella, crested auklet
Agelaius phoeniceus, red-winged blackbird
Aimophila quinqueistriata, five-striped sparrow
Aix galericulata, mandarin duck
Alauda arvensis, skylark
Alca torda, razorbill
Alcedinidae, kingfishers
Alcedo atthis, common kingfisher
Alcidae, auks
Alectoris spp., see partridges
Alectura lathami, Australian brush-turkey
Anas clypeata, northern shoveler
Anas platyrhynchos, mallard
Anatinae, ducks
Anser anser, greylag goose
Anser indicus, bar-headed goose
Anseriformes, geese
Aphelocoma coerulescens, scrub jay
Aptenodytes forsteri, emperor penguin
Aptenodytes patagonicus, king penguin
Apteryx australis, brown kiwi
Aquila audax, wedge-tailed eagle
Ara ararauna, blue and yellow macaw
Archaeopteryx lithographica, extinct
Ardea alba, great egret
Ardea cinerea, grey heron
Asio flammeus, short-eared owl
Asio otus, long-eared owl
Aviceda subcristata, Pacific baza

Balearica regulorum, crowned crane
Bonasa umbellus, ruffed grouse
Bubo bubo, northern eagle owl
Bubulcus ibis, cattle egret
Buceros rhinoceros, rhinoceros hornbill
Bucerotidae, hornbills
Bucorvus leadbeateri, ground hornbill
Burhinus oedicnemus, stone curlew

Cacatua galerita, sulphur-crested cockatoo
Cacatua leadbeateri, Major Mitchell's cockatoo (also pink cockatoo)
Cacatua roseicapilla, galah
Cacatuinae, cockatoos
Cactospiza pallida, woodpecker finch
Cairina moschata, Muscovy duck
Calidris alba, sanderling
Calidris alpina, dunlin
Calidris canutus, red knot
Calidris maritima, purple sandpiper
Calidris spp., sandpipers

Calyptorhynchus banksii, red-tailed black cockatoo
Calyptorhynchus funereus, yellow-tailed black cockatoo
Calyptorhynchus lathami, glossy black cockatoo
Calyptorhynchus spp., black cockatoos
Camarhynchus (also *Geospiza Certhidea*), Galápagos finch
Campylorhynchus brunneicapillus, cactus wren
Campylorhynchus nuchalis, stripe-backed wren
Caprimulgidae, nightjars
Caprimulgus europaeus, European nightjar
Cardinalis cardinalis, northern cardinal
Casuarius casuarius, southern cassowary
Catharacta skua, great skua
Catharacta spp., skua
Cathartes aura, turkey vulture
Caudipteryx spp., extinct
Centrocercus urophasianus, sage grouse
Centropus phasianinus, pheasant coucal
Certhiidae, Climacteridae, treecreepers
Chalcophaps indica, emerald dove
Charadriidae, plovers
Charadriiformes, waders, shore birds
Chrysococcyx basalis, Horsefield's bronze cuckoo
Ciconiidae, storks
Cinclus spp., dippers
Circaetus gallicus, short-toed eagle
Circus aeruginosus, Eurasian marsh harrier
Circus macrourus, pallid harrier
Cistothorus palustris, marsh wren
Clamator glandarius, great spotted cuckoo
Colinus virginianus, northern bobwhite
Columba livia, domestic pigeon, rock dove
Confuciusornis, extinct
Coraciiformes, kingfishers
Coracina novaehollandiae, black-faced cuckoo shrike
Corcorax melanorhamphos, white-winged chough
Corvidae, ravens, *Corvus* spp.
Corvus caurinus, northwestern crow
Corvus corax, common raven
Corvus coronoides, Australian raven
Corvus frugilegus, rook
Corvus monedula, Eurasian jackdaw
Corvus moneduloides, New Caledonian crow
Coturnix japonica, Japanese quail
Coturnix spp., quails
Cracticus spp., butcherbirds
Crex crex, corn crake
Cricaetus gallicus, short-toed eagle
Cyanoramphus spp., parakeets
Cygnus atratus, black swan
Cygnus columbianus, Tundra swan
Cygnus spp., swans

Dacelo leachii (blue-winged kookaburra), kookaburra
Dacelo novaeguinea (laughing kookaburra), kookaburra
Diatryma, extinct
Didunculus strigirostris, tooth-billed pigeon
Dinoris maximus, moas
Diomeda exulans, wandering albatross
Dolichonyx oryzivorous, bobolink
Diomedea, albatross
Dromaius novaehollandiae, emu
Dromornis stirtoni, extinct
Dromornithidae, thunderbirds (extinct)

Enantiornithines, extinct
Ensifera ensifera, sword-billed hummingbird
Ephthianura albifrons white-fronted chat
Ephthianura tricolor, crimson chat
Erithacus rubecula, Euopean robin
Eudocimus ruber ruber, American white ibis
Eudynamys scolopacea, common koel
Euryapteryx spp., moas
Eurystomus orientalis, dollarbird

Falco berigora, brown falcon
Falco peregrinus, peregrine falcon
Falco tinnunculus, common kestrel
Falconiformes, raptors
Ficedula albicollis, collared flycatcher
Ficedula hypoleuca, pied flycatcher
Ficedula spp., flycatchers
Fratercula artica, Atlantic puffin
Fregata magnificens, magnificent frigatebird
Fringilla coelebs, chaffinch

Gallirallus australis, weka
Gallirallus spp., wood rails
Gallus gallus domesticus, domestic chicken
Gallus gallus spadiceus, Burmese red junglefowl
Gallus gallus (red junglefowl), junglefowl
Gallus lafayettei (Ceylon junglefowl), junglefowl

Gallus sonneratii (grey junglefowl), junglefowl
Gallus varius (green junglefowl), junglefowl
Gavia arctica, black-throated diver
Gavia immer, great northern diver
Geococcyx californianus, greater roadrunner
Geophaps lophotes, crested pigeon
Geophaps plumifera, spinifex pigeon
Geopsittacus occidentalis, night parrot
Geospiza spp. (also *Camarhynchus* and *Certhidea*), Galápagos finches
Gerygone chrysogaster, yellow-bellied gerygone
Gerygone palpebrosa, fairy gerygone
Gerygone spp., gerygones
Glareolidae, pratincoles
Glossopsitta spp., lorikeets
Grallina cyanoleuca, magpie-lark
Gygis alba, white tern
Gymnorhina tibicen, Australian magpie
Gypaetus barbatus, lammergeier
Gyps fulvus, Eurasian griffon vulture
Gyps spp., vultures

Haematopus spp., oystercatchers
Haliaeetus leucocephalus, bald eagle
Haliaeetus leucogaster, white-bellied sea eagle
Haliaeetus vocifer, African fish eagle
Hieraaetus morphnoides, little eagle
Himantopus himantopus, black-winged stilt
Hirundininae, swallows
Hirundo rustica, barn swallow
Hydrobatidae, storm-petrels

Indicator indicator, black-throated honeyguide
Ixobrynchus sinensis, yellow bittern

Lagopus spp., ptarmigan
Lanius ludovicianus, loggerhead shrike
Larus argentatus, herring gull
Larus marinus, great black-backed gull
Leipoa ocellata, malleefowl
Limosa lapponica, bar-tailed godwit
Lonchura striata, Bengalese finch
Lopholaimus antarcticus, topknot pigeon
Lophopsittacus mauritianus, broad-billed parrot (extinct)
Lophorina superba, superb bird of paradise
Luscinia megarhynchos, common nightingale

Malurus cyaneus, superb fairy wren
Malurus spp., fairy wrens
Manorina melanocephala, noisy miner
Megalurus pryeri, Japanese swamp warbler
Megapodiidae, megapodes
Megapodius reinwardt, orange-footed scrubfowl
Megopodius freycinet, dusky megapode
Meleagris gallopavo, turkey (wild)
Meliphagidae, honey-eaters
Melopsittacus undulatus, budgerigar
Melospiza georgiana, swamp sparrow
Melospiza melodia, song sparrow
Menuridae, lyrebirds
Mergus serrator, red-breasted merganser
Merops apiaster, European bee-eater
Merops ornatus, rainbow bee-eater
Merops viridis, blue-throated bee-eater
Milvus migrans, black kite
Mimus polyglottos, northern mockingbird
Molothrus ater, brown-headed cowbird
Molothrus spp., cowbirds
Morus bassanus, northern gannet
Mycteria americana, American wood stork
Myiopsitta monachus, Monk parakeet

Nectarinia coccinigastra, splendid sunbird
Nectarinia mariquensis, Marico sunbird
Nectariniidae, sunbirds
Neophron percnopterus, Egyptian vulture
Ninox connivens, barking owl
Ninox novaeseelandiae, southern boobook owl
Nucifraga columbiana, Clark's nutcracker
Numenius arquata, Eurasian curlew
Numididae, guinea fowl
Nyctea scandiaca, snowy owl
Nyctibius grandis, great potoo

Oceanites oceanius, Wilson's storm-petrel
Oceanodroma leucorhoa, Leach's storm-petrel
Opisthocomus hoazin, hoatzin
Orthotomus sutorius, common tailorbird
Otus asio, common screech owl
Otus kennicotti, western screech owl

Pandion haliaetus, osprey
Paradisaea raggiana, raggiana bird of paradise
Paradisaeidae, birds of paradise
Pardalotus punctatus, spotted pardalote
Pardalotus spp., pardalotes

Paroaria coronata, red-crested cardinal
Parus atricapillus, black-capped chickadee
Parus bicolor, tufted titmouse
Parus caeruleus, blue tit
Parus carolinensis, Carolina chickadee
Parus major, great tit
Parus palustris, marsh tit
Parus spp., tits
Passer domesticus, house sparrow
Passer montanus, tree sparrow
Passeriformes, perching birds
Passerina cyanea, indigo bunting
Pavo cristatus, common peafowl
Pelecanus erythrorhynchos, American white pelican
Perdix spp., partridges
Pernis apivorus, European honey buzzard
Petroica australis, New Zealand robin
Pezoporus wallicus, ground parrot
Phalacrocorax aristotelis, Eurasian shag
Phalacrocorax bougainvillii, Guanay cormorant
Phalacrocorax carbo, great cormorant
Phalacrocorax olivaceus, olivaceous cormorant
Phalaropus lobatus, red-necked phalarope
Phasianidae, pheasants
Philetairus socius, sociable weaver
Phoebetria spp., albatross
Phoenicopterus ruber, greater flamingo
Phorusrhacos, extinct
Phylloscopus collybita, common chiffchaff
Pica pica, black-billed magpie
Platycercus elegans, crimson rosella
Platycercus eximius, eastern rosella
Ploceinae, weaverbirds
Ploceus cucullatus, village weaver
Pluvialis spp., golden plovers
Podargidae, frogmouths
Podargus strigoides, tawny frogmouth
Podiceps cristatus, great crested grebe
Polemaetus bellicosus, martial eagle
Polyplectron bicalcaratum, grey peacock pheasant
Pomatostomus temporalis, grey-crowned babbler
Porphyrio mantelli, takahe
Probosciger aterrimus, palm cockatoo
Protoaxis texensis, extinct
Psittaciformes, parrots
Psittacula eupatria, Alexandrine parrakeet
Psittacula spp., parakeets
Psittacus erithacus, Grey parrot
Ptilinopus magnificus, wompoo fruit-dove
Ptilinopus regina, rose-crowned fruit-dove
Ptilinopus superbus, superb fruit-dove
Ptilinorhynchidae, bowerbirds
Ptiloris victoriae, Victoria's riflebird
Ptilorus spp., riflebirds
Puffinus gravis, great shearwater
Puffinus griseus, sooty shearwater
Puffinus spp., shearwaters
Puffinus tenuirostris, short-tailed shearwater
Pygoscelis papua, gentoo penguin
Pyrocephalus rubinus, vermilion flycatcher

Rallidae, rails
Ramphastidae, toucans
Raphus cucullatus, dodo (extinct)
Recurvirostra avosetta, pied avocet
Rheidae, rheas
Rhipidura leucophrys, willie wagtail
Rhipidura rufidorsa, grey-breasted rufous fantail
Rhipidura spp., fantails
Rissa brevirostris, red-legged kittiwake
Rynchopidae, skimmers
Rynchops niger, black skimmer

Sagittarius serpentarius, secretary bird
Sayornis phoebe, Eastern phoebe
Scenopoeetes dentirostris, tooth-billed bowerbird
Scolopacidae, sandpipers
Scolopax minor, American woodcock
Scolopax rusticola, Eurasian woodcock
Scopus umbretta, hammerkop
Scotopelia peli, Pel's fishing owl
Scythrops novaehollandiae, channel-billed cuckoo
Serinus canaria, island canary
Somateria mollissima, common eider
Sphenisciformes, penguins
Spizaetus coronatus, crowned eagle
Steatornis caripensis, oilbird
Sterna albifrons, little tern
Sterna hirundo, common tern
Sterna nereis, fairy tern
Sterna paradisaea, Arctic tern
Strepera graculina, pied currawong
Strepera spp., currawongs
Streptopelia decaocto, collared dove
Strigops habroptilus, kakapo
Strix aluco, tawny owl

Strix varia, barred owl
Struthidea cinerea, apostlebird
Struthio camelus, ostrich
Sturnus roseus, rose-coloured starling
Sturnus vulgaris, common starling
Sula dactylatra, masked booby
Sula nebouxii, blue-footed booby
Sylviidae, old world warblers, common chiffchaff

Tachycineta bicolor, tree swallow
Tadorna spp., shelducks
Taeniopygia guttata, zebra finch
Tallegalla spp., black-billed tallegalla (brush-turkeys)
Tallegalla fuscirostris, yellow-bellied brush-turkey
Terathopius ecaudatus, bateleur eagle
Thalassoica antartica, Antarctic petrel
Thryothorus ludovicianus, Carolina wren
Thryothorus nigricapillus, bay wren
Titanus walleri, extinct
Todirhampus (Halcyon) sancta, sacred kingfisher
Toxostoma rufum, brown thrasher
Trichoglossus spp., lorikeets
Tringa glareola, wood sandpiper
Trochilidae, hummingbirds
Tryngites subruficollis, buff-breasted sandpiper
Turdinae, thrushes
Turdus iliacus, redwing
Turdus merula, common blackbird
Turdus migratorius, American robin
Turdus philomelos, song thrush
Turnix suscitator, barred button-quail
Tyto alba, barn owl
Tyto capensis, grass owl

Upupa epops, hoopoe

Vanellus vanellus, northern lapwing
Vidua spp., whydahs
Vultur gryphus, Andean condor

Wilsonia citrina, hooded warbler

Zonotrichia leucophrys, white-crowned sparrow
Zosterops lateralis, silvereye

INDEX

Numerals in ***bold italics*** indicate figures